RABBONI

Which Is to Say, Master

Other books by W. Phillip Keller

God Is My Delight
His Way to Pray
Joshua—Mighty Warrior and Man of Faith
Outdoor Moments with God
Sky Edge
Songs of My Soul
Strength of Soul
Triumph Against Trouble
What Is the Father Like?
Wonder O' the Wind

RABBONI

Which Is to Say, Master

W. PHILLIP KELLER

kregel
PUBLICATIONS

Grand Rapids, MI 49501

Rabboni: Which Is to Say, Master

Copyright © 1977 by W. Phillip Keller

Published in 1997 by Kregel Publications, a division of Kregel, Inc., P.O. Box 2607, Grand Rapids, MI 49501. Kregel Publications provides trusted, biblical publications for Christian growth and service. Your comments and suggestions are valued.

For more information about Kregel Publications, visit our web site at http://www.kregel.com.

Cover design: Alan G. Hartman
Cover photo: Copyright © 1997 Paul Stepanovich

Library of Congress Cataloging-in-Publication Data
Keller, W. Phillip (Weldon Phillip), (1920–1997).
    Rabboni: which is to say, Master / W. Phillip Keller.
        p.   cm.
    Originally published: Old Tappan, N.J.: Revell, © 1977.
    1. Jesus Christ—Biography. I. Title.
BT301.2.K44   1998   232.9'01—dc21   97-30359
                                                                        CIP

ISBN 0-8254-2991-9

Printed in the United States of America

2 3 / 03 02 01 00 99 98

IN MEMORY of my mother,
who
dearly loved Christ
and
introduced me to Him

An Explanation

Rab "A teacher, or any master."
Rabbi "The teacher, master, one well known."
Rabboni "My teacher, my master, the one for whom I hold the very highest esteem."

Contents

In Appreciation

As intimated elsewhere, there is a deep debt of gratitude owed by anyone who writes about our Lord to those who have gone before. It is inevitable that some of their views, insights, and impressions should have become ours. And to all such I express my genuine thanks.

Many of the thoughts in this book were first shared with my church. It was they who listened patiently, week after week, for more than a year, while a layman labored to bring some of these truths to life.

They were generous enough to record the messages. The tapes of those talks, along with my own prolific notes, are the basic material, drawn directly from God's Word, upon which this book has been based.

It was also gracious of my church to grant me leave of absence during winter to go away and write. Freed from the constant demands of teaching Bible-study groups, or personal Christian counseling, almost full and undivided attention could be given to the manuscript of this work.

My dear wife, Ursula, a fellow adventurer under God, has worked diligently to type the manuscript. We have shared in the excitement, labor, and anguish of bringing this book to birth.

Most important has been the very real presence of our Lord Himself, by His Spirit. Again and again I have turned to Him in the quiet hours before dawn, seeking guidance in what to put on paper. In truth, a large part of this work has been possible only because He is here.

W. PHILLIP KELLER

Why This Book?

It is reasonable to ask why yet another book should be written about Jesus the Christ. Surely by now, after so many scholars, theologians, and other writers have applied their talents to this character, the subject should be exhausted.

But it is not.

Better to say, *He* is not.

For in dealing with Jesus Christ we are dealing with the greatest person to appear on the world's stage: He is the Almighty, the Infinite God, the One who is from eternity to eternity and who is therefore inexhaustible.

What is more: So majestic, so great, so utterly overwhelming is this person that no man in a brief lifetime can begin to grasp all there is to knowing Him. At best all that any author can do is to portray in faltering fashion his own picture of the Christ from his particular viewpoint.

To use a simple illustration, it is something akin to men who live at the foot of a mighty mountain. Each, depending upon the particular spot where he spends his life, will hold a distinct, positive, but different impression of the same mountain. I was reminded of this when, as a young man, I spent a good deal of time on the Kenya side of Mount Kilimanjaro.

From that easterly aspect, the craggy, shattered rock pinnacles of Mount Mawenzi were on the left side of the mountain's lofty saddle. On the right side towered the massive, smoothly rounded, icy dome of Mount Kibo.

At a later date I had to make a trip around the mountain to the Tanzania side. There I found the majestic, snowy Mount Kibo on the left, while the jagged peak of Mount Mawenzi stood on the right. It was the same mountain and the same man viewing it. The diametrical difference in its appearance lay in the direction from which I was looking.

And so it is in coming to look at Jesus Christ. The view given in the pages which follow is from that of an ordinary layman. It is an honest and sincere attempt to put on paper, in word pictures, my own personal impressions of Jesus the Christ.

No attempt is made to delude the reader into believing that I have had formal training in theology. I have not. But this is not to say that I have not read widely in the Christian field, for I have. And, strange as it may seem, no books have ever gripped or stirred me more than those dealing directly with Jesus Christ Himself.

Indeed, I owe a great debt of thanks to those writers courageous enough to share with me their insights into the life of this wondrous Person.

But beyond the books there has been my own, intimate, personal acquaintance with Jesus Christ. From my earliest childhood up until the present day, well over half a century later, He has been the most prominent character sharing my years on earth. No one else has made such an enormous impact upon me. No one else do I more admire. No one else has known me as intimately. No one else has, despite knowing the worst about me, accepted me so completely in total affection. No one else has so captured my heart and mind. And no one else has conveyed to me the meaning and direction and purpose in living as the Living Christ.

It is, therefore, in large measure, out of a deep and genuine sense of gratitude to Him that this book has been written. It is my most sincere hope that in turn it will help someone else to see Him in a new, dynamic, and inspiring dimension. It is my prayer that through the pages which follow, Jesus Christ may become to the reader a living, winsome, wondrous Person, who, though very approachable, is also able to lift one to new levels of noble, lofty living.

CHAPTER ONE

Before the Earth Was

Our Lord did not have His beginning at the little hamlet of Bethlehem. His story does not start with a stable. This may be the common concept of the Christ, but it is not the correct one. He cannot be confined to the limitations of earthly time and space. For before the earth was, He existed.

This means that our finite understanding of Him must be opened wide and expanded to the farthest horizons of human comprehension. Our concepts must be projected back beyond the birth of our own planet, earth. They must envisage the endless eons of eternity. Somehow we must grasp with the deep intuition of our spirits the realm of the supernatural, where time and space and our physical senses are no longer the basis of our observations. This region of the spirit is just as real, just as sure, just as valid as is our everyday world of earth, water, trees, sky, plants, and living creatures. Because so many of its attributes are abstract in form, most of us find it hard to envisage them. But let us try.

For lack of a better term, I call this other region of the spirit *eternity*. It might be equally well referred to as "the everlasting region," "the realm of the infinite," "the supernatural world," "God's heaven," "the eternal home," "paradise"—or even just the *outer,* or *other,* world.

All these terms, in one way or another, are used to describe that magnificent domain of the divine.

This supernatural world of eternity is peopled with beings who have distinct personalities. They have definite characteristics which are familiar to us. Their attributes are love, courage, faithfulness, joy, integrity, wisdom, beauty, justice, compassion, strength, and serenity. These form their pattern of life. They are as real to them as they are to us. These elements of good emanate from their realm directly into ours, touching the common lives of us common men on earth.

This is the realm which is home to Christ.

It is a realm of harmony, of serenity, of love.

Because of our human birth and lifetime of conditioning to this planet, we have enormous difficulty comprehending God's eternal, unseen world. But that is where His story began, and somehow it is imperative that we get some sort of picture of that paradise.

I used the word *paradise* on purpose. Not to conjure up a picture of a beautiful region with gorgeous trees, silver streams, golden streets, and angels playing harps, but to portray a more authentic picture. For paradise is not just a pretty place. It is much, much more. It is a realm of rest, a state of tranquillity, a world of wholesomeness.

It is exceedingly hard for us humans to even imagine such a world. After all, with our earthly makeup, we can scarcely even think of a world without sorrow, pain, death, separation, evil, misunderstandings, or selfishness. We are so accustomed to our lifelong struggle with these difficulties that it seems impossible there could be some place without them. But there is. It is where God the Father has complete control. This is the eternal residence of the righteous. It is Christ's abode.

To grasp something of the grandeur and glory of that realm, it helps us to contrast it with our earthly world.

Here we have to contend with pain, with both physical and mental suffering or stress. There one is set free from this perplexing and agonizing problem.

Here we experience sorrow and sadness both emotional and spiritual. Life is beleaguered by disappointments, grief, frustrations, and heartache. In that eternal region there is rest from all remorse and anguish of spirit or mind.

In this world we all must face the somber prospect of death. It is a common denominator to all human experience. In eternity, death does not exist; gone are the foreboding and dread with which it haunts so many here.

Upon this planet we stumble through the darkness searching for light, groping for ultimate truth, seeking to understand and be understood. In the bright and brilliant dimension of eternity there is no night. The searching has ceased. There is complete understanding. Satisfying illumination of both intellect and spirit is experienced.

Here we humans wrestle unremittingly with the down drag of evil. It dogs our steps and blights our best intentions. We struggle with sin but we are stained in the encounter. In the presence of God there is no sin. It is an area of existence where no temptation thwarts or tantalizes the spirit of good. It is a region of repose from self and selfishness.

On earth we are engaged in an endless contest with the Enemy of our souls which ultimately decides our destiny. In the realm above he has been banished from view and rendered inoperative.

Here we are inured to, yet often hurt by, painful separation. We endure alienation between man and man, man and woman, man and his Maker. But over there lies the wondrous world of unity: complete harmony and everlasting acceptance.

This was the other world that was our Lord's home. It was the realm in which He moved completely at ease. He had been there from the beginning . . . for He, too, was from the beginning. He always was. He was and is the eternal I AM. It was this environment which was His native abode and natural air.

In those distant eons of eternity, billions upon billions upon billions of years ago, Christ moved effortlessly: the Prince of Peace in His majestic realm, one with God His Father, yet distinct in personality.

With our finite minds we can probe but a short distance into the vastness of His preearth existence—but with the enlightenment that comes to our spirits by His Spirit, we sense and feel the magnitude of His enterprises in arranging and governing the universe.

Such enlightenment, I said, comes from His Spirit. He—the Eternal Spirit of the Infinite God, the same Spirit of the Eternal Christ—was simultaneously in everlasting existence with both the Father and the Son, our Christ. He, like them, was engaged in the enormous activities that long preceded even the appearance of the planet earth.

In all the enterprises which engaged this tremendous triumvirate, there was perfect coordination of concept and ultimate unity of purpose in their planning. Unlike human endeavors, it was never marked by discord. Friction was unknown simply because there was no selfish self-interest present. Between God the Father, God the Son (Jesus Christ), and God the Spirit there flowed love in its most sublime form. In fact, this love was of such purity that it constituted the very basis of their beings. It was the essence of their characters.

We earthmen can barely conceive of a relationship so sublime that it contains no trace of self-assertion, no ulterior motive nor self-gratification. But that is the secret to the strength of God. Here was demonstrated the irresistible force of utter selflessness. In the total giving of each to the other, in profound *caring* for each other, lay the love of all eternity. This was love at its loftiest level. This was love at its highest source. This was love, the primal source of all energy.

Just as there is stored within an atom enormous power because of the interaction between neutrons, protons, and electrons, likewise there was inherent unlimited energy in the Godhead because of the interrelationship between Father, Son, and Spirit. And the essence of this energy was love.

In that outer world love was the moving force behind every action. Love was the energizing influence at work in every enterprise. It was the very fiber woven into every aspect of Christ's life. It was in fact the basic raw material used ultimately to fashion and form all subsequent matter.

To the reader this may all seem a bit obscure, a bit beyond belief. But if we pause to find parallels upon our planet, earth, we may soon see the picture in practical terms. What is the most irresistible force upon the earth? Love! What pulverizes strong prejudice and builds enduring allegiance? Love! What binds men together in indestructible devotion? Love!

What underlies all generous and magnanimous actions? Love! What is the source of strength for men and women who gladly serve and die for one another? Love! What energizes the loftiest and most noble enterprise of human hearts and minds? Love! If this be true of selfish mortal men, then how much more is it the very life of God—and this is the life of Christ.

It was in the setting of a realm permeated by love that the generous thought of sharing it with others came into being. Of course, it could scarcely be otherwise; for if heaven was such a happy home it would scarcely have been consistent for God to want to keep it to Himself. Love insists on sharing.

So the concept was born of love that other sons and daughters should be brought into being who could participate in the delights of paradise. That such a remarkably generous endeavor was even considered is in keeping with the character of God. He chose to do this in love and out of love simply because of who He is.

> Praise be to God and Father of our Lord Jesus Christ for giving us through Christ every spiritual benefit as citizens of Heaven! For consider what he has done—before the foundation of the world he chose us to be, in Christ, his children holy and blameless in his sight. He planned, in his love, that we should be adopted as his own children through Jesus Christ—this was his will and pleasure that we might praise that glorious generosity of his which he granted to us in his Beloved.
>
> Ephesians 1:3–6 PHILLIPS

Like all other divine enterprises, it undoubtedly first found expression in the mind of God the Father. Yet it was agreed to completely by God the Son and fully endorsed by God the Holy Spirit.

Insofar as we human beings can ascertain, it was possibly one of the most daring ideas ever generated in the council chambers of God. And we may be quite sure that when the scheme was made known a wave of excitement swept across the expanses of eternity. None of the angels or other ministering spirits had ever dreamed of such a stirring project.

God was determined to reproduce Himself.

He would bring into being and sonship others like Himself.

He was intent on populating His heavenly home with freewill beings fashioned in His own character.

They would be heirs and joint heirs with Christ, His Son, entitled to enjoy eternity in ecstasy.

The thought must have been a tremendous thrill to God the Son. Now He would have brothers and sisters to share the joys of eternity with Him. No longer would He be the only child. It was a challenging endeavor. To Him would fall the responsibility of carrying it through to completion.

Of course He would have the full cooperation of God the Holy Spirit in this enterprise. Still He knew assuredly that upon Himself would devolve most of the responsibility for the ultimate success of the scheme.

He cherished the idea and gave Himself to the project unhesitatingly.

CHAPTER TWO

A Planet in Preparation

We are not given to understand exactly why God would take the time and trouble to prepare a unique part of the universe for His new project. I say *new* in a relative, human sense, because He had been in existence for eons of time before ever the earth began to take form.

No doubt it is a mark of our finite limitations that we consider this new creation of His involved both time and trouble. For really, with God time does not exist as such. He totally transcends time simply because He is not limited by the physical or geographical bounds of a single planet the way we are.

> But this one thing, beloved, you must not forget. With the Lord one day is as a thousand years, and a thousand years are as one day.
>
> 2 Peter 3:8 WEYMOUTH

Still the fact remains that looking at it from a human viewpoint the processes set in motion to produce the planet earth did require tremendous spans of time. At very best we can only hazard the roughest estimate of when the sun (a relatively small star) and its solar system began to be brought into being. Nor can it be stated unequivocally how the earth was formed and flung into orbit around the sun. Such matters have been debated and still are the subject of intense study by some of our finest minds. Relatively little is known for sure; much remains locked in the immensity of space.

One fundamental fact of which we are now confident is that matter could be and was produced from pure energy. This truth, first propounded by Einstein, opened wide the doors to our comprehension of how the universe was brought into being from the apparent emptiness of space.

The original source of energy resided in the very life and love of God. It became apparent through the activity of Christ, who has always been the artisan actively engaged in carrying out divine designs. This is seen as we observe His role in all the ongoings of history.

Always behind the scenes there stands the majestic person of God the Father. He is the author, the originator, the architect applying His thoughts, impulses, and plans to both the seen and unseen worlds. His influence, design, and energy are everywhere apparent, both in the supernatural and natural worlds.

The implementation and actual accomplishment of all His Father's purpose and plans—known more often as His will—remain the responsibility of Christ, God the Son. This applies as much to the material realm as it does the spiritual. It was the actual, personal activity of the Christ which set in motion the chain of events that have produced the physical universe as we know it. And the ultimate production of a planet capable of supporting intelligent life was His special interest.

I do not assert, from the selfish standpoint of human pride, that Christ's preparing earth for human habitation was something men merited because of any special status of their own. Rather, the emergence of the earth was of great significance because it demonstrated the magnanimous and overwhelmingly generous character of God. It was entirely His initiative!

This, incidentally, is not something that we earthmen care to admit. For untold centuries the pride of the human intellect has held that man in himself was something very special. In fact for a long time our philosophers were sure that man stood at the center of the universe.

It is exceedingly difficult, even today, with our rapidly expanding horizons of knowledge of outer space, for men to accept the view that man is of secondary consequence.

It requires a certain element of intellectual honesty and humility to admit and recognize God's master mind in the universe. It is even harder to concede the energetic activities of Christ in creating and sustaining the universe.

Uniquely it is the official work and responsibility of God's Spirit to transmit this information to us. He acts as the agent at work enlightening our minds and arousing our understanding to grasp precisely what God was, and is, doing.

Though God the Spirit is eternally active, He does not draw attention to Himself. He endeavors always for us to see the work achieved by the Christ. He centers our interest in Him. Basically this is because God has chosen to make Himself articulate through Christ.

So it is that when it was decided to prepare the planet earth for human habitation, it was Christ who carried out this daring concept. I use the word *daring* deliberately, simply because we have no knowledge of any other such sphere in space capable of supporting human life. It may well be that far out in the enormous expanses of distant galaxies, or perchance even in our own Milky Way, other beings exist who, like us, have a capacity to correspond with the infinite God. But no definite evidence of this has ever been deposited with man.

On the contrary, we are given to understand by God's Spirit that the planet earth was a unique place prepared with meticulous care for a peculiar new people: people with a very pronounced capacity to communicate and associate with God Himself.

Just how long Christ—God's Son—and His coworker, God's Spirit, were actually engaged in preparing the planet remains a mystery. What we do know is that it was He who set in motion all the physical, chemical, and biological forces that were to fashion it. Scholars, scientists, and theologians have debated for years about the possible duration of time required to produce the planet and the people on it.

As with so many unanswered questions which confront mankind in the universe, I see no reason to be unduly agitated about the length of time or precise techniques required to prepare the earth.

For after all, if we are to be realistic, it must be admitted that God's work with this world is still not done. The original systems Christ set in motion from its inception are still in action. The seasons come and go; day and night pass; new mountains are made; old ranges are worn away; rivers rise and fall to change the landscape; continents drift apart; tides ebb and flow, while the sea ever sculpts the shore.

It is my contention that we have insufficient data to become dogmatic about the birth of this planet earth. I say this in sincerity. The scriptural account given in the first chapter of Genesis is very brief. At best it provides only a bold outline of the basic events which took place in an orderly sequence. It is indeed a meager amount of data on which to propound prolonged arguments, as so many have endeavored to do. Undoubtedly there are inherent in that brief résumé certain basic concepts still beyond our finite comprehension. Only the ultimate revelation of having this explained to us in detail at some later date by the Christ who was there in person will finally settle the matter of just how it all happened.

Likewise I would remind the skeptics and self-assured scientists, who may tend to scoff at the scriptural record, that even the best of human minds have only very limited data on what transpired in those titanic times when earth took shape. The multiplicity of theories advanced and the debates which still rage over the origin of the earth, life itself, and all subsequent species of plant and animal forms later to emerge, are evidence of our relative ignorance.

For my part, I am prepared to accept the idea that making the earth was a very long and painstaking process. Seldom do I see much to make me feel that God is ever in a great hurry as men are. Somehow, everything He does bears upon it the stamp of careful thought, precise procedures, endless effort, and tremendous attention to minute details. This is true whether it be the majestic grandeur of a mountain shaped under the relentless rasping of giant glaciers for thousands of years, or the growing of a tree that gently adds ring to ring of wooden layers with the passing seasons.

Christ touched on this theme when He Himself later came to reside on the planet for a short spell. He pointed out, for example, that even the number of hairs on a head is known to God. He emphasized that no fledgling sparrow fell from the nest without its being of direct concern to the One who had brought it into being. In other words, none of the objects of the natural earth world were just mere "things" to Him. Rather, they were all of personal and intimate interest simply because from their beginning He had been intimately involved in their production. They were what they were because of the basic concepts originally conceived in His mind and later put into operation by His enterprise.

To view the planet earth from this standpoint is to see it in a dimension of great beauty and wondrous unity. Even the astronauts when looking at the earth from outer space have exclaimed again and again over the unique breathtaking splendor of their earth home. It is doubtful indeed if any other body in all the universe is so wondrously wrapped in wraiths of white clouds, iridescent blue oceans, warm brown landscapes, and refreshing green mantles of vegetation.

Precisely how all of this masterpiece of terrestrial architecture emerged out of the emptiness of space—which, in reality, is not truly empty—must remain to us an enigma. But we may be quite sure that the Christ was there, actively engaged in its orderly development. For it bears upon it everywhere the indelible imprint of sublime order and unity and integrity. Here the Master Craftsman was at work, fashioning a superior piece of workmanship.

> Now Christ is the visible expression of the invisible God. He was born before creation began, for it was through him that everything was made, whether heavenly or earthly, seen or unseen. Through him, and for him, also, were created power and dominion, ownership and authority. In fact, all things were created through, and for, him. He is both the first principle and the upholding principle of the whole scheme of creation.
>
> Colossians 1:15–17 PHILLIPS

We need pause only a few moments to examine under a microscope the breathtaking beauty of a butterfly's wing, the fastidious fabric of a feather, the intimate structure of a snowflake, the exquisite symmetry of a seashell, and we sense deep down, instinctively, the imprint of One who cares—and cares very deeply. This was the impact of Christ's touch upon the planet as it came into existence.

Are we surprised to see the same principles, the same underlying laws, the same forces that functioned so wondrously well in His outer world of eternity, applied equally to this little earth world? Are we not glad to think He confirmed these same principles when He later chose to use such ordinary objects as wheat, salt, flowers, soil, and sheep in His parables to help our dull hearts and slow minds to grasp something of the grandeur and glory of God and heaven?

His parables were precise statements of spiritual truth made apparent in physical form.

It is one thing to state, rather casually, that Christ created all things. It is quite another to try to come to grips with the enormousness of such a concept in our minds and hearts. If we honestly believe He was before all things, and by Him all things came into being, we are forced to some astonishing conclusions.

First we must accept that His knowledge, understanding, and familiarity with all scientific and mathematical disciplines exceed anything known on earth. We must concede that He is the supreme mathematician, the ultimate physicist, and the most erudite chemist. For by these disciplines He not only produced the universe but maintains it in all its infinite intricacy. We must face the awesome reality that He is the absolute astronomer and at the same time the most profound philosopher. For ultimately He alone has the capacity to fully comprehend and embrace the full enormousness and rationale of the universe.

When we come to ponder this same Person—the Christ—in relation to our planet earth, we are obliged again to rethink our thoughts concerning Him.

In order to fashion it as He did, with its incredible array of plants, animals, insects, birds, fishes, reptiles, microorganisms, and man himself, demanded the attributes of deity. His insight into science staggers our imaginations. He is the greatest botanist, zoologist, and biologist of all time. And so we could go on to enumerate all the fields of knowledge in which He alone holds all prior knowledge and absolute prime position.

It is no wonder that the epithets bestowed upon this Person in the Bible tend to exhaust human language. Little marvel that men, when inspired by God's Spirit to write about Him, eventually end up with phrases which at their best are rather earthbound. For instance, *King of Kings, Lord of Lords, Maker of heaven and earth, Alpha and Omega, the Beginning and the End, from everlasting to everlasting*—all demonstrate our inability to fully encompass the overwhelming Person of Christ.

Yet, for me, as an ordinary layman, perhaps the most moving aspect in the preparation of the planet lies in the painstaking care applied to the project. My meager mind cannot grasp the greatness of God in trying to understand the stars. The enormous expanses of outer space boggle my imagination. But something of the strength and tenderness and thoughtfulness of Christ comes through to me every time I stand awestruck by a sunset or a sunrise. When I pluck a wild flower and sense the smooth, satin texture of its petals, when I inhale the delicate fragrance of its perfume, something of His special skill and care and artistry touches my heart. Or when I go to walk upon the grass, springing green after rain, shining iridescent with silver droplets under golden sunlight, I know that He put a special part of His own careful thought and planning into every aspect of the earth. Back and beyond every bird song, every tumbling leaf in the wind, every cloud soaring across the sky, lie the wondrous, eternal laws and principles which He applied methodically to the planet.

I am completely convinced that as He saw it first taking shape from a formless mass of whirling gases in outer space there stirred within Him a thrill of expectancy. As each successive stage was successfully initiated under His definite direction, a deep sense of divine satisfaction swept through His being. It was all meticulously programmed and all systems were progressing on schedule. Not only did the actual ongoing of the plans provide pleasure, but also the exquisite beauty and incredible diversity of life emerging must have delighted Christ enormously.

He touched on this when later in His human experience He referred to wild field lilies as being so extraordinarily beautiful. They still impressed Him with their splendor. Yet He had been the first to see them thrust themselves up from the raw virgin soil of the primeval planet.

The appearance of all subsequent species of insects, fishes, reptiles, birds, and mammals, must have excited Him.

He knew them all firsthand. He was familiar with precisely how they had been formed and fashioned. The Master Artist and Artisan looked on His work and was glad to comment, "It is good."

It is important for us to appreciate that not only was He deeply concerned about the detailed development of the planet but also equally pleased with the end product. Of course in one sense we cannot say that the earth was finished, for it is still undergoing enormous changes—the reasons for which will be touched on in a later chapter. But basically the work of preparation was completed when the earth was fit for human occupancy.

Before man appeared on the scene, we must realize, a great, overmastering sense of harmony and serenity characterized the scene. It could not have been otherwise. The balances and counterbalances of natural processes were in perfect poise. The interplay and interaction of natural laws were of such order that there was complete harmony within the biota. All of them reflected the character and mind and personality of their Innovator.

Admittedly this is not easy for us to picture. In rather simple layman's language we might refer to it as a pristine paradise. But this is a bit beyond us, for we are totally conditioned to a world which is anything but a paradise. Every place we turn, if we are at all sensitive in spirit and mind, we sense stress, tension, death, and deterioration. In the context of our present-day world we stand by utterly dismayed at the increasing devastation wreaked upon the earth. Even the most callous individuals are becoming aroused and alarmed over the pollution and despoliation of the planet. We find in almost every realm of life, from the most primitive marine organisms of the oceans to the most sophisticated human societies resident in great cities, destructive and dangerous forces at work. All the biological systems of the biota are subjected to enormous stresses and strains. So overwhelming are the implications of all these trends that many leading thinkers insist the end of the earth is imminent. But away back before the advent of man, the planet was breathtakingly lovely. It was a supreme achievement of divine diligence. In design, in operation, in appearance, it bore the stamp of the great Artisan and Artist—Christ Himself.

CHAPTER THREE

And Then, Men

The appearance of man upon the planet was a momentous event: not only because of what he would *do,* but even more important, from God's standpoint, because of what he *was.*

Momentarily we must go back in our minds and remind ourselves that the reason for man's arrival on the scene was to satisfy God's own heart-hunger for children. He longed to share His own life of love with others like Himself. It is tremendously important to keep this clearly in view. Without this basic understanding, all that follows may only bewilder the reader.

This being the case, we must conclude that the first humans were fully able to communicate with God. There was no barrier between them and their Father in heaven, no misunderstanding between them and their Creator, the Christ of God.

They were totally and absolutely complete in their manhood. They were likewise totally and absolutely complete in their divinity. This is what is meant by true *man* standing unstained and unsullied in his original state.

It is not the least surprising that God would derive personal pleasure from communing and conversing with such people. In fact we find Him coming to consort with the first couple in the cool of the evening, eager to share Himself with them in a most remarkable manner—by walking with them.

There is something distinctly unique in the realization that all through subsequent human history God very often chose to approach people when they were walking or traveling. Somehow Christ just loves to come alongside and have a chat. That is when many people seem to sense His presence best.

It was during these early conversations with the first human beings that Christ imparted some of His Father's will and wishes to them concerning the world in which they found themselves. Not only did He clearly delineate what their responsibilities and privileges were, but also He conveyed to them precisely some of His own basic concern for the wondrously complex world He had fashioned.

To be true to Himself, Christ had no alternative but to be the supreme conservationist. What He had brought into being He was concerned should be preserved. And the initial picture of man painted for us in Scripture is that of one placed in a magnificent environment with definite instructions to tend and husband it with care.

> The Lord God placed the man in the Garden of Eden as its gardener, to tend and care for it.
>
> Genesis 2:15 LB

Contrary to much distorted teaching on the subject, early man had no need to subdue nature. He found himself a harmonious part of the whole scheme of creation. That he was endowed with an intellect superior to that of other life forms in no way implied it was for the purpose of subjecting them to his personal whims. The sense in which he was given "dominion" over all the earth implied, rather, a profound responsibility for the preservation and perpetuation of his earth, with all its beautiful life forms.

This is an enormously important point. It completely escapes most scholars and theologians. Yet it is inherently true to the very person and nature of Christ. The very essence of His character is *to care*. And by this I mean to care very deeply, with intense feeling. After all, the inner heart of selflessness and divine love is caring. So it was natural, and to be expected, that when man was made in God's likeness the cardinal aspect of his character, too, would be that of concern and caring.

Of course we can scarcely conceive of such a serene setting. We earthlings, who are now so completely conditioned to the chaos and carnage that characterize the present planet, cannot imagine a natural world not red in tooth and claw. We find ourselves left limp trying to even picture a plant and animal community in which there are no predators nor those preyed upon, no death and no decay following in the wake of the endless struggle to survive.

But if we are true to the character of God and if we are consistent with the person of Christ we have no other alternative but to accept the idea of a delightfully durable world, free of death, free of decay, free of deterioration, free of destruction. I am quick to concede that this is not an easy thing for us to envisage. The first impulse is for us to dismiss the thought with a shrug of our shoulders as pure fantasy.

We cannot, simply because the subsequent teachings of Scripture are replete with very positive assertions from God Himself that such a setting will eventually be re-created. This is generally referred to as the "new heaven and a new earth." What is more, Christ Himself has made it His personal part in God's program of redemption not only to restore man but also to remake heaven and earth in this former condition of utter perfection.

The very first thing entrusted to the care of early man was his own environment—that is to say, the whole world around him in which he had been placed. Put in modern language, his entire outlook and attitude was to be that of a conservationist. This is made very clear to us in the opening chapters of the Bible. I confess it baffles me a bit how men have, in the history of our race, been able to use these passages as a mandate for exploiting the earth. One of the grievous charges levied against Christianity by its opponents is that the Book of Genesis has been the basis for appalling ruination of the planet by supposedly pious people, carried out in the name of so-called progress.

It is significant that early man was given to understand that he could use any fruit or vegetation for his own sustenance. From this we must conclude that it was all beneficial and therefore completely integrated with his need of nourishment. In no sense was there the terrifying struggle to survive which has subsequently become the theme of so much modern thought.

There were two other attributes of early man which are essential for us to understand. That he was made in the likeness of God does not mean simply similarity of appearance as much as it means similarity of character. Not only was he one who "cared," but he was also one who inherently was to be *creative,* just as Christ was creative.

Whatever man did was, by virtue of his very inheritance of divine life, intended to be useful and constructive. At the very core of God's thinking when He brought human beings into existence with Himself was the idea of doing something beneficial. In other words, the major imprint of the Maker on man was that he in turn should be a maker, a creator—one who did good, who accomplished something constructive. This whole outlook was bound up tightly with the concept of caring, or, as has been noted earlier, of loving. For in fact to love is to care, and to care is to love. And, strange as it may seem, the opposite of love is not hate, as is so often imagined; rather, its opposite is *not to care.*

It follows as a natural corollary to this that the man who loved, cared; and because he did care, he would wish to be creative and constructive in a positive way. We later see this carried out so clearly in the life of Christ when He became a man and lived amongst us. He went about "doing good."

These two attributes of caring and creating were in turn bound together with a third attitude—that of cooperation. Put in another way, it was essential to the harmony and serenity of the early paradise for all there present to be persons who cared, who were creative, and who cooperated for mutual benefit. It being understood, of course, that the cooperative enterprises would always be those in accord with the wishes and will of God Himself.

Actually it could not be otherwise. For from eternity there had been complete harmony between God the Father, God the Son, and God the Holy Spirit. They were three in one not only in love but also in purpose and unity of mind. Heaven above and man's early earthly paradise below were what they were simply because of the exquisite environment in which each cared for the other; each was constructive and each cooperated fully in carrying out the will of God. And that will was and is simply the magnificent harmony of heaven.

CHAPTER FOUR

Problems in Paradise

There is no one but God Himself who knows how or why problems should have arisen in paradise. No doubt the trouble first started in heaven itself, and at a much later time was transferred to the paradise of earth. We are told very little about how the dark clouds of dissension and division began to cast their gloom across the glorious realm of God.

Human beings have pondered this problem of evil all through human history. They have searched ardently for its origin but without real success. We know it, like gravity, is a force with which we must grapple, but how it came into being originally and why it should continue to desecrate the universe remain an enigma.

Probably the best we can do as common people is to accept the idea that for every positive force there must be a negative counterpart. We must realize from the evidence all around us that in the very nature of things what one does, another undoes.

The information given to us by God's Spirit in this matter of the origin of sin or evil is extremely scanty. We understand that the problem began with pride. Pride, of course, is simply self-interest. It is self-*ishness*. It is the precise antithesis to self-*lessness*, or self-sacrifice. And since the latter is the essence of the character of love and therefore of God Himself, it stands in direct opposition to Him.

It is obvious that pride and love are mutually exclusive. The two cannot keep company. They are inherently repellent. So it follows that the instant pride became apparent in paradise a problem of major proportions had arisen. And if we are to grasp fully all that God the Father, His Son our Saviour, and the gracious Holy Spirit have endeavored to achieve ever since that awesome hour, we must understand their abhorrence of pride.

Pride found first expression in the person of Lucifer, son of the morning, chief archangel in heaven. We conclude that because the angels and other ministering spirits are of a lower order than God, they are prone to pride. For Lucifer alone was not the only angel to succumb to selfishness. Many others like him, with selfish self-interests, were ultimately to join his ranks. These are referred to in Scripture as evil spirits.

> How art thou fallen from heaven, O Lucifer, son of the morning! how art thou cut down to the ground, which didst weaken the nations!
>
> For thou hast said in thine heart, I will ascend into heaven, I will exalt my throne above the stars of God: I will sit also upon the mount of the congregation, in the sides of the north:
>
> I will ascend above the heights of the clouds; I will be like the most High.
>
> Yet thou shalt be brought down to hell, to the sides of the pit.
>
> Isaiah 14:12–15

Those beings belonging to Satan and his entourage are in direct opposition to Christ and God. The difference being so diametrical that Satan, or the devil as he is sometimes called, is referred to as the Prince of Darkness.

It is important at this point for us to recognize the enormous implications that the attitudes of such a one as Satan had in heaven. Here was a person who because of selfish self-interest did not care what chaos his conduct created. Instead of being positive and constructive in character, he was totally negative and destructive. He was diametrically opposed to God. He refused to cooperate or in any way comply with the will and wishes of God.

We know very little of the tremendous upheaval that took place. But Scripture does inform us that such a personality could not be permitted in paradise. He was banished from the beautiful realm in which he had been so significant a member and then exiled to the planet earth. This was to produce enormous problems for Christ. But even more so, Satan's presence was to produce continuous conflict for human beings who had to cope with him. My personal impression is that a sense both of dismay and foreboding must have swept through eternity when Satan began to make his first overtures to men. It may well have been a foregone conclusion that men could not meet the subtle subversion of such a schemer without being victimized. After all, God's archenemy, who before had been His archangel, would now seek some measure of revenge for his own personal downfall. He would endeavor to drag others down with him.

I do not think it is presumptuous for us to wonder why God the Father would allow Satan such latitude. Its attendant risk to His own plans for producing children was enormous, and He must have been aware that the human race on whom His heart had been set would be subverted.

The only reasonable conclusion which we, as mere human beings, can come to, is, of course, open to debate. But it was a demonstration—a sublime demonstration—of His own essential love. It was to be the ultimate proof of His personal willingness to go to the very extremes of self-sacrifice in order to deliver His children from the entanglements of Satan which would bedevil them.

It follows that if the presence of such a person as Satan created problems in heaven, that same personality would produce enormous difficulties in the earthly paradise. There man, at first, was a freewill agent able to enjoy his exquisite environment in complete harmony with his Creator, the Christ. He knew nothing of dissension or division. His desire was to do God's will and comply with His wishes. It was a serene state of affairs but it was not destined to last long.

No doubt Christ Himself was acutely aware of this. And he knew moreover that if men submitted to the wishes of the devil, then from that point on there would be a continuous confrontation between Himself and Satan. This confrontation would continue all through human history.

It was essentially a spiritual war in which there would be no pause or letup until ultimately He Himself had triumphed. There could never be an armistice. There would be no cease-fire. The end would be total and complete annihilation of Satan with all his cohorts. It could not be otherwise, simply because ultimately it is impossible for God to tolerate the presence of evil. Complete love cannot countenance the existence of sinister selfishness. That which is positive and constructive abhors that which is negative and destructive. The forces of cooperation are greater ultimately than those of division and rebellion. In short, goodness ultimately must triumph over evil, simply because God is good!

But the agony and anguish of the ensuing struggle is the story of human history. And it is only as we view the pathetic pageantry played out upon the planet against this gigantic backdrop of Christ and Satan in conflict that the drama makes any sort of sense. Apart from this concept, the earth, its people, and all their painful stories are but a meaningless mockery. It is absolutely impossible to discover either point or meaning to the horrendous history of the human race except in the context of a gigantic battle between good and evil—between Christ, God the Son—and Satan, His archenemy.

Scripture sometimes refers to it further as the conflict between light and darkness—life and death—good and evil—love (selflessness) and self (selfishness)—spirit and flesh—the old nature and the new nature. Essentially, the struggle that ensued for thousands of years was a spiritual struggle. It has been a struggle for the souls and destinies of uncounted millions of men and women. It is a struggle on God's part to produce children like Himself despite the most devilish designs of Satan to thwart His purposes.

We cannot, from a purely human point of view, begin to grasp the enormousness of the spiritual war that has raged on unabated for so many centuries. It completely dwarfs and overshadows the most appalling wars perpetrated by earthmen—though we must also understand that in part the latter are but a by-product of the former. For it delights the devil to create chaos and confusion in every human situation. This makes his own destructive interests and ambitions more readily realized. He gloats over global upheavals. He revels in human misery. He chortles over every crisis that will turn men away from God to choose evil.

Amid all this carnage we can detect the presence and personality of Christ, God's Son, and His gracious Spirit at work counteracting the forces of evil. It is true His approaches are less spectacular, less bombastic, less obvious than Satan's. Still they are there, and ever as of old, there comes the quiet, unpretentious appeal to the will in man. For after all, man was made with a free will—able to choose, able to respond, able to cooperate with God or Satan, with good or evil.

In essence this was the enormous risk God ran in making men. Perhaps He did not see it as a risk, but rather as a means of revealing Himself in human history. In any case, we do know that when the chips were down and Satan had his first encounter with man, Adam, the outcome was cataclysmic. Instead of being willing to forgo his own selfish self-interests, he chose to exercise them and exert his own will, contrary to the best interests of both himself and God.

Precisely at this point there was a duplication on earth of what the devil had already done in heaven. In other words, Satan had his first son (Adam) and daughter (Eve), simply because they had demonstrated the identical behavior pattern that he himself had demonstrated in heaven. Instead of cooperating with God's explicit wishes and instructions they had chosen to act against them. Self had asserted itself in direct opposition to the declared will of God.

The upshot was, as might be expected, the setting in motion of destructive forces. Death became a dire reality. Decay and deterioration immediately came into play. Labor, toil, pain, sorrow, suffering, separation, disease, and all the attendant evils that make up so much of life on earth as we now know it were initiated at this point. It was inevitable. In the very nature of things it was quite unthinkable that those who had chosen to be selfish and uncooperative and in antagonism to the will and purposes of the eternal God should be able to live forever. Just as Satan had deliberately doomed himself to eventual death, so, too, had those who willfully disobeyed God's instructions and chose knowingly to be identified with the devil's family.

This is a fearsome fact. Yet it is supremely logical. At no time has God our Father ever condemned any man or woman to death. Rather, by virtue of their own choices and own decisions—whether or not they determine to cooperate with God—do men decide their own destinies.

Christ when He later moved amongst men in human form emphasized this point repeatedly.

> For God sent not his Son into the world to condemn the world;
> but that the world through him might be saved.
>
> John 3:17

Yet in spite of all His assertions, men will not believe Him.

So it was that in the initial epic encounter between Adam and Satan, sin came into being as a sinister force upon the planet, as inexorable as gravity itself. Just as the earth's gravitational pull drags everything down to the lowest level, so sin acts as a perpetual down drag on every person born. In man's very makeup there lies an inherent and inescapable tendency to "go down," to choose evil rather than good, to prefer darkness to light, to cooperate with selfishness rather than to do what God desires.

It was in this setting and because of deliberate disobedience or lack of cooperation that the sudden acute awareness came over this first couple that they had in fact cut themselves off from their heavenly Father. When He came, as was His habit, to have a friendly chat and happy conversation in the cool evening air, they were in hiding. His cry of "Adam, where are you?" is the first conversation recorded for us between God and man. In it we are hearing the eternal, unchanging call of God our Father to His wandering, self-willed, lost children. It was a refrain to be repeated all through human history. It was not that He did not know where they were. He did, all too well—with terrible pain. Rather the call implied "O man, do you know where you are—away from Me, cut off, separated, lost, doomed by your own decision to do your own thing and go your own way out into darkness, facing death with the devil as company?"

Perhaps this is the place to pause a moment and consider the enormous implications of death's sudden appearance on the planet.

First we must understand what death is. It is the cessation of life. But what is life? Even our most brilliant minds cannot fully define it. The best we can do is to say it is a condition or state in which any person or organism is said to be in correspondence with its environment. Or put another way, when an organism is actually absorbing and deriving strength and sustenance from its surroundings, so that it can survive, it is said to have life.

The first couple cut themselves off from God by their deliberate choice to go counter to His will. This ruptured the harmony of their relationship. Correspondence between them was severed. And from that moment the shadow of impending death hung over their future. Prior to this it was in the very presence and person of God that they had moved, lived, and enjoyed their eternal being.

Their continuous communion with God implied unending and eternal life of a most bountiful sort.

But now their disobedience led to death. An unwillingness to cooperate, to comply with the wishes of God simply produced its own consequence—death. It was a very straightforward case of cause and effect.

Because of this cataclysmic break between God and men, a whole chain of related events was set in motion. Obviously God could not and would not dare to tolerate the idea that those who were opposed to Him—who willfully chose to be selfish, destructive anarchists—should live forever. So He took prompt action to insure that all of earth would be subject to control and limitations imposed upon it by death and decay.

The net result was a paradise totally perverted because of the diabolical behavior pattern of its prince, Satan. Men now found themselves cut off and alienated from God their Father and Christ their companion brother. The earth itself became subject to destructive forces of death, decay, and deterioration. The energy-conversion cycle of birth, life, death, decay, rebirth, life, death, and decay came into play. All life upon the planet found itself shackled to the wheel of death that would grind on relentlessly for untold centuries.

Of course for the devil this may have seemed at the time a tremendous triumph. He had quite dramatically thwarted the immediate plans and purposes of God. He had prevented people from being identified with God their Father. Instead they had been debased to become his own followers, children of the devil. From now on human beings would wrestle with evil, with the wiles of Satan, with their own selfish natures. It was to prove a horrendous ordeal for millions of men and women.

Are we surprised then to see Christ's concern at the awful darkness, death, decay, and despair that had settled menacingly over His supreme masterpiece? Is it any wonder that Satan should become His implacable enemy? It was a desperate, devilish situation that demanded a divine solution.

CHAPTER FIVE

God's Rescue Operation

From God's viewpoint the planet earth was no longer a peaceful paradise in which human beings could live in pleasant perpetuity. Now it was a doomed spaceship hurtling through history, destined for ultimate destruction. Its inhabitants, though endowed with a capacity to communicate with Himself, would turn rather to their own devices to decide their own awful destinies. Amid death and decay, destruction and degeneration, they would lie and kill and sin and struggle selfishly to survive the awful darkness of their despair.

It was a dreadful picture.

God grieved, and still does grieve deeply, over the plight of the planet and its people. Again and again He was to be plunged into remorse by the selfish, self-willed stubbornness of the human race. There would be times when He even regretted that He had made men. The pain they brought Him far outweighed the pleasure. His most persistent and patient overtures to men would be rebuffed and ridiculed.

In spite of all this, true to His own gracious character, He formulated a plan to rescue and redeem men from their predicament. His very nature of loving concern simply demanded it. So He put into action the divine rescue operation whereby it was possible for men and women, otherwise destined to perish, to find immortal life that transcended their own death: That those alienated from Himself, the living God, could be restored to an intimate, vital personal relationship with Him: That in very truth His own eternal, never-ending life could be transmitted to mortal men: That they might still become, as He had always envisaged, His own sons and daughters. Drastic situations demand divine solutions.

To God it was self-evident that He Himself, at enormous personal cost, would have to intervene directly in human history. He would have to become intimately identified with man in his dilemma in order to deliver him.

The Scriptures of the Old and New Testament are the report of that story. They reveal the never-ending enterprises of God, through Christ, executed to rescue and restore faltering and fallen human beings.

Being absolutely just, God in mercy continually gives men opportunity to turn back and be reconciled with Himself. With enormous long-suffering and patience He pursues men down the long corridors of time inviting them to repent and walk with Him in contented communion. He pleads with people, as a Father with His children, to enjoy the wondrous relationship of His family.

Yet, in spite of such generous overtures, most men would reject Him. Throughout history only a few would turn toward Him and deliberately choose to enjoy His companionship. Their lives dominated by sin and selfish desires and the subtle deceptions of Satan, they preferred to pursue their own proud path of perverseness.

This was demonstrated clearly in the very first hostility that arose between Cain and Abel. In a fit of selfish, jealous rage Cain murdered his brother. When queried by God about his brutal behavior, his crude, evasive retort was—"Am I my brother's keeper?"

With that one stabbing sentence he laid bare the inner motives of men. It revealed the selfish, destructive, divisive character of human conduct. He simply did not care. He couldn't care less!

This was in direct and dramatic antithesis to the very character of God. There in man's first atrocity lay the preview of all his subsequent performances that would be played out upon the planet in pathos and pain.

Meanwhile God, in Christ, the first begotten amongst many sons, our elder brother, looked on stricken with anguish . . . for He cared deeply.

In fact it was something of Christ's own character in Abel which initially aroused the hatred and anger in Cain. Abel's attitude of humble contrition had been acceptable to God. His offering of a lamb to atone for his own failures found favor with his Maker. Not because there was any intrinsic merit in this animal sacrifice itself, but because of what it represented. The death of this first innocent lamb was the symbolical advance notice that all subsequent sacrifices were but forecasts and feeble foreshadowings of Calvary. For, in due course, there on the cross, Jesus Christ, God's own Lamb, God's own Son, in a divine act of selfless self-sacrifice would pay the supreme penalty for all men's perverseness for all time.

This was a titanic event of tremendous proportions toward which all the Old Testament sacrifices pointed. It was the infinite God atoning for finite men in order to rescue and restore them.

It is important to see this. Further, with our finite comprehension we must still endeavor to grasp the fact that Christ suffered as much at the hands of Cain as He did at Calvary, or as He suffers today when selfish, sin-driven men do Him to death by their misdeeds. This is because He lives outside the time/space concept which conditions our earth life. He is the eternal, ever-enduring I AM, who suffers on behalf of sinning, fallen, fierce men. John, the aged Beloved Apostle, discloses this clearly in Revelation where he points out that men's names are written and have been written in the book of life from the foundation of the world because of *the Lamb slain.*

Abel's initial rite of slaying a small lamb was but the first of the millions upon millions to be performed during the ensuing centuries. Between the offering of the first innocent lamb by Abel and Christ's own subsequent death on a crude cross thousands of years later, men of pre-Christian times would attempt to make atonement for their sins in this manner.

All the Passover lambs offered by Israel in Egypt under Pharaoh's bondage, all the thousands of lambs slaughtered in the desert camps where a movable tabernacle replaced an altar of uncut stones, all the millions of lambs butchered in the courts of the magnificent temples erected in Jerusalem were but repeated previews pointing to the Christ, the Lamb of God, offering Himself on Calvary's cross for wayward, willful men.

It is a measure of the majestic generosity of God that He would accept such sacrifices as a substitute for the penalty which perverse men should otherwise have paid with their own lives. Something of the love and concern of Christ comes to us clearly as we see Him suffering, sorrowing, and agonizing for the sins and selfishness of the stubborn human race, while they go free, acquitted by the atonement made on their behalf by the sacrificial lambs . . . lambs that were but symbols of His own suffering Self.

It had been commonly held and naively supposed that after man fell in the Garden he was more or less abandoned and left to his own devices. But this is simply not so. God just is not like that. In tender compassion He pursued every possible means to maintain an intimate relationship with man. And an intrinsic part of that endeavor lay in His own enormous suffering—screened from human view by the substitutionary sacrifices offered on ten million crude altars across uncounted centuries of time. Yet amid all this carnage Christ came in quiet, unostentatious suffering to be identified with sinning, struggling earthmen, who were His lesser brothers.

That this was actually so is borne out by the bold assertions and forecasts of the Old Testament prophets. Both in their psalms and in their prophecies they spoke of their Redeemer—their Messiah—their Coming King who one day would be revealed. Yet much of the language in which these utterances were couched spoke of a suffering Saviour—of a lamb bearing away the sins of the people, of a substitute dying in their stead. Many of the Old Testament stalwarts, moved upon by the presence of the Spirit of Christ, were brave and bold enough to bear the reproach of Christ, God's Lamb, slain from the foundation of the world. For example:

> By faith Moses, when he was come to years, refused to be called the son of Pharaoh's daughter;
> Choosing rather to suffer affliction with the people of God, than to enjoy the pleasures of sin for a season;
> Esteeming the reproach of Christ greater riches than the treasures in Egypt: for he had respect unto the recompence of the reward.

By faith he forsook Egypt, not fearing the wrath of the king: for he endured, as seeing him who is invisible.

Hebrews 11:24–27

In the writings and thundering of the great prophets there is drawn in bold lines a dramatic portrait of Christ as man's Redeemer and substitute Saviour:

He is despised and rejected of men; a man of sorrows, and acquainted with grief: and we hid as it were our faces from him; he was despised, and we esteemed him not.

Surely he hath borne our griefs, and carried our sorrows: yet we did esteem him stricken, smitten of God, and afflicted.

But he was wounded for our transgressions, he was bruised for our iniquities: the chastisement of our peace was upon him; and with his stripes we are healed.

All we like sheep have gone astray; we have turned every one to his own way; and the Lord hath laid on him the iniquity of us all.

He was oppressed, and he was afflicted, yet he opened not his mouth: he is brought as a lamb to the slaughter, and as a sheep before her shearers is dumb, so he openeth not his mouth.

He was taken from prison and from judgment: and who shall declare his generation? for he was cut off out of the land of the living: for the transgression of my people was he stricken.

Isaiah 53:3–8

He shall see of the travail of his soul, and shall be satisfied: by his knowledge shall my righteous servant justify many; for he shall bear their iniquities.

Isaiah 53:11

By the intuition of their spirits, enlivened by the Spirit of Christ Himself, they saw and knew and understood that He was with them. They were aware of God in a way much more profound than most of us realize. Ancient men were not all groping in the dark, as some modern poets and writers would lead us to believe.

If, without bias or prejudice, we study carefully the accounts of numerous Old Testament characters, we discover that they were keenly aware of the presence and person of Christ. Of course they did not call Him Jesus Christ. That was a name conferred upon Him during and after His birth and life in Palestine. It was not until He began His public ministry amongst men that they recognized Him as the Christ—God's anointed One, God in human form, Jehovah God—the Lord of the Old Testament. This He Himself endorsed by confirming that even before Moses was, I AM.

It is deeply moving to observe the winsome and wonderful way in which men of old sensed the presence of the Lord. To them He was exceedingly real, exquisitely near, and very cognizant of their affairs. He walked with them. He talked with them. He was a counselor. He was a companion with whom they communed in the privacy of their own spirits. He was their captain. He was their comforter. He was their spiritual leader. He was their ruler. He was their inspiration. He was their idol—in short, He was their God.

It is virtually impossible to read the Old Testament record without being overwhelmed by the intimacy that existed between the Lord and those who sought His companionship. The Lord God Jehovah—Yahweh of the Old Testament—was none other than Jesus Christ of the New Testament, but under another appellation.

Again and again this One came to His people. Over and over He appeared in person and under various guises to those who sought Him earnestly. God in Christ has ever done this with the human race. Even at Bethlehem, when born amongst us as a little child, He came unknown, unrecognized—the King disguised, God in mufti—the Saviour, who is Christ the Lord. God incognito!

We see Christ coming to commune with Abraham as Melchizedek, king of Salem. But we also see Him coming to Abraham as the Angel of the Lord, being none other than the manifest presence of Christ Himself. This is made transparently clear for us in Isaiah 63:8, 9:

> For he said, Surely they are my people, children that will not lie: so he was their Saviour. In all their affliction he was afflicted, and the angel of his presence saved them: in his love and in his

pity he redeemed them; and he bare them, and carried them all the days of old.

Immediately after Abraham had shown his willingness to offer up his son Isaac as a sacrifice on Mount Moriah, we are told of the remarkable manner in which the Angel of the Lord—none other than Christ Himself—intervened to assure Abraham of His presence with him.

> And the angel of the Lord called unto him out of heaven, and said, Abraham, Abraham: and he said, Here am I. And he said, Lay not thine hand upon the lad, neither do thou any thing unto him: for now I know that thou fearest God, seeing thou hast not withheld thy son, thine only son from me.
>
> Genesis 22:11, 12

Events similar to this occur throughout the entire Old Testament. Christ was continually coming to men in various forms and guises. Sometimes it was in the form of men, sometimes in the guise of an angel; on other occasions by visions, dreams, or revelation, by a voice speaking directly from heaven, and sometimes through the impulse of His own Spirit.

As we recognize this fact a great serenity steals over our hearts. We see that at no time has Christ ever withdrawn Himself from the world of men. Always He has been present, powerful and active on behalf of those who endeavored, even feebly, to comply with His wishes and desires.

The great promises of God made to Moses and Joshua, to David and Isaiah, that He would be with His people so long as they walked in His way are no less stirring than the same promises made by the same Lord to His disciples in the New Testament. Always, throughout all of human history, Christ has been coming and coming and coming to men. Today He comes to us by His own gracious Spirit. He draws near to us through His Word, He speaks to us through His own people, in whom He resides.

Yes, the Christ is always close as the air around us. He envelops us with His presence. Most men and women—now, as in the Old Testament times—are simply not responsive to Him nor eager to make His acquaintance. But to those who do, He is ever there!

Over and beyond all of this there ran all through pre-Christian times the clear conviction that this One—this Lord, this Christ, the Anointed of God, the Messiah—would one day make Himself manifest in human form upon the planet as a regal resident. This theme of the "Coming King" runs like a royal thread of gleaming gold all through the dim pages of ancient history.

It began with the assertion made by God to Satan, in the Garden, that Christ would come to conquer him: That despite his worst efforts to pervert the planet and men upon it, his devices would be defeated by the coming of the Christ.

This forecast and promise found a hundred different forms. It was the great hope. It was the word of the Living God to struggling men. Enoch lived by it and walked with God in perfect harmony for three hundred years. Likewise it was a lodestar for Noah, Abraham, Isaac, Jacob, and Joseph, to whom it came as a covenant between God and men that enabled them to exercise implicit faith in God's veracity: That in due course a Redeemer—a Saviour—would appear on the world scene.

Moses, Joshua, Gideon, Samuel, David, and scores of other godly men and women of great spiritual insight and stature saw afar the shining prospect of the Messiah—the Christ—who would step onto the world's stage in person. They were called the *seers*—those who could "see" with eyes of spiritual discernment and faith. And what they saw stirred their hopes, enlivened their confidence in God, and empowered them to transcend triumphantly the darkness and despondency of their times.

The prophets and poets of God, during the long centuries before the advent of Christ, spoke and sang of His coming like birds whose early morning calls announce the glory of a new day long ere dawn dispels the darkness. Even throughout the long centuries of silence during and after the captivity in Babylon, a strange, still, awesome expectancy stirred in men's spirits.

The Messiah—the Christ, God's anointed—would come . . . but when?

> For unto us a child is born, unto us a son is given: and the government shall be upon his shoulder: and his name shall be called Wonderful, Counsellor, The mighty God, The everlasting Father, The Prince of Peace.
>
> Isaiah 9:6

CHAPTER SIX

The World in Waiting

Rarely does God rush.

Unlike impatient, impetuous, hasty humans, He carries out His plans and accomplishes His purposes with majestic precision, unhurried and unflurried. Whether it be the awakening splendor of a sunrise spreading its light across the earth or the breaking of divine illumination into a darkened human spirit, His methods are precise, painstaking and perfect.

So, when in fullness of time He felt human history, darkened by the deepening despair of hardhearted men, was at last in need of special light, He made preparations for the coming of the Christ. It was He who would come quietly, gently onto the world scene like dawn across the eastern sky.

That celestial light of the living Christ, when spread over the earth, would flood across all the artificial frontiers and barriers of men. No longer would it be the glimmering light enjoyed by a favored few. It would be the splendor of the Son of God Himself becoming available to all men everywhere.

This simply had to happen.

Perhaps the most important reason it had to take place was simply that men did not understand God. Their ideas of Him were often grotesque and false. As the centuries rolled by, their view of God became ever more distorted. He was looked upon as an austere judge standing over His created earth beings in anger and wrath. They envisaged God as stern, relentless, and vindictive. To most men God was someone very remote, very detached, very indifferent to the dilemma of struggling earthmen. He was an august being almost impossible to approach except with apprehension. He was served only in fear. He was an ominous being in need of appeasement.

In brief, the concept of God's true character was but a cruel caricature.

Therefore it followed that if He was to be seen and known as He truly is, it was imperative that He appear in person on the earth's little stage.

That He was willing to condescend to such a lowly role is a majestic mystery. It is a mark of divine generosity. In no other way could finite men with their finite limitations of seeing or understanding spiritual values ever comprehend God. In no other way could they grasp the innate goodness of God. In no other way could they appreciate the love, concern, justice, mercy, and grandeur of God's character and conduct.

So, now that He was to appear in person to play a part on the world's stage, He took great pains to prepare that stage for His coming. While He waited in the wings, as it were, and while the world waited for His debut, careful preparations were in progress. Not only did these go on here on planet earth, but also out in the infinite immensities of the unseen world.

First of all, as pointed out in the previous chapter, God had been, through the poets and prophets of His chosen people, foretelling the coming of the King. The announcement had gone out. A handful of men and women actually did anticipate that such an event was in the offing. Always there was a tiny remnant who, with true hearts and pure purpose, anticipated His arrival. For the most part these were the prophets and priests and holy men of Israel.

Yet this advance knowledge was not restricted to Israel alone. We see the wise men, the ancient rulers or monarchs, drawn from the distant desert kingdoms of the East, drawn to the scene of God's advent on earth. Nor was the stupendous arrival of heaven's royalty restricted only to special, spiritual people. For humble shepherds of the southern Palestinian hills would have a part in this premier performance. God, then as now, was open and available to any receptive human heart wherever it be found, no matter how lofty or lowly its station in human society.

But the fact remained that the coming of the Christ had been a special message, borne by a specially chosen race with whom God had chosen to closely identify Himself. For not only was it their special honor to be entrusted with the heralding of His coming, but also to contribute the greater part of the human lineage through which He would condescend to enter the world scene in disguise.

It is important for us to recall, however, that this human lineage was not purely and only from Israel. In it we find names like Ruth and Rahab, women drawn into this line from pagan races by God's Spirit. God does not and will not deprive anyone of deity who truly seeks Him. Rather He delights to be identified with any who search for Him in spirit and in truth.

The coming of the Christ was also prepared for in the sphere of human society as a whole. The Greek civilization that had flowered and flourished across the then-known world had faded. Greek culture and Greek thought had had its day. But behind these had been left one of the most expressive, most beautiful, most precise human languages of all time. Greek was the lingua franca of the world. Greek was the international medium in which the exciting drama of God's great act on the human stage would be played out to the whole wide world. It was a language by which God's character and conduct would be clearly communicated to all men everywhere.

Not only were the preparations restricted to spiritual and social aspects of society, but also to the very strategic essentials of spreading the action far and wide for all men to see. For though the events of Christ's life were to take place upon the very limited stage of tiny Palestine, they would be reported worldwide. Without the benefit of mass media of communication—without printing presses, without newspapers, periodicals, radios, televisions, telephones, or space satellites—the report would still run all over the earth. How? By the power and might of the great Roman Empire.

Rome was at the pinnacle of her prestige. It was Caesar Augustus who declared that all the world should be taxed. Because of this edict Joseph took Mary to Bethlehem along a Roman road. It was along those same Roman roads, under the safety of Roman rule that men, and commerce, and news, and power, ran freely all across the world. It was along those roads and under Rome's iron rule that all the reports of God's arrival on earth would reach all men rapidly.

But even more important than the divine preparations under way on earth were the supernatural arrangements being made in the unseen realm of the eternal Godhead. There waves of excitement and expectancy swept through the angelic hosts of heaven. God, very God, in Christ the Son, was to take up residence upon the planet earth.

This time He would visit the race of earthmen—minute as specks of sand, adhering tenaciously to their tiny spaceship that hurtled through the immensity of the Milky Way—for a matter of thirty-three years. He would not come to them in overwhelming majesty as a giant deity. He would not come as a shining angelic visitor. He would not come as a mysterious spirit of sublime import. He would come as a *mere man*—nor would it be even as a man of royal human lineage, but of humble birth to peasant parentage.

This was not a game for God.

He was not participating in some party masquerade.

This was no playful performance to indulge human beings.

God's coming to men in human form was the most profound and poignant demonstration of genuine humility—of utter selflessness—ever enacted in history.

Because of the very essence of God's character and person it had to be so. Here the very Christ, creator and sustainer of not only the planet earth but—much more—of the entire majestic universe, would lay aside His majesty, His might, His prestige, His immense power to become a mere mite of humanity.

When I use the word *mite* I do so advisedly, carefully, and with enormous respect. I do so with an awesome sense of wonder, adoration, and humiliation upon my spirit.

To think that He, the Christ—who, by the enormous energy and might of His eternal deity, spoke the stars and their planets into being, who by the self-same grandeur of His godhead position sustained all the universe in meticulous precision of which the complex and multitudinous life forms on earth are but a part—*that this One would divest Himself deliberately of all such power and position, limiting Himself to a single cell,* completely staggers me.

For it had to be a single cell, a single spermatozoon, bearing the character of deity, which, by the very Spirit of God Himself, would be implanted in the uterus of a young virgin girl on planet earth.

That God in Christ would allow Himself to be so constricted—that He would accept the restrictions of becoming the smallest single common denominator of human life—is a profound and moving mystery. We are overwhelmed by this majestic magnanimity of our God. If we meditate upon it but for a moment we are humbled by the distance God has gone to deliver us in our human dilemma. The depth to which He descended to redeem men overwhelms our hearts.

To become a man—a true man, a man of human parentage but divine origin—He had no alternative but to lay aside His heavenly estate. He had to assume the same beginnings whereby we humans begin within a woman's womb in order to truthfully call Himself "Son of man"—His own favorite appellation. Yet He was also "Son of God"—the title conferred upon Him by God Himself.

So it was that the world went on watching and waiting. Men were wondering when the Coming King, so long promised by the prophets and poets of old, would appear. In the meantime the Christ of God lay gently cradled, resting in the warm womb of a shy Galilean girl for nine mysterious months.

There He waited in the wings, so to speak, for the precise moment when He would emerge upon the world's stage. There would be no blowing of human bugles to announce His birth. There would be no pomp or pageantry on planet earth to proclaim His arrival. There would be no fanfare to declare that in fact "the King had come!"

For He would be the King in disguise.

He would be God in mufti.

He would be but a babe.

Whatever declaration there would be that in truth Christ—the Messiah, the Saviour, the King of Glory—had emerged on the world's stage would have to be announced from heaven above. There they knew the good news. The angelic hosts would broadcast it with joy! Joseph and Mary were too shy to say anything.

CHAPTER SEVEN

Bethlehem and Before

This is an appropriate point to pause briefly and reflect upon the events surrounding the birth and boyhood of Christ. It is commonly supposed amongst some Christians that the unusual circumstances of Christ's coming to earth and His childhood days are believed because they were written in the record of both Matthew and Luke.

This is not really the case.

Actually the events surrounding His birth were incorporated into the two Gospel accounts because they were in fact the common property and knowledge of the early Church in the first century. The details given to us by both biographers were secrets shared with her contemporaries by Mary, the mother of Jesus, after His Resurrection and return to glory. Mary was a shy, retiring, reticent woman. She did not prattle about her private, personal affairs. And it was only after the risen, ascended Christ was recognized by His contemporaries to be none other than God very God, who had dwelt amongst them as a man, that Mary unlocked her heart's door to disclose the divine secrets God had shared with her in the coming of His Son—and her son.

It is tremendously important for us to bear this in mind. The manner in which God chose to come to earth is believed not because men wrote it up that way. It is not a fabrication. It is not a piece of poetic fiction. It is believed simply because it is so. That is how it actually happened. This was the very natural, very humble, very beautiful yet very wondrous way God chose to come and reveal Himself to us. It was the manner He decided would best suit His whole plan for His redemption and rescue of the human race. It is true its details were dramatic. The pathos and winsome pageantry of His advent have stirred the souls and spirits of men for nearly two thousand years. But nonetheless, the events before and after Bethlehem took place in precise order and sequence just as they had been prophesied and foretold centuries before. The possibilities of so many details following in such precision give them a mathematical accuracy within the laws of probability that dispels any doubt about their authenticity.

The chances that Christ would come as He did, where He did, when He did, in the way He did, all foretold long centuries before, are one in millions upon millions. In such knowledge our spirits are still: Our minds are at rest that the record is reliable.

And so we are told that one day young, lovely Mary, then a virgin maid of perhaps fourteen years, was visited by an angel. Her home was in Nazareth, a busy trading town located astride the main trade routes that crisscrossed Galilee in northern Palestine. Mary's hand had been spoken for in marriage by a respected carpenter-tradesman of the town, named Joseph. He was a man somewhat older than his little bride to be, no doubt in his very late teens or early twenties. In those days average life expectancy for hardworking peasant people was quite brief. Many people, men especially, were dead by thirty-five. So if they were to be married and raise a family it was important to start early. That is why most girls were betrothed at puberty and bore children at the tender age of fourteen or fifteen years.

In Galilee people were much more relaxed and free in their lifestyle than down in dour Judea. In Galilee it was common for young couples to consort together and revel in their early romance. No doubt barefooted Mary, with her glistening black hair, gorgeous big dark eyes, and clear, shining complexion kissed by the sun, had often stopped by Joseph's shop for a lighthearted chat. She would twiddle her toes in the soft fragrant sawdust and shavings on the floor and laugh lightly when Joseph looked at her with love in his eyes. Her cheeks and throat would flush with a gorgeous blush when he spoke tenderly of his admiration for her beauty. And her pulse would race and her heart hammer when they shared together their secret hopes of a home and family.

But now the angel visitor stood before her as she sat alone. And what he said troubled her simple soul. Why should she, of all the girls in Galilee, of all the women in the world, why should she be selected to share the secret of the Most High? Who was she to be chosen to bear the Messiah of her people, the Saviour of the world?

The angel's reassurance was comforting. It was God Himself, it was Christ Himself, it was the Lord, Jehovah, who was standing with her sharing this momentous news. He Himself, in angel guise, was announcing to this gentle girl the titanic implantation of His own life into hers. "The Lord is with thee! I am here. I am present with you in person. Be at peace."

But unanswered questions raced and surged through Mary's mind and emotions. "How can this be? I am a virgin, spoken for, but yet not married. How? How?"

By the presence and power of God the Holy Spirit.

By Him, Mary would conceive and bear the child who would be called *the Son of God.*

Gentle in disposition, cooperative in spirit, Mary, the little maiden, acquiesced. In her acceptance there lay peace.

This was a tremendous secret.

It was too startling, too stunning, too special to be broadcast. She was even too shy to share it with Joseph. But it had to be shared—shared with someone special.

In true womanly intuition Mary left Galilee to find a confidante. Who could be better than aged Elisabeth, her cousin, a mature woman who would and could understand the young girl's excitement? A spiritual soul mate who, like Mary, was herself undergoing an incredible transformation because of God's special touch on her life.

So Mary threw together a few things for a protracted visit to her cousin down in stiff, staid old Judea. Both of them were expecting. Both of them were bearing very special babes, Elisabeth's already six months on the way. They would have a great deal in common.

Three months later, Elisabeth, wrinkled with age and lined by long years under the southern sun of Judea's blasted hills, bore her first child—John the Baptist. On the day of the infant's circumcision, his father, Zacharias, stricken dumb previously because he simply could not believe his aged wife would ever conceive as the angel had said, wrote in plain language upon a tablet of clay, *"His name is John."* And therewith he began to speak.

Perhaps young Mary was midwife to Elisabeth at John's birth. We do not know. In any case, her visit was over and she returned home to Nazareth—but heavy in heart.

There now hung over Mary's soul a cloud of pain which was but the first of many pains she would endure. For when she returned to Nazareth and to her beloved Joseph, she was heavy with child.

Cruel, piercing questions raced through Joseph's mind.

He was in an agony of indecision.

Had his betrothed been unfaithful to him down in the Judean hills? What would people in Nazareth think? Should he put her away from him and break off the betrothal? Wouldn't tongues tattle now?

Then one night, as he tossed and turned on his bed in torment of mind, an angelic messenger came to him.

"Don't discard Mary. Don't distrust the girl. She is innocent. That one to be born of her was conceived of the Spirit of the Most High God. Take her as your own."

And so he did. Despite the wagging tongues. Despite the whispered gossip. Despite the sneering jests of neighbors. It took courage of the highest caliber. It was a measure of the man that he was more responsive to what God said than to what the people of Nazareth said.

So for the remaining months that the little virgin girl bore the Christ, she and Joseph carefully kept their secret of the Saviour: kept it as carefully as the reverence and respect of this man of honor kept himself from exercising his masculine rights as a married man. For when the babe was born He would emerge from a womb that was sacrosanct, never entered or touched by a male organ. It was a virgin who would present the King of Glory to the waiting world.

The time of her delivery and the Roman decree by Caesar that the whole empire be taxed, virtually coincided. The earth's greatest kingdom was extracting all it could from its subject people.

Meanwhile the kingdom of heaven was presenting earth's people with their greatest gift—freely, gladly.

Patiently, quietly without complaining, Mary on a little ass, Joseph walking by her side, the two set out from Nazareth for Bethlehem. It would be a rough ninety miles over winding rocky roads that wound through the hot Judean hills. Even if they only took the trip in easy stages it would mean five or six days of torturous travel for a woman nine months pregnant. The increasing heat as they moved ever south toward the Negev desert, the endless jogging of the surefooted little donkey, the crowds and commotion of other taxpayers jostling back and forth across the country were wearing and wearisome for Mary.

By the time they reached Bethlehem it was later than most people who had come there to be registered under Caesar's tough decree. In vain desperation and growing despair Joseph searched for a spot to stay. The rough, rude hostelry was already overcrowded with clamoring guests. As a last effort he turned to the countryside—barren, blasted by the southern sun, and riddled with rock outcrops of limestone ridges. There amongst the limestone caves he stumbled upon a crude underground stable where normally shepherds would keep their sheep at night. Now it stood empty because drought conditions forced the owners to graze their flocks afield by night.

The sheep corral, filthy as only an Eastern animal enclosure can be, reeked pungently with manure and urine accumulated across the seasons. Joseph cleared a corner just large enough for Mary to lie down. Birth pains had started. She writhed in agony on the ground. Joseph, in his inexperience and unknowing manly manner, did his best to reassure her. His own outer tunic would be her bed, his rough saddlebag her pillow. Hay, straw, or other animal fodder was nonexistent. This was not hay- or grain-growing country. Stock barely survived by grazing on the sparse vegetation that sprang from the semidesert terrain around the town.

Mary moaned and groaned in the darkness of the sheep shelter. Joseph swept away the dust and dirt from a small space in one of the hand-hewn mangers carved from the soft limestone rock. It was covered with cobwebs and debris fallen from the rock ceiling. There, as best he could, he arranged a place where Mary could lay the newborn babe all bundled up in the swaddling clothes she had brought along.

There, alone, unaided, without strangers or friends to witness her ordeal, in the darkness, Mary delivered her son. A more lowly or humble birth it is impossible to imagine. It was the unpretentious entrance, the stage entrance of the Son of man—the Son of God, God very God in human guise and form—upon earth's stage. In the dim darkness of the stable a new sound was heard. The infant cry of the newborn babe came clearly. For the first time deity was articulated directly in sounds expressed through a human body. Those sounds brought cheer and comfort and courage to Mary and Joseph. These peasant parents were the first of multiplied millions upon millions who in the centuries to follow would be cheered and comforted by the sounds that came from that voice. God is come. God is with His people. Immanuel.

Outside the stable that night all had been still, except perhaps for the distant call of a scavenging jackal. The stars, bright, intense, pulsing, desert stars, cast a pale glow across the countryside. In the faint starlight little clusters of sheep accompanied by their watchful owners moved across the barren landscape in search of grass to graze or brush to browse. It was always preferable to pasture the feeble flocks at night when dreadful droughts ravaged the countryside. At least they did not have to contend with the desperate heat and thirst of the midday sun. Nor were they troubled by flies or parasites that tormented sheep in the daytime heat.

But the shepherds were troubled men. Day after day, week after week, they watched the pastures shrivel and die. Their sheep too wasted away. The older ewes with worn-out teeth could not survive on the hard herbage. Finally they would collapse in utter weakness. Starved and sickly, their carcasses littered the landscape. Vultures, crows, and ravens fed upon the corpses by day. Jackals fought over the offal by night.

And the shepherds turned their troubled eyes to search the skies for clouds or hint of rain. There was none: only drought . . . drought . . . drought.

But even that was not all. Each man wrestled with the anxiety of his own heart. He struggled with himself wondering if he could survive. Had Jehovah, the Lord of Israel, forgotten His people?

Were the heavens shut up against His children that there was neither rain to refresh their land nor dew to refresh their flocks?

Still more—as if to add insult to injury: Had not Rome—that hated, despised, pagan power that ruled Israel with an iron fist—had not Rome demanded once again that all should be taxed? How could they pay? Where could money be found when their flocks were decimated by drought and they themselves were driven into abject poverty? For the shepherds outside that night things were terribly dark and terribly black. It was a tough, rough world into which Christ came.

But into the blackness of the shepherds' despair, into this dark night of their ordeal, there suddenly burst a new light. It was a terrifying sight. These watchers of the desert skies had never before witnessed such a spectacle. A brightness far surpassing stars, planets, or even the glory of the full desert moon engulfed them. They threw up their hands to shield their eyes from the glorious splendor of the angelic visitor. His radiance completely enveloped them. The whole countryside lit up. Their flocks fled, scattering in wild panic.

Then those wondrous words *"Fear not"*—eternal words that always fall first from God to man—words that still our spirits and soothe our souls. *"Fear not"*—words that would be spoken again and again from this first night to the last night that Christ came to His dearest friends in that room where they were locked in fear after His Resurrection.

Always, ever, God comes to men with good tidings, good news, of great joy and good cheer.

And for these desperate, driven, destitute shepherds the angelic announcement was doubly significant. A Saviour, a Redeemer—perhaps from the tyranny of Rome—had come. He was born that night in Bethlehem, in one of their own filthy, crude, empty stables. If they went now they would find Him lying peacefully in a manger, wrapped in swaddling clothes.

Then suddenly, the whole night sky seemed aglow and alive, pulsing with the presence of hundreds of heavenly beings. There came from them joyous sounds of praise and adoration. It was a jubilant chorus from a choir that had never been matched on earth before. The angelic hosts of heaven were announcing to simple, humble shepherds the debut of deity.

But why to shepherds? Why should an impoverished handful of sheep men be the first to know that Christ—the Messiah—the Saviour of not only Israel, but all the world, had come? Why hadn't His arrival been broadcast to the high priests, or the Sanhedrin, or the politicians—or even the bankers and businessmen? Why humble shepherds?

For two good reasons.

All of Israel's history had been closely identified with sheep and shepherds. From Abel, the first shepherd, who offered the first lamb as an acceptable sacrifice to God, many of Israel's outstanding leaders had been shepherds. Abraham was a shepherd; so was his son Isaac and his grandson Jacob. Moses had been a shepherd for forty years before leading Israel out of Egypt. David, Israel's greatest king, was a shepherd. Isaiah, the venerated prophet, spoke freely of the coming King as a Shepherd who would tend His sheep.

So it was appropriate and in keeping with this great and noble theme that the shepherds of Bethlehem should be the first to know their Shepherd King had come.

The second reason is perhaps even more important. Always, ever, the sacrifice of spotless lambs, without blemish, had served as the symbol of atonement and appeasement between God and men. The sins of men had been propitiated for by the death of an innocent lamb.

Now the Lamb of God—God's own Son, of whom all the other lambs had been but a symbol—had appeared on the scene, to be offered in due time as a sacrifice at Calvary. So what the angelic messengers were announcing really was, Here is God's Lamb—slain from the foundation of the world—whose life and death will atone for all men of all time.

Therefore it was proper that the shepherds of Israel, those who up until now had provided the sacrifices for Israel, should know God had supplied His own sacrifice. His own spotless, sinless Lamb had been born that night in one of their own simple stables. Was not the setting in order?

Later in His life, when Jesus, the Christ, began His public ministry amongst men, this truth was validated by John the Baptist. John, who was born of Elisabeth and was not only a first cousin to Jesus but also His divinely appointed forerunner, shouted when he first saw Jesus coming to him, "Behold, look; there is the *Lamb of God* who takes away the sin of the world."

The shepherds, on that still night, standing awestruck under the desert skies, knew fully what the angel's message meant. They may have been simple plain men but they were informed men saturated in the teachings of the Scriptures of the Old Testament prophets. And the significance of the events that night was not wasted on them.

Quickly they gathered together, forgetting their flocks for the present, and hurried to the stables in Bethlehem. A quick search soon led them to where the newborn babe lay cradled in a manger. Being goodhearted, generous country folk, they no doubt heaped their hearty congratulations on Joseph and Mary in awe and wonder. They would tell ecstatically but with restrained excitement about the visit and proclamation of the angel and his attendant choir.

In the bighearted, happy way that sheep men have, they would insist that Mary and Joseph bring their tiny mite of a newborn child into one of their own humble homes. Not for another hour would they think of leaving their newfound friends in the stable with all its stench and filth.

Excitedly the good news swept along the shepherd lines of communication. Each shared with others the happy news of what had happened in and around the tiny town of Bethlehem that night. Visitors came by the score, bearing their simple birthday gifts of white milk, white cheese, white wool, and perhaps even the odd white lamb.

These were but tokens of esteem and gratitude to the Lord God who alone could bestow on them the gift of His own Lamb, bearing His own white righteousness for His people.

CHAPTER EIGHT

The Child Jesus Stirs Jerusalem

Joseph and Mary, in strict compliance with Jewish custom, had their infant circumcised at the very tender age of eight days. This rite was an ancient custom initiated by Abraham almost two thousand years before the birth of the Christ child. It was a mark of special distinction separating God's chosen people, who lived by implicit faith in Him, from their pagan neighbors who worshiped false gods.

According to Israelite tradition, a newborn child had no personal identity for the first seven days of its life. But on the eighth day it was given a name—and if it was a male child, circumcised at the same time. Thus Mary and Joseph, in implicit obedience to the instructions given to them by the angel who had visited them in Nazareth months before, called Him *Jesus*—meaning *Saviour*—for He shall save His people from their sins.

From that point Jesus, the Christ, was known, recognized and identified as a member of the children of Israel. His lineage traced back directly to famous forebears. It included both well-known and obscure characters. Yet in very truth it enabled Him later in life to rejoice in His favorite name for Himself—*the Son of man*.

Five weeks after the babe had been named, His parents took the short trip from Bethlehem to the great temple in Jerusalem. There in strict adherence to the Mosaic laws they would present their son to Jehovah God. The mother would complete her rites of purification. Two small turtledoves would be offered in sacrifice to seal and confirm the ritual.

All of this would mark the beginning of a boyhood in which Jesus would be reared most rigidly in total allegiance to Jewish law and tradition. There would be no glossing over obligations or slipshod carelessness in His upbringing. Whatever had been decreed of God would be carried out in meticulous detail by these devout young parents. They had no ordinary child in their care.

When they entered the great temple, so prominent in Jewish life, they were met by an aged veteran named Simeon. Simeon was amongst the very last of the Old Testament "seers." Upon him the Spirit of God reposed in rich manner. To him the Spirit of God had given promise that he would, before his death, set eyes upon the Messiah—the Christ.

The moment Mary, with Jesus in her arms, stepped through the giant doors into the temple, Simeon knew immediately—"Here is the Messiah!" Tenderly he took the infant in his thin, bony arms. With eyes uplifted in glowing wonder and gratitude he gave thanks to God. Here in his hands he held the Christ, who was the glory of Israel. Here before his dim old eyes that had waited so long, *he saw the Light of the World*—a light to enlighten not only his own people but all the gentile world.

It was a moving moment, not only for the withered, gnarled old man but also for the awestruck parents. Out of the thousands of children that Simeon had seen pass through the temple doors, Jesus—their little Jesus—was selected and recognized as "God Incognito." He was the One who had been awaited for hundreds of years. He was *God in Man*. He was *Salvation* for fallen men of all time everywhere.

Apart from John the Baptist, who a few years later was to prophesy about the Christ, Simeon was the last of the Old Testament prophets to speak glowingly of God's promises to His people. He confirmed completely, "He that was to come, has come."

But as though this in itself was not evidence enough to Mary and Joseph, who cast furtive, knowing glances to each other, another special person appeared. It was Anna. Anna was even more ancient than Simeon. She was at least 105 years old. If married at 14, then widowed at 21, she had since spent eighty-four years serving the temple. This would give her 105 years of age, most of them spent devoutly in prayer, fasting, and meditation.

Dear, wrinkled, sweet old Anna was in close communion with God. His Spirit rested on her as surely as it rested on Simeon. And she likewise knew immediately that the tiny infant still held tenderly in Simeon's gentle embrace was none other than the Redeemer—The Christ—who would bring deliverance.

In her elation and ecstasy she broadcast the good news to all her friends and associates in the city. Anyone who with anticipation expected and looked for the Coming King was reassured by Anna that in fact He had arrived.

But, strange to say, the witness and testimony borne by these two devout old people as to the identity of the Christ child scarcely stirred the surface of busy life in Jerusalem. Their outbursts of joy and gratitude to God for fulfilling His promises to His people barely rippled the spiritual atmosphere of the ancient city. Jerusalem—steeped in tired traditions; cynical with its cunning, contriving priests; material minded with its temple traffic and trade—was not ready yet to receive its Redeemer and its proper King.

Let Simeon prophesy if he wished, through his long white whiskers. That was but the babbling of an old, feeble man. Let Anna praise God if she so desired with her croaking, feeble voice and bent body. She was but a deluded old lady.

Meanwhile Mary and Joseph, overwhelmed with quiet awe and inner wonder, completed the dedication of their child—then quietly left the city.

The record is not clear, nor are all the details given of what transpired during the next few years. It is thought by some that Joseph and Mary had received such a warm and royal reception from their newly made shepherd friends in Bethlehem that they returned there to live for a short interlude.

Joseph no doubt set up shop to make plows and yokes and tables and benches for his shepherd friends. And in any case it would be a relief to be away from the idle gossip, false fabrications, and stinging insults of Nazareth. Time takes care of many things. People would, in time, forget the strange betrothal between Mary and Joseph.

Meanwhile the Spirit of God had moved upon the hearts and minds of wise and powerful men far, far to the north of Bethlehem. Away up in the remote regions of the Caspian Sea, hundreds and hundreds of miles removed from little Bethlehem, sage astrologers scanned the night skies with searching eyes. For uncounted years they had meticulously monitored the movements of celestial bodies. Their knowledge of the sun, moon, stars, planets, and great constellations was immensely accurate. Without the advantage of telescopes or other sophisticated optical instruments they had studied and plotted the course of heavenly bodies for untold centuries.

In amazement they observed the conjunction of the planets Saturn and Jupiter. But even more startling was the sudden appearance between them of an evanescent star. It was a unique phenomenon. Only rarely did it ever occur. Centuries later it was to be confirmed both by Kepler, the great German astronomer, then by Humboldt, the famous naturalist and scientific writer.

The wise men set out to follow the star. They were wealthy men, potentates in their own right, more powerful than most kings. To them monarchs and rulers turned for insight and direction in their empire affairs, just as Nebuchadnezzar had in ancient times turned to his wise men for counsel. Yet it remained for Daniel, upon whom the Spirit of God reposed, to disclose the meaning and accurate interpretation of the king's dreams.

So the wise men set out to search for the new Monarch, the new King, whose star they had seen rise to shining brilliance in the night sky. He it was whose rule would usher in a new era for men upon the planet. Find Him they must. Honor Him they must. At any cost, anywhere.

No one knows how many wise men set out upon this quest. Simply because they bore three kinds of gifts does not denote there were only three magi. There may have been three, five, ten, or even twenty. For long months, with profound patience, their caravans moved across the wind-blown sands and rocky hills of the Middle East . . . searching . . . searching for a new Sovereign.

Gradually they drifted ever southward. From oasis to oasis across the burning deserts they moved. Every night their eyes traced the movement of the star leading them persistently into Palestine. Eventually they stood in Herod's court, seeking knowledge of where the new King might be found.

Herod's wretched heart of bitter hatred and flaming jealousy trembled in terror. "Another king? One who would usurp my throne? Where? Why? When was He born?"

Few were the tyrants more terrible that ruled any people than this profligate monster from the Arabian desert. He was neither Roman, Greek, nor Jew. He was an Idumean who by graft and treachery finally ascended the throne of Jerusalem. He murdered his first wife, murdered his mother-in-law, murdered all his own sons born to him by his first wife, murdered his brother-in-law, and burned alive a number of Jewish leaders.

He was a match for the cruel Caesar who ruled in Rome. There corruption, decay, and awful licentiousness prevailed. Young men and women grew old before their times, sotted with sensuality. The aged were crippled and broken, with wretched lives wasted on debauchery.

It was into this kind of world, under these kinds of monarchs that Christ, the King of Glory, entered human society as a child. It was a society rotten to the core, riddled with intrigue, rife with hatred, malice, and envy.

And now Herod, with cunning, hoping for swift action to wipe out this new contender for his crown, inquired of the chief priests where He might be found.

Little did he know that this very King had already paid his royal city a brief visit. But the news of His arrival had barely stirred a hair.

Now, however, when the news came from afar, brought by foreign gentiles of great prominence, not only Herod's heart but all of Jerusalem was stirred with fear and grim foreboding. It is ever thus. The lowly are despised, the proud and mighty favored.

Advised that the newborn infant King could be found in Bethlehem, the wise men quickly resumed their trek. As prophesied by Micah of old, they found the young child, now some months old, and His mother in their home. Joseph was away, perhaps on a short trip to buy up a supply of tough acacia wood from some lone woodcutter in the hills.

The potentates prostrated themselves in humble, devout adoration before the tiny tot. He was presented with precious gifts of gold and frankincense and myrrh, each of enormous worth.

Yet, strange as it may seem, each of these priceless presents represented material, passing values which Christ Himself would later denounce as of no value. What was a man profited if he gained the whole world with its glittering wealth, its special religious rites, its pomp and pageantry, yet lost his own soul? But the gifts were received with gratitude. They came from hearts that searched for heaven's own best gift to men. For God had so loved the world that He gave His only begotten Son, that whosoever believed in Him, both as Saviour and Lord, might not perish but save his own soul and have everlasting life.

Warned in a dream that Herod's intent was to destroy and murder the King of heaven, just as he had murdered all other rivals, the wise men went home another route. They skirted around Jerusalem and retraced their long journey back to the land of the Chaldeans.

Herod was furious! Double is the heated vengeance of a fox who has been outfoxed. He had been double-crossed. His cruel rage flamed out fiercely. He would not be outwitted even by the wise men of the East.

What he did not know was that he was being outwitted by God Himself.

For the angel of the Lord warned Joseph in a dream to flee to Egypt with Mary and their child. This he did without delay. The precious gifts of gold and frankincense and myrrh would be their means of support during the long stay in the foreign land.

Herod's mercenaries moved in on Bethlehem. Under their cruel swords scores of innocent children, two years of age and less, perished. Parents wailed. And Herod relaxed—but in vain.

CHAPTER NINE

Formative Years

The record left to us of Christ's formative years is very meager. Often, so often, I have longed for more insights into the boyhood and early manhood of Jesus Christ. It is as though a curtain of silence had been drawn across the nearly thirty years spent in Nazareth. So the best that can be done is to base our ideas on the temper of His times: to see the typical manner in which a Jewish lad of those days would be reared.

It is not known exactly how long Joseph and Mary lived in exile in Egypt with their infant son. The cruel Herod died in A.D. 4. After that it was deemed safe for them to return home. Is it not strange that this King Incognito should recapitulate the precise history of His people? Just as Abraham, the founding father, fled to Egypt, then later returned to the land promised him by God; just as Israel with his household of seventy souls sought shelter in Egypt, then four hundred years later a nation of two million made the great Exodus under Moses back to Palestine; so now the Christ reenacted those ancient episodes. It was total identity with His people.

Joseph, as head of this tiny household, now decided to return to Nazareth. Not only was that home to him and his wife, but even more important it was to become home to the boy Jesus. The ancient seers had forecast that even though their Messiah, their Coming King, was of the seed and lineage of David, that though His royal descent would be from the tribe of Judah, still He would be known as a Nazarene.

To be a Nazarene was no honor. To be a Nazarene was to be despised by the devout and haughty Jews of Judea. Later in life when Philip found Jesus of Nazareth and sensed with deep spiritual intuition that He was the Christ, the Messiah, he ran to share the good news with his friend Nathanael. The latter's incredulous reply was, "Can any good thing come out of Nazareth?" Was it possible that out of a town held in such contempt, with such a terrible reputation, anything divine could come?

God's ways are not man's ways. Nor are His thoughts our thoughts. His Son would not grow up sheltered from the rough and tumble of His times. He would not be walled around with soft, sanctimonious surroundings. He would not be nurtured within the safe seclusion of a spiritual ivory tower. He would not be the product of some exclusive religious school like the Sanhedrin.

God's Son—God in man—would grow up fully exposed to the abrasive stresses and strains of His day. He would mature as a man amongst men. He would be One who had tasted and drunk deeply from the stream of human struggle, labor, and sweat, just to survive.

This is one of the great glories of our God. He is not a remote being detached from our desperate earth days. He is not a sublime deity who never entered the turmoil of our earth struggle. He is God, very God, who took on Himself the form of a man. He lived amongst us most of His earthly life as a carpenter's child who became a skilled craftsman in His own right. Our life was His life. Our delights were His delights. Our sorrows were His sorrows.

This makes Him so approachable. This endears Him to us. This draws us to Him with the quiet reassurance that He knows, He understands, He identifies with us in all our difficulties.

Nazareth, where Jesus spent most of His years, was a rough, rowdy crossroads town. It sat astride the main trade routes that crisscrossed northern Palestine. Trade, commerce, and caravan traffic were its lifeblood. Here men and merchandise from all across the Middle East and around the Mediterranean world moved in restless, ceaseless, creaking caravans. Not only did the merchants bring the finest of their countries' wares, but also the poorest and most profane of their pagan customs. Their saddlebags bore jewels, spices, perfumes, and fine carpets. Their crafty, cruel minds brought bestial habits and licentious longings. Prostitution, slavery, and narcotic traffic swirled through Nazareth like raw sewage, spilling over its streets, polluting its shops.

This was where Christ grew up.

Somehow I always picture the boy Jesus as a sturdy, strong, barefoot lad with cheeks and arms kissed by the sun. With coal black hair and piercing bright eyes He was a picture of eager youth and energetic vigor. No doubt in company with other boys His age He climbed and explored all the hills that surrounded Nazareth like a giant amphitheater. There He watched the wind blowing the wild flowers. He followed the hill farmers as they raked their hay and harvested their grain. He stealthily stalked the wild foxes and found their secret dens. He came across bird nests in the shrubby hedgerows and trees. Perhaps once or twice He picked up a fallen fledgling from the ground, tenderly replacing it in its nest.

The sights and sounds familiar to the Galilean countryside were some of the fine fabric woven into His early years. They obviously made an enormous impression on Him. Later in life when He spoke profound and imperishable truth in common layman's language it was always couched in terms of trees and grass, seed and soil, sparrows and foxes, vineyards and vinedressers, weeds and wheat, wind and weather.

The manner in which He used natural phenomena to demonstrate supernatural truth was both winsome and wonderfully effective. To His hearers it was clear that He spoke with knowledge, authority, and conviction because these elements of the countryside were familiar to Him. But even more remarkable, though of course most of His audience never caught on, was that He was the Supreme Artisan who had initially brought them into being. Is it surprising that this One who was thought to be but another common Nazarene later spoke with such startling authority yet disarming simplicity?

I am sure that often when He returned home after an exhilarating scramble in the hills, He would bring a bunch of wild flowers for Mary. Or perhaps an armful of dried grass and twiggy thorns for fire beneath her cooking pots. And here or there He would pick up a broken branch from which Joseph could fashion a crude candlestick.

He would have His chores to do at home. He was the first of seven children to be borne by Mary. As the eldest son, the responsibility for His siblings would rest heavily on His strong, broad shoulders. In fact He had to shoulder the full responsibility for the entire family when Joseph died at a comparatively early age. So He knew what it was to work long hours, to have menial jobs and sweat-stained hands.

But before that we are given a glimpse into the quiet life of this lad. We are told that He grew to be strong—not weak, emaciated, or effeminate as so many artists have portrayed Him. We are told that He increased in wisdom. He was not slow or dull or simpleminded. His intellect was alert, His mind keen, His perception acute. We are told that the grace and favor of God were upon Him. His was a blessed boyhood. He moved toward manhood in quiet strength, bright awareness, and godly behavior.

He was a balanced boy who because of His strong inner resources did not have to bluster about or misbehave to attract attention to Himself. He did not have to put up a front or show off to prove His prowess. His magnificent manly physique, His keen intelligence, His gracious spirit endeared Him to His contemporaries as well as to His Father in heaven.

In fairness it must be said that Joseph and Mary no doubt had a prominent part to play in the shaping of His character. In a Jewish home it was the father's solemn responsibility to instruct his children in the Scriptures. The greatly venerated book of Deuteronomy gave explicit and detailed instructions about how children were to be taught God's commandments. This was not a casual, hit-or-miss procedure. The parents took it dead seriously. The Scriptures were read, recited, and discussed every day. This was done whether one was at home, sitting up, lying down, or walking in the countryside, be it morning, noon, or night. Scriptures were wrapped around the posts of the doorway. They were worn on the hands. They were suspended around the head. In short, a Jewish child grew up surrounded and saturated with the laws of God.

And Jesus was no exception.

Even when He went off to the local synagogue to take His schooling, all of it was closely bound up with the Old Testament.

Until the age of ten, practically the only textbooks Jesus ever saw were the Old Testament scrolls handled with enormous reverence by the rabbi.

The first poems or writings Jesus ever memorized were from these sacred scrolls. The reciting done in unison was drawn from these Scriptures. The only text ever used to teach Him how to read was the Old Testament. When His childish fingers began to copy out the first Hebrew letters and words, they were following the lines written long ago by the Old Testament prophets and poets.

Are we surprised that His mind and emotions and will were steadily impregnated and molded in total conformity to the Scriptures? As He read, recited, wrote, and studied those ancient writings, there stirred within Him an awesome response to their truth. His Spirit was acutely aware that many of those great prophecies and poems pertained to Himself. There stole over Him an ever-increasing realization that He was the central character around which they would be consummated.

Perhaps the old bearded rabbi in Nazareth found it a bit awkward to have such a spiritually precocious boy in his classes. No doubt from time to time Jesus raised His hand to ask penetrating questions that were utterly beyond the old man. After all, the brightest and wisest rabbis always gravitated to Judea. It was a common saying that "if you wanted to be wise in God's Word you went to Judea. If you wanted to become rich you stayed in Galilee." So the level of spiritual learning and enlightenment in Galilee—especially in an uncouth town like Nazareth—was pretty poor and very low.

Consequently the boy's questing spirit and soaring soul went unsatisfied. Neither could Mary, His mother, nor the simple, gentle Joseph find adequate answers to the penetrating questions coming from this lad now nearly twelve.

Then an exciting event took place. His parents would take Him with them to the great temple in Jerusalem for the annual Passover feast. Not once since He had been presented there to God as an infant in Mary's arms had there been a chance to see the temple, much less enter it. This was a special privilege reserved only for older boys, who at the age of twelve were initiated into the temple ceremonies, thus becoming "Sons of the Law." Roughly, it resembled the rite of confirmation carried out in many churches.

For Jesus this was to be one of the great highlights of His youth. Along with thousands of other religious pilgrims, He and His parents pushed their way along the hot dusty roads leading south toward Jerusalem. Jews from all over the then-known world congregated at Jerusalem. They came from Libya, Egypt, Arabia, Persia, Mesopotamia, Greece, even as far as Rome, and naturally from all over Palestine. The hordes multiplied as they converged on the city. Roads and trails were clogged with the chanting crowds. An air of electric excitement gripped the people as they sang the great psalms of ascent approaching the glistening city on its high hills. Praises to Jehovah swept through the streets. And amid the million or more devout Israelites, one lad of twelve literally trembled with exultant expectation. It was His first visit as a maturing young man to this mighty temple in this mighty city.

O Jerusalem, Jerusalem! If only Jerusalem could know that her greatest hour of opportunity was approaching. If only she could recognize that this lad Jesus who now gazed upon her with wondering eyes and racing pulse was her rightful ruler. If only she could see that by spurning and rejecting Him her own dreadful destiny would be sealed. But she could not! Jerusalem was drunk, blind with the desire for power, fame, and gain. Gold was her god. She had sold herself for shekels. Her heart was not ready to receive the King of Glory.

Jesus knew and sensed this at once.

Quickly and surely, once the Passover feast was over, Jesus found His way to the leading temple rabbis. Here were the most brilliant, most learned, most spiritual of all Israel's teachers. If anyone had answers to His questions it would be these august scholars. Their entire lives had been immersed in studying the Scriptures.

For three full days He plied them with questions. His insight into spiritual truth astounded them. Where would a youth of twelve gain such a broad grasp of God's Word? Surely no second-rate rabbi in Nazareth could impart such spiritual understanding! They in turn put difficult questions to Him . . . questions that they themselves had never resolved . . . questions tinged with doubts, misgivings, and perhaps even skepticism. Swiftly, surely He replied, dispelling their doubts and assuring them of the absolute veracity of God's Word.

So engrossed were student and scholars in their discussions that the days sped by. Where Jesus slept and who provided His meals has often interested me. Did no one stop to wonder where His parents might be? It is a measure of the depth and intensity of their dialogue that secondary considerations hardly entered their thoughts. Suddenly Mary and Joseph, both very distraught, showed up in the temple searching for the lad.

Mary's remonstration about His behavior seemed to puzzle Jesus. His gentle reply—*"Did you not know I had to be in My Father's house?"*—both reassured her and rebuked her. He was where He should be. And what was more, He now recognized clearly and fully that it was God who was His Father, not Joseph.

Mary and Joseph, slow of spirit and heavy of heart, seemed quite unable to understand. Mary, fallible Mary, admitted as much to Dr. Luke, years later, when he wrote the record of this incident.

Jesus for His part, much enlightened, spiritually stimulated, was content to go home. He would still be subservient to these two plain peasants. Yet on into manhood He matured, ever gaining in wisdom, spiritual understanding, and favor with God and men.

For the next eighteen years of our Lord's life we really know only one thing: He was a carpenter! There is nothing demeaning about being one who works with wood. But it is surprising that God would see fit to have His only begotten spend most of His earthly sojourn at a simple workbench in a dusty shop on one of Nazareth's side streets.

It does tell us one thing: Honest work, well done, no matter how humble, is of eternal worth. It bears great dignity and it is every bit as sacred as sermons from a pulpit or prayers from a priest. With God there is no distinction between the sacred and the secular. It is the spirit in which they are performed that proves their merit.

From His later life it is evident that Jesus was a gregarious man who loved all sorts of people and who in return was loved by many. No doubt children loved to call at His little shop. They would run their hands through the soft shavings and smell the sweet fragrance of the fresh-sawn wood. Meanwhile Jesus would talk to them tenderly of eternal things.

Because there fell on Him the enormous responsibility of providing for His mother and younger brothers and sisters, He never felt free to leave home and establish one of His own. He deliberately denied Himself the privileges and pleasures of a married man. It was part of His great selflessness.

In His daily toil of handling, hewing, and shaping the tough wild olive wood and hard acacia common to the region, He developed tough sinews and hard muscles. He knew what weariness and work and sweat and strain took from a man.

In buying His lumber and selling His finished yokes, plows, chests, tables, benches, and candlesticks, He had to barter or deal in hard cash. He was exposed to all the whims of a busy, boisterous, brutal world. Amid that world He came to be known as *the carpenter of Nazareth*. If one wanted excellent workmanship at an honest price, he went to Jesus. His craftsmanship was first class. His price was right. But best of all He loved people and could become your friend.

Then quietly one spring day He laid down His tools. He dusted off His strong hands. He walked out of the shop never to return to it again.

CHAPTER TEN

The Desert Firebrand

About a year before Jesus the carpenter set aside His hammer and saw, chisels and plane, His famous forerunner, John the Baptist, son of the desert, stepped on center stage. Israel had not seen nor heard such a flaming prophet for over four hundred years. The long silent years before the advent of Christ had been devoid of divine pronouncements from God. There had been no great seer to stir men's hearts.

When John, burned black with the desert sun, his long, uncut raven locks hanging loose like a shaggy mane, shouted his mighty warnings to Israel, all Jerusalem and Judea were alerted. Could this be their long-awaited Messiah? Was he the promised King? Perhaps this was the Christ.

John flatly denied it. He was not the Christ! He was but a voice in the wilderness calling God's chosen people to prepare for the reception of their royalty. But much more than that: He was calling a decadent people sunk in despair, deceit, and debauchery to repent and turn to God again.

His cries did not go unheeded. His flaming eyes and fearless courage startled Israel wide awake. His uncompromising stand against evil wherever it was found—whether in Herod's palace, the Roman legions, the priesthood, or even amongst powerful ecclesiastical people—met with wide acclaim. He did not pussyfoot around issues of the day. People of every class and stratum of society streamed out to the desert valleys beyond Jordan to hear him. They came from all of Jerusalem and Judea. It has been estimated that in the short, lightninglike flash of his eighteen months' ministry he addressed some six or seven million people.

No prophet in all of Israel's long history had ever approached John in prominence. Without benefit of any public-relations program, without mass media of communication except the common human grapevine, without any religious or political backing— simply alone and single-handed, under the Spirit of God—he shook Israel. The winds of his message swept the country like a raging brush fire.

Again and again this firebrand sent from God shouted across the desolate desert dongas: "Repent, for the kingdom of heaven is at hand! Prepare the way of the Lord. Make His paths straight!"

It would be difficult to imagine two men of greater contrast than John and Jesus. Yet their lives were, in the plan and economy of God, inexorably intertwined. They were as complementary to each other as night and day, winter and summer.

It will be recalled that John's mother, Elisabeth, and Jesus' mother, Mary, were cousins. Elisabeth was a very aged woman, living quietly with her aged husband, Zacharias, in a small Judean village where he was priest. When told by the angel of the Lord that his wife, who had never borne children, would conceive and bear John, he simply could not believe it possible. Because of his lack of faith he was made dumb for the next nine months.

When she was six months into her pregnancy, Elisabeth was visited by her little cousin Mary, still just a virgin maid, betrothed to Joseph up in Nazareth. When Mary came into the house, John leaped with elation in his mother's womb, aware that Mary was bearing the Lord of Glory in her body. Under the inspiration of God's Spirit there had been this prenatal recognition by John of whom Jesus was. It is a unique phenomenon in human history.

John preceded Jesus at his birth by six months. When presented to the Lord at eight days, onlookers asked the stricken Zacharias what his name should be. Unable to speak, he wrote out deliberately as instructed by the angel of God, "His name is John!" And with that act of obedience his speech was restored.

John's upbringing was diametrically opposite to that of Jesus. He was the only child of very aged parents. He grew up in the quiet, religious atmosphere of a priest's home. In large measure he was sheltered from the struggles and strains of the working world. He gradually grew into a solitary sort of man who preferred solitude and serious, still meditation to mixing with crowds. Eventually John gravitated to the life of a desert recluse. The forbidding wasteland of sand, rock, scrub thorn, and blazing sun was in keeping with his stern and solitary nature. But more than that, John was deliberately prepared by God for special service. It is noteworthy that this was a divine pattern of dealing with men that proved very effective. Abraham, Jacob, Moses, Joshua, David, John the Baptist, and later Paul were all men with desert years. Years during which they were brought into intimate, prolonged contact with God. Years in which God could in the stillness and solitude and isolation of the desert convey His innermost thoughts and intentions to His special servants.

In the desert John lived as an ascetic for the greater part of his formative years. He was a Nazarite, not a Nazarene. A Nazarite was one set aside especially for service to God. John's hair was never cut. He abstained from indulging in rich foods or any drink derived from the fruit of the vine. He was deprived of the joys of marriage. His clothing was coarse—of camel's hair. And his diet consisted of the common large prolific desert locusts that swarmed in huge clouds across the barren landscape. Locusts were one of the few insects not forbidden to be eaten under the old Levitical law. They could be easily caught in huge quantities when the migrating swarms moved across the countryside on their way south to Arabia and Africa. To this day locusts are looked upon as a delicacy by desert tribes.

John augmented the fat and protein-rich fare of locusts with wild honey. This was collected from wild bees that nested in rock crevasses and old hollow stumps scattered here and there amid the desolate wadis. Much of this wild honey was made by the foraging bees from the nectar of desert acacia trees. The honey is very dark, sometimes almost black, pungent and strong in flavor. Like the locusts, it was highly nourishing food that provided a delicious adjunct to his Spartan diet. On this sparse fare John developed into a powerful, strong-muscled man. His mental faculties were clear and alert. His spirit was uncluttered by his simple life-style. He was an individual uniquely prepared for powerful use under God.

John's two great themes were: (1) genuine repentance that would produce permanent fruits of change in a person's life, (2) the imminent arrival of the Messiah, the Redeemer of Israel, who would usher in His kingdom.

John's fiery preaching presented the people with a form of repentance more than skin deep. It was not just a superficial sorrow for misconduct. His repentance was a radical and permanent about-face in which the sinner turns from his old life-style to that of serving the living God in sincerity. Evidence that men and women had truly repented had to be seen in their willingness to quit, once and for all, their old behavior. It entailed making proper restitution for their former misdeeds. And it meant men and women had new values, new attitudes, new priorities in their personal lives. Anything less than this simply did not satisfy the stern demands of the fiery prophet.

The net result of his preaching was to prepare thousands of people for the coming of the Christ. John made no great boast about his own prowess. Yet he continually eulogized the Coming King. He said bluntly that he was not worthy to undo His sandal straps. He made it clear that his own star would soon set, while the bright and morning star of God's Anointed would rise to its zenith. In sincerity and honest humility he accepted his own lower station. He warned his devotees: "He [Christ] must increase, but I must decrease." And when, in due course, Jesus Himself did come down to the Jordan to be baptized of John, the flaming spokesman shouted aloud, "Behold, look, the Lamb of God who takes away the sins of the world."

Are we surprised that the accolades conferred on John by Jesus are the noblest ever earned by mortal man? For it was God in Christ who said of John, "He was the greatest man ever born of woman." On another occasion Christ commented, "He was a bright and shining light"; and again, "He was much more than a prophet."

Though a man of the desert—rough and tough—John was a giant in God's economy and plans for planet earth.

When the day came for Jesus to gently close the door to His

carpenter shop for the last time, He knew exactly where to go. With firm footsteps and quiet determination He set off directly to see John. Following the winding roads from the hill country of Nazareth, He headed down into the burning heat of the Jordan Valley where John was baptizing in the running river. Jesus, too, like His contemporaries, insisted on going through this rite. At first John protested, pleading he was not worthy of so great an honor as to baptize the Son of God. But Jesus prevailed upon him.

As Jesus came up out of the murky Jordan waters, a voice—the voice of God the Father—spoke from above: "This is My beloved Son in whom I am well pleased." Thus the action Jesus had taken in humble submission to John was endorsed by deity. Evidence, apparent to all standing there, was not only in the words from heaven, but also in the visible descent of the dove of God's gracious Spirit upon the person of Jesus. This was indeed His special endorsement, His special anointing, with the Holy Spirit, for special service.

From this point on in His earthly sojourn, Jesus was not only God's Anointed in name, He was also the Christ, God's Anointed, in reality and truth. All that He thought, said, or did would be under the direction of His Father in heaven, empowered by the presence and person of the Holy Spirit. It was the mode whereby His entire life would be absorbed in one single objective—perfect obedience to God's will in the world.

The thoughts He thought would be His Father's thoughts. The words He spoke would be His Father's words. The things He did and the works He worked would be His Father's works! He and His Father were irrevocably one in their common pursuits and common purposes on the planet.

In being baptized by John, Jesus had put the stamp of divine approval on John's mission. The prophet had thoroughly prepared his people for the coming of the King. And now the Messiah had stepped onto the stage of public life amongst His people. Would they receive Him with honor as royalty?

It was a moot question at this particular point in Israel's history. For even the most learned and astute of Jewish people hoped and dreamed of the day when God's kingdom would be established on earth. To most devout Israelites this was nothing more or less than

the restoration of Israel as it had been at the pinnacle of its powe₁
under David and Solomon.

Then the might of the Jewish empire extended from the Eu-
phrates River in the east to the Mediterranean on the west. It
stretched from the borders of Egypt on the south to Lebanon in the
north. It was a world power embracing and dominating almost the
whole of the Middle East, with a million and a half men under
arms. And the Jews longed for, pined and waited impatiently for
that mighty monarch, the promised Messiah, who would restore to
them the pride and prestige of such an earthly kingdom. In their
mind's eye they could see the power of Rome crumble. They could
see themselves flinging off the grievous yoke of military oppression
and exploitation that ground them down into abject poverty and
humiliation. They could see themselves rising again to grandeur
and glory. If any king would appear on the world's stage to do this
for them they would surely receive him with honor and follow him
with loyalty.

So it is not the least surprising that whenever one like Jesus
stepped into public view declaring "The kingdom of God is at
hand!" or "The kingdom of heaven has come!" their pulses quickened, their hearts raced and their hopes soared.

But the kingdom of which Jesus spoke and taught so often was
not an earthly empire. Rather it was the *government of God,* being
established in individual human hearts. It implied simply that as in
His own life, the Spirit of God invaded a man's spirit, there to
establish His divine sovereignty. And gradually under God that
sovereignty would be extended to take over the entire territory of
the person's total being. His mind, his emotions, his will would
come under the direct control of the incoming King of Glory.
Where this happened, God's values, God's standards, God's
views, God's priorities and purposes would be paramount.

Jesus said, "The kingdom of God is within you—amongst you."

But very few would or could ever understand this spiritual concept.

CHAPTER ELEVEN

Beginning Great Things

God's ways and men's ways of doing things are totally different. If it had been human enterprise which was to launch the King of Glory on His lifework there would have been fantastic fanfare. His presence would have been proclaimed publicly to the whole wide world. People and cities and towns everywhere would have been alerted for His arrival.

Instead of that we read the stark, simple record that "He was led of the Spirit into the wilderness to be tempted of Satan." There in the wastelands of rock and sand and brush, beyond Jordan, Jesus was to undergo enormous testing for forty days and forty nights. Something of the severity of this ordeal can be judged from the fact that in this desolate region daytime temperatures, in the shade, commonly reach 120 to 130 degrees. The sun was a blazing ball of fire beneath which the scorched desert panted with burning thirst.

Here, all alone, this gregarious, sociable individual had to face the forces of evil arrayed against Him and His lifework. Jesus was not a John the Baptist who felt at ease and at one with this harsh environment. He had not come there because it was a restful retreat from the crowds. Later in His life He would do this, but not at this point. No, rather He was there for a face-to-face encounter with Satan, who would endeavor, at the very outset, to thwart the plans and purposes of God for the rescue of humanity.

Again and again we must remind ourselves that there are at work in the world two enormous wills. There is the will of God our Father. That will is that none should perish: That all men should be redeemed and restored to righteousness: That people should repent, turn from evil, and be reconciled to God: That in newness of life they should become mature sons and daughters of God who delight in doing His will: That men will flourish in the joyous fellowship of His family: That they live lofty lives.

Opposed to all of the foregoing is the will of the Evil One. His desire is to have the human race sink down in despair and death. He endeavors to undo all the good which God does. He attempts to enslave men to sin, selfishness, and himself.

Consequently it really is not surprising that at the very outset Christ's archenemy would endeavor to undermine Jesus' mission to redeem men. That he even had the audacity to do so reveals how desperate was his desire to destroy the divine rescue operation.

Jesus was not the first person to fast for forty days. On previous occasions men had endured such an ordeal. Moses, when given the law of God on Mount Sinai, had been without food and water for forty days. But he had been ever in God's presence, upheld by that inspiration. Elijah had fasted forty days, but was meanwhile ministered to by angels. But here in the desert, alone, Jesus endured His ordeal in conflict with Satan: a tremendous test of physical, mental, and spiritual stamina.

Since Jesus, the Christ, was tempted along the three lines of approach generally presented to us, it is helpful to look at them briefly.

Satan appealed to the soul life of Jesus. He approached Him first through the realm of His emotions—of His feelings, of His sensations. He was hungry—what a pleasure food would be! Why not satisfy that insistent appetite for something pleasing? Turn stones into bread. If He were the Son of God this was a simple step to take.

To do so would have been to succumb to self-pleasure. To capitulate would have been to become a servant to self-gratification. Jesus refused. He routed Satan with the stabbing reply "Man does not live by bread alone." A spiritual man lives by the Word of God—in accord with the will of God.

Next, Satan with great subtlety appealed to Jesus' rationality. He suggested that if He were indeed God's Son and performed some spectacular feat like flinging Himself from the pinnacle of the temple in full view of thousands, He would be acclaimed. Especially when the angels preserved Him from being pulverized on the pavement below.

This would be a dramatic display of self-preservation. And after all, isn't life so precious we all want to save ourselves? But Jesus simply would not be trapped. He knew that if a man were to save his soul forever he had to be ready to lose it, to give it up, to give it away. That was the very purpose for which He Himself had come to earth. He would give His life freely for men.

"No. No. No. Satan, you will not tempt, you cannot tempt, the Lord God that way!"

The archenemy, however, was persistent. He was determined that somehow he would undo Jesus before ever He began His public ministry amongst men.

His third attempt was a direct appeal to Jesus' will. He had tried to trap Him through His emotions—self-pleasure; through His mind and rationality—self-preservation; now, through His will—self-prominence, self-assertion.

He was shown all the mighty empires of the earth. All of them could be His at a whim. All that He needed to do was gratify His self-desire, self-will for prominence and power. Simply capitulate to the Prince of the Power of the Air, the evil imposter who had usurped the position of power on earth, and He could have it all in His hand.

Jesus simply would not take this shortcut to reestablishing His own kingdom on earth. It would have so easily bypassed all His earthly agony, His earthly endeavors, His cruel death on the cross. But He refused to exercise His self-will for self-realization. He simply would not set His will against God's will. He would not pursue prominence or power or prestige this way. Instead in that terrible moment of terrific temptation He determined to do only His Father's will. The path He would pursue was complete obedience to the will of God. And because of that obedience, because of His humiliation, in due time He would be hailed as King of Kings and Lord of Lords, to whom every knee would bow, and every tongue, including the Tempter's, would declare that Jesus Christ is Lord (Philippians 2:5–11).

"Satan—never, never, never would the Son of God, the Son of

man, submit to you or your wishes. Instead, *you* must and will submit, and eventually fully surrender to the will and wish of God." Righteousness would reign! Truth would triumph!

And with that, Satan was gone.

The titanic conflict was a glorious victory for Jesus, the Christ. It would not be the last encounter with the devil, but it displayed the pattern of triumph upon triumph that marked the whole subsequent life of our Lord.

Unlike the first Adam, God's son who when tempted fell, this second Adam, God's Son, the Christ, conquered. And because of His obedience, His righteousness, many would be made righteous. You and I.

When Jesus came striding strongly out of the Transjordan wastelands, He came in enormous strength. Angels had ministered to Him. No doubt this included both physical food and drink as well as mental and emotional refreshment. In spirit He was stimulated and mightily empowered by His tremendous spiritual conquest. There was about Him a majestic magnetism that would attract the attention of lesser men.

He returned to where He had left John. And when John saw Him approaching he cried out exultingly, "Behold, look; the Lamb of God who takes away the sins of the world." It was the public proclamation that the kingdom of God was about to be established.

Amongst the very first to follow Jesus were some of the ardent young fellows who had previously followed John. These were not old decrepit men with gray beards and bent backs, so often depicted in paintings and pictures of Jesus' disciples. Rather, they were rough, tough young men at the powerful peak of early manhood, either in their late teens or early twenties. Of all Jesus' disciples, only Peter was married, and even he could not have been much more than twenty-three or twenty-four.

It must be remembered, too, that of the twelve who subsequently stayed with Jesus the longest, several were directly related to Him. James and John, the sons of Zebedee and Salome, were His cousins. Salome was a sister to His mother, Mary. She was a very aggressive, ambitious woman unlike her quiet, gentle sister Mary. Some of her drive had been transmitted to her two sons, James and John, who, because of their bombastic characters, had been dubbed the Sons of Thunder.

Peter was a powerful, hard, impulsive man. He was never short of words or slow to act. He was an abrasive individual. He covered up his own inner weakness by a bold show of bravado. All it took to tear the mask from him was the taunt of a little servant girl in the high priest's house. There in a moment of weakness he disowned his Master, not once but several times, finally to go out into the darkness and dissolve in tears.

These three—James, John, and Peter—were Jesus' closest intimates. Perhaps it was a case of opposites attracting each other. One thing is sure: The impact of Christ's own life and Spirit upon them produced an amazing transformation in their characters. They were diametrically changed into men of wondrous strength and love.

John, as the years moved along, came to be known by everyone as John the Beloved, a winsome person whose three Epistles and famous Gospel constitute the most wondrous commentary on love the world has ever known. James, the other "Son of Thunder," at one point was determined, with his brother, to call down fire from heaven to destroy a whole community, yet later, like his Lord, was led into a position of powerful leadership in the early Church. His Epistle is probably the most practical document in all of Holy Writ for men who would walk with God in a way that convinces a skeptical world that Christianity works. Peter, up-and-down Peter, the crude, coarse, cursing fisherman from Galilee, under the impact of Christ's Spirit and love became the stable, brilliant spokesman for the early Church. His fearless sermons after Pentecost, his breaking of the good news to the gentile world, showed a man who had become as mighty as a lion, steady as a rock.

These were the sort of men—ordinary men like you and me, with lights and shadows, strengths and weaknesses—who came to follow Christ. Always Jesus looked at them with enormous perception. His piercing eyes and penetrating spiritual intuition could see clear through their souls. The Master was not one to assess men and women on the basis of their external behavior. He appraised them from the standpoint of their ultimate potential. He knew what could come from the coarse young comrades He chose to be His companions. He knew sinners could become saints.

Some of His followers were more gentle souls. Andrew, Philip, and Nathanael were lovable characters. Judas Iscariot, the only

Judean in the crowd, was a scheming, crafty character. Yet no matter who they were or where they came from, Jesus saw them as those who would help begin to build the kingdom of God on earth.

Andrew may well be regarded as one of Jesus' most attractive disciples. In contrast to his older brother Peter, he was a quiet young man. He could be relied on to turn others to Christ rather than attract attention to himself. It was he who initially brought Peter to meet Christ in his early and eager excitement. He was sure Jesus was the Christ, so he shared this news with his brother. It was Andrew who brought the lad with his sardines and buns to Jesus to have them blessed and broken and shared with hungry crowds. It was Andrew who, when Greeks from afar came looking for the Lord, happily led them to Jesus, sharing Him with gentiles.

Andrew had discovered the key to the kingdom of God. Simply lead others to the Master. Leave them with Him. He would do the rest. There was nothing complicated about this young fisherman. He could capture men for Christ as readily as catch fish for his father, Jonas.

Philip resembled Andrew in his enthusiasm for spiritual things. He was ever in search of spiritual truth. He, Andrew, Peter, James, and John all grew up in the coastal fishing village of Bethsaida, a twin town to Capernaum. Capernaum with its little whitewashed homes on the shores of the Lake of Galilee, was where Peter had his home, now that he was married. And eventually Capernaum was to become the main center for Jesus' public ministry.

Philip's closest chum was a very devout young fellow named Nathanael in John's record. In the other Gospels he is called Bartholomew. Of the twelve followers who stayed with Jesus, Nathanael was the greatest Zealot. He steeped himself in the Scriptures, hoping and praying for Israel's early emancipation. He was in the habit of secreting himself in the dense foliage of a favorite fig tree. There, where the branches grew to the very ground, screened from prying eyes, he would meditate over the Old Testament and pour out his soul in prayer.

Jesus, with His deep, instinctive intuition knew this. When introduced to Nathanael by Philip, He told him so. It startled the young fellow. And he, who, before meeting Jesus, had wondered if anything desirable could come out of Nazareth, now exclaimed,

"Rabbi [Teacher], You are the Son of God. You are the King of Israel."

Nathanael, in that burst of acclamation, substantiated what others had said from the time of Jesus' birth. Here was the Messiah! Simeon, Anna, John the Baptist, and even Andrew recognized that Christ was no ordinary man. He was God amongst men. How else could He have possibly known he was hiding in the fig tree, much less discern the very thoughts he was thinking about Jacob of old and the angelic stairway to heaven?

In that flash of spiritual insight Nathanael found a truth that escapes most men. He realized that God knows all about us, that really nothing is hidden from Him. We may be able to bluff other human beings; we may be able to screen and shelter ourselves from other people's prying curiosity. But not with Christ. To Him all things are open and revealed, even men's most intimate secrets. So we might as well drop the facade and come to Him in open honesty. He knows us at our best and He knows us at our worst. Yet the earnest, searching, seeking soul discovers that God in Christ is willing to take him as he is, provided he comes in honesty without phony pretense or playacting.

It was soon after these half dozen young men had fallen into Jesus' company that they were invited to a merry wedding in Nathanael's hometown of Cana. The rather loosely knit band of seven men welcomed the chance to share in the festivities. Perhaps the little girl bride or her handsome young groom was a friend of Jesus' family, because Mary, His mother, was also invited.

Unlike our Western culture, in the East it is the groom's family who host the wedding ceremony and provide the banquet. The groom's friends go to the bride's home and fetch her for the groom. She would be brought to his home amid great gaiety, singing, and celebration.

Jesus, being a gregarious individual, loved these happy occasions. He enjoyed eating and drinking with His friends around the festive tables. He was a man of good cheer. Later in His life His detractors accused Him cruelly of being both a glutton and winebibber. Anything to humiliate Him! The very same people claimed His cousin, John the Baptist, because of his abstinence from wine or rich food, was possessed of a devil.

No matter what a devout man did, it wasn't right. It was quite literally impossible to please all the people. Some human beings can find fault with God Himself, and heaven forbid that they should ever enter its realm, for even there they would find plenty to complain about. Happily their own deep discontent and cruel criticism forever bar them from its joyous environment. They would be dreadful misfits. That is why if a man does not feel comfortable with heaven's company in this life, he most surely would be even more miserable with it in the next.

As the gay wedding festivities progressed, a most awkward and embarrassing thing happened. The wine ran out. In concern for the host, Mary bustled over to Jesus and whispered her anxiety in His ear. For years now she had turned instinctively to her oldest son in every difficult situation. Jesus had always come up with a solution. He had always managed to meet any emergency. He was never without an answer to the most awkward question. Surely He would know what to do now.

His reply to Mary has been sadly misconstrued by multitudes. It was not a hasty or discourteous rebuttal. It was rather a simple statement of spiritual import. In layman's language it would be put this way: "Lady [a term of honor and respect], I really do not share your anxiety in this situation. I have the solution."

Mary appreciated and understood. With enormous relief she turned to the distraught servants who had drained the wine casks to their dregs. "Whatever He tells you to do, just do it!"

Without fuss or fanfare, Jesus simply, quietly, calmly instructed them to fill six huge stone jars with roughly 120 gallons of water. They complied at once. Then Jesus told them to draw off delicious wine and take it to the master of ceremonies. He was startled by its exquisite taste and delicate bouquet.

"Whence such choice vintage?"

From the Christ. From the One who can fill these stony hearts of ours with the water of His own life. Then have that same life passed on to others in the wine of refreshment, blessing, and rich benefit. All are His miracles of grace!

CHAPTER TWELVE

Jesus Challenges Jerusalem

In the early events of our Lord's public ministry the scenes shifted swiftly. He was a powerful, potent person whose presence was soon to be felt all over Palestine. Because the Spirit of God moved in Him mightily He was a highly charged magnetic man. People who came in contact with Him were immediately polarized by the enormous influence of His character and conduct. Either they were strongly attracted to Him or, conversely, repelled. One could not remain neutral. He Himself, without apology, declared, "Either you are for Me or against Me."

It has been thought, very wrongly, that Jesus the Christ simply moved very quietly through the gentle countryside doing only benevolent deeds. That He went about doing good is not denied. But because of the corrupt culture of His times, laced through with deception, graft, greed, and phony duplicity, it was inevitable that His coming produced enormous storms of protest from those in positions of power and privilege.

Jesus, because He had grown up in pleasant, gay Galilee, naturally felt more at home there. He was quite at ease amongst His comrades, most of whom were rough-and-ready young Galileans. He loved the warm sunny hills and glistening lake of Galilee. It was a region that drew Him back again and again to His tranquil boyhood memories.

Yet it was inevitable that His coming into public view was bound to produce enormous clashes with the deeply entrenched ecclesiastical hierarchy of Judea and Jerusalem. Jesus never saw nor regarded Himself as a political power, though ultimately His death would be engineered by the priesthood, using political men and means to achieve His execution. No, the kingdom He came to establish, of which He was the Monarch, was spiritual. The challenge which He brought was to the corruption of the religious life of His era. The confrontations which would mark His whole public life were with the scholars, the priests, the Pharisees and Sadducees, who professed to be the spiritual elite of Israel.

The great central stronghold of spiritual life had been Jerusalem. Jerusalem was the very heart of Judaism. And in Jerusalem the great temple stood as the symbol of the culture and climate of spiritual life throughout all of Jewry. If Jesus was going to make known God's will and wishes for the world, it would not be enough to quietly speak about them up on the sunny shores of the Lake of Galilee. His mighty message would also have to be proclaimed aloud on the very porches that encircled the awesome temple in Jerusalem.

Jesus refused to be restricted to the favorable climate of Galilee, where He soon became a popular figure with an enormous following. Word of His mighty deeds soon swept across the countryside along the human grapevine. No, He was determined again and again to make one assault after another on the entrenched forces in Jerusalem. His devoted disciples sometimes endeavored to deter Him. But His determination was as hard as flint. Nothing could deflect Him from His mission.

Ever since Jesus had been inducted into the spiritual life of His people as a "Son of the Law" at the age of twelve, He had made an annual trek up to Jerusalem for the great Passover feast. For eighteen years, on eighteen occasions, His sensitive soul and divine spirit had been grieved and wounded by the wicked traffic that went on in the temple. No doubt when He returned to toil at His carpenter's bench during this long quiet interlude, He had turned over and over in His mind how one day He might overturn the terrible trade He witnessed in the temple.

And now the time had come for Him to put into action the hot thoughts that had burned within Him for so long. When He left Capernaum with its quiet waters lapping on the beaches, He was bound for the temple stronghold in the heart of Jerusalem. He was coming now not just as a "Son of the Law" but as the Son of God. And what His eager young comrades would witness was the greatest challenge ever flung down before a wicked and perverted priesthood. The bold blazing action of their leader would not only stir their own spirits but also shake the whole city in fury.

The atrocious wrongs and devilish deeds done in the temple defy our imagination. It is hard to realize that some twenty thousand priests and helpers in and around Jerusalem survived like parasites draining the lifeblood and hard-earned savings from the people who came there to worship. It has been estimated that the average annual income derived from the temple trade exceeded thirty-five million dollars. On this the hierarchy of priests and scholars lived in pompous, pious ease and luxury. Some were so skilled at manipulating money that they had become inordinately wealthy. Their hearts' affection was supposed to be in heaven, but they made very sure their sensual souls were glutted with silver on earth. They banqueted in abundance, wrapped in their rich gowns of gold brocade, while hungry beggars and poor peasants lay prostrate in their rags on the temple steps.

Some poor pilgrim may have marched a hundred miles or more to reach this citadel of his spiritual hopes. Through rain and snow, summer heat and desert thirst he may have trudged to reach the temple of his God. In his arms, cradled gently all that way, there may have been a gentle lamb or a pair of doves to offer in contrite and humble sacrifice for the atonement of his sins. When he reached the temple his heart would flame with joy, his eyes brighten with eager hope.

Then the priest would speak. His words were worse than sword thrusts: "Your lamb is not fit for the Most High! Can't you see the blemish on his front foot? You will have to buy a better lamb. Spotless lambs are available from the priest on the outer porch!"

What could he do? Where would he go now? At best perhaps he could sell his own pet lamb for a shekel or two. To purchase a "perfect" one would cost him twenty. The difference would be pocketed by the crafty vendor. For in turn he would take the pilgrim's little spotless lamb and sell it at an exorbitant profit to the next gullible victim who ventured to come and worship Jehovah.

This sort of abuse and dozens more, some even more diabolical, were part and parcel of the priesthood trade. Jesus saw it and His blood boiled. His spirit flamed white hot. Yes, He—God very God, yet man very man—could not, would not stand by any longer. His utter justice, His intense integrity, His consuming compassion burned in blazing indignation. Anger impelling Him, He swiftly braided a whip from cords of rope. He stormed into the temple, eyes flashing. His strong-muscled arms lashed out with the whip. He drove out the livestock, traders, money changers, and all their accomplices. Commotion and excitement swept through the temple porches. People tumbled out into the streets shouting and cursing. Small urchins scrambled for the coins that rolled away from the overturned money changers' tables. The beggars and peasants who had hung around the steps smiled slyly. Some even dared to cheer in open defiance of those who had ground them into hopeless poverty.

"You will not make this temple, My Father's home, a trading center!" Jesus shouted above the din and uproar. "Get these things out of here!" He roared, tossing the sacks of coins, bird cages, and trading tables out onto the pavement.

"My Father's house!" They were the same identical words, the same familiar phrase that sprang from His lips and from His heart eighteen years before as a boy of twelve.

Yes, in very truth . . . God was His Father. His mother and Joseph had heard Him say it. Now all the priests in the temple and the throngs outside heard the same clear declaration: "God is My Father—I am His Son." By His own proclamation and in public hearing He had stated who He was.

The news electrified Jerusalem. Word of the upheaval swept up and down the narrow dusty streets of the city like a desert storm. In anger and fury the priests reacted violently. Their position, prestige, power, and prominence were imperiled! Who was He? Under whose authority did He dare such a revolutionary action?

Jesus knew that day His earthly death was near and sure.

He knew no stone would be left unturned to destroy Him.

He knew the bloodhounds of Jerusalem would dog His footsteps until His own blood stained a cruel cross outside these city walls.

The priests shouted and screamed at Him. They were a band of pariah dogs bent on tearing Him to pieces. "Prove Yourself!" they yelled in anger. "Let us see some sign that will convince us You are the Christ!"

Men of all times, of all cultures, and all creeds—in colossal self-conceit—call on God to prove Himself. Sotted with their own spiritual importance or intellectual arrogance, they challenge God to show Himself. But God is not about to demean Himself by indulging their stupidity. On every side they are surrounded by irrefutable evidence of His existence. Natural beauty, the majestic order of the universe, flawless precision in the movement of the stellar bodies, the insatiable aspirations and deep longings of our human spirits are but a few of the unmistakable proofs of His presence and person.

But on this stormy day in the temple, stormy hearts and hot heads saw none of this. All they saw was this man from Galilee, this unknown mendicant who posed a powerful threat to all their schemes. What if He was God? What if He was the Messiah? What if He was their King? They would not have Him! "A thousand times no! We will not have this man to rule over us!" Why? Because His way and their way, His life and their lives, His truth and their deception were diametrically opposed.

He was light and they were darkness. He was life and they were death. He was the way to God and they were the way to destruction.

Light—the light of the very life and character of God—had come into the world, but men steeped in their own perverseness, pride, and greed preferred darkness; actually loved it, because their deeds were evil.

The lines of conflict were clearly drawn that cataclysmic day in Jerusalem. Jesus fearlessly flung the challenge of God's justice and righteousness into the face of the phony religious hierarchy of His time. He did it deliberately at the very outset of His public ministry. He knew what the consequences would be. Certain death.

His opponents picked up the challenge. And, just as surely as the Christ, *they* knew there could be only one answer. Certain death—*His death!*

Amongst those most deeply stirred in Jerusalem was

Nicodemus. His brother, the famous historian Josephus, tells us
Nicodemus was one of the leading Pharisees of the day. He was a
member of the notorious and august Sanhedrin. He was also repu-
ted to be the third richest man in Jerusalem. So he wielded enormous influence. Yet he was a man of mixed motives.

Stealthily, by night, wrapped in his cloak, walking in the
shadows where he would not be noticed, he came to see Jesus
privately. No doubt he remembered Jesus as the precocious
youngster of twelve who had come to the scribes and teachers in
quest of spiritual enlightenment. With the intervening years the
young man had matured into a powerful prophet and teacher.

Nicodemus addressed Jesus with due respect and courtesy.
"Rabbi, you are a teacher, come from God." Perhaps in that simple statement of half truth lay the secret to the whole puzzle of
Nicodemus' peculiar, paradoxical nature. Like uncounted millions
of other men and women throughout the world, to him Jesus was
only, and never more than, a teacher. He simply did not see that
this One who now spoke to him gently of the kingdom of God, was
none other than God, very God Himself, in human form.

At best Nicodemus was only a halfway believer. He was too
embroiled with his wealth, his position of prominence in the city,
his personal ambitions for greatness, to turn his back on them.
With one hand he reached out tentatively to this "teacher." With
the other he clung tenaciously to his temporal possessions. He
wanted the best of both worlds—heaven and earth—seemingly un-
aware that he was attempting the impossible.

His subsequent behavior after this secret encounter with Christ
clearly demonstrated his lack of courage to commit himself to the
King of Glory. Once later he used his influence to divert his fellow
Pharisees from lynching Jesus and killing Him without a proper
trial. But this did not deter them from finally having the Romans
crucify Christ, which was just as cruel. Then when that noble
Person, so abused by brutal men, hanged as a corpse on the cross,
he undertook to embalm His body. But always his actions were
only halfhearted and half effective.

But, during this secret interview with Jesus, the Christ, there
was unlocked to Nicodemus truth which across the ensuing two
thousand years has unlocked more hearts and freed more spirits
than any other portion of God's revelation to man. In their conver-

sation it was made very clear that no one who wished to enter God's family did so by his own self-effort.

Jesus, using very familiar natural phenomena, disclosed that night to Nicodemus that it was God who reached down to earth to touch and transform lives. It was the will of God, the energy of God, the work of God to remake, regenerate, and restore men to His family. It was God's enterprise by His Spirit, God's initiative, that enabled fallen men to be reborn in spite of their sins and selfishness. It was God imparting Himself by His Spirit to man's spirit that quickened and made him come alive to His Father. This was to be born from above.

Jesus went over the ground twice with Nicodemus. He seemed spiritually dull, even though steeped in the ancient Scriptures of the Old Testament. Nicodemus was typical of the thousands, yes even millions, of human beings who somehow feel sure they can make it with God on the basis of their own good behavior. He felt that his self-righteousness was sufficient to satisfy the righteous requisites of a holy God.

What he failed to see was that if he failed to comply with even a single requirement of God's laws, he failed completely. And, of course, he, like all men, had actually transgressed in many areas. So that at best, his most commendable behavior was regarded by God as little more than a contaminated outer cloak for a corrupt inner heart.

It was a man's interior that had to be remade. This was the special work of God's Spirit. He came as a fresh, cleansing wind to clear out the accumulated chaff and cobwebs of the old wicked ways. It was He who would enable the seeking soul to see that it was God's love for the world that enabled Him to lay down His own perfect flawless life for lost men. It was God's generosity that imputed and credited Christ's own perfect obedience and righteousness to sinful men. It was God's grace that imparted and shared that very life, the eternal life of the eternal God, with men by His Spirit. It was all of God. God had come in Christ not to condemn men but to redeem them.

For poor old Nicodemus, it was all too simple, yet at the same time too difficult to believe. He never really did cast in his lot wholeheartedly with Christ. To become a child of faith seemed a bit beyond him.

CHAPTER THIRTEEN

The Woman at the Well

Leaving Jerusalem and Judea, with their rigid, angry, and antagonistic attitudes toward Him, Jesus turned His footsteps northward toward Galilee. This travel, to and fro, north and south, back and forth between Jerusalem and Galilee was to be the warp and woof of His public life. Hundreds and hundreds of miles of tough trekking would be done this way. With His little band of loyal youths, under blazing sun, starry nights, and along hot trails, He would crisscross the country with incredible endurance and relentless energy.

This in itself would have demanded the best in physical stamina from any man. But added to it were the endless, heart-wrenching demands made upon Jesus to heal the sick, to feed the hungry, to cast out evil spirits, and to teach the crowds that came to hear Him. To serve one's fellows in any one of these fields is a full-time occupation. Yet this One, without fanfare or public support, without any organized religious society, without any financial backing, without any charitable foundation to underwrite His enterprises, set out in simple assurance to minister to uncounted multitudes.

His life during the next three years would touch thousands upon ten thousands of other lives. His healing would bring relief to countless sufferers. His forgiveness would restore dignity to the downtrodden. His presence would give hope to the hopeless and life to the lifeless. His compassion would come as a pure selfless stream of empathy that soothed and healed a thousand broken hearts. His Spirit would bring uplift, inspiration, and enlightenment of spirit to those in darkness and doubt. His teaching would lay the foundation for a whole new society of men upon earth—men who first started out as His followers,who became His friends, who in the end He regarded as His brothers.

But though Jesus the Christ was God, very God, with the resources of God at His disposal, He was also man, very man, who could grow weary, thirsty, and tired.

On the way to Galilee He had decided to travel through Samaria. The more devout and sanctimonious Jews avoided this country. They regarded the Samaritans with contempt. They wanted nothing to do with such a crude crowd of immoral people. Somehow they were sure the loose living and coarse conduct of the Samaritans would rub off on them, to besmirch their own supposedly white and sinless souls.

There was none of that about Jesus. True to His own impeccable character, He would walk anywhere, go anywhere that men and women were in need. And it is typical of His great generous heart that He always had a soft spot for the downtrodden, despised underdog. He told the winsome, wonderful story of the man who fell amongst thieves. The hero in that drama was a humble Samaritan. He healed ten lepers, of whom one was a Samaritan—yet only the Samaritan was grateful enough to return and give Him thanks.

And now one day as He and His disciples trudged across the brown, hot hills of Samaria, Jesus, weary with the road, sat down beside a well to rest. He was more than tired though. He was also thirsty and hungry. His younger companions went off to the village shops in search of something to eat. Meanwhile the Master waited at the well. Someone would come along with a rope and bucket to draw water so He could slake His burning thirst.

The ancient well where He sat was about 150 feet deep. It was a very unusual well, dug by hand by Jacob's servants nearly 1750 years before. Its walls were smooth, worn slick with the raising and lowering of countless containers of water. It was the only well in a region renowned for its springs. Jacob had been compelled to dig it when denied the use of the natural springs by the local people amongst whom he came to live so long ago. But once that well began to flow it never ceased. And now Jesus sat on its low lip of stone, waiting for the woman whom He knew would come to draw water.

Despite what so many have said about her coming at noon, there really was nothing unusual about the hour. She was no worse a woman than most of her neighbor ladies. Most of them lived loose lives. She was there because she wanted water. It was that simple. What was not so simple was the amazing conduct of the man who sat upon the stone rim of the well. After all, men just didn't converse with strange women. And most certainly a Jewish gentleman would not normally condescend to engage a Samaritan lady in conversation.

She was really very surprised and puzzled.

But so, too, were Jesus' young companions.

Gradually they were beginning to see that Jesus was no conventional character. He was not a run-of-the-mill man. Whether He was in Jerusalem creating a general uproar in the temple with His furious anger, or sitting here alone talking softly to a solitary Samaritan, His conduct and character were remarkably unique.

In a direct, straightforward way Jesus asked her for a drink. In her surprise she expressed astonishment that He would even do this. Jesus' counterreply was that perhaps if she so wished they could make a trade. He would give her something to satisfy her thirsting spirit, while she gave Him water to quench His thirsting body.

It was an intriguing idea. They were obviously on common ground, but how did one go about this? He had no rope or bucket, and as far as she was concerned only this hole in the ground could satisfy their needs. Where was His supply? Did He have another source? If so, where was it? Could there possibly be any better well than this one left to posterity by Jacob?

Perhaps her perplexity makes us smile. We know the outcome of this brief encounter. The woman, for the first time, drinks a draught of life-giving water from the eternal fountain of God's own life-giving Spirit. She is satisfied in spirit, refreshed in soul. A cleansing has occurred. Her former life-style, lived out passionately with five common-law companions, is completely converted. She makes a clean break with the past. And her newfound refreshment of spirit stirs her whole community.

This incident, reported with such precise pungency by the dear old apostle John near the end of his long, long life, was a powerful memory. It had made an incredible impact on John as a young man. It was nearly as great an insight into the character of Christ as had been the exciting events in Jerusalem: the cleansing of the temple, the midnight talk with Nicodemus. Obviously, the Master would meet anyone, anywhere, anytime. And, even more amazing, He always had the answer to the questing spirit of humanity. From the most respectable and richest of men to the poorest and lowliest of despised women, He came without reservation. Why? Because He knew them through and through. With all men of all time, He knows our deepest cravings, our innermost yearnings.

The spirit of man was created with an enormous capacity for God. Nothing less than God Himself, by His Spirit, can or ever will satisfy that thirst for spiritual refreshment. Like a body, which when athirst must be resupplied from a source outside itself, the spirit of a man can be satisfied only by eternal spiritual sustenance from outside itself. Foolishly and persistently men endeavor to satisfy this thirst by drinking from earth's unsatisfying cisterns and wells. Yet in despondency and dismay, from each, men turn away in despair. Men will try wealth, power, fame, knowledge, science, art, literature, travel, sport, gaiety, luxury, comfort, and ease to satisfy their thirst. All leave them panting, searching, unfulfilled.

Most men and women, like the woman at the well, are preoccupied with their particular old hole in the ground. So earthbound are our eyes that we seldom lift them to see our God standing by us. Despite the fact we come back ten thousand times with our ropes and buckets, hoping to be satisfied from self-dug cisterns, we turn away still distraught in spirit.

Meanwhile the Master is here. His invitation is so simple, so sincere, so straightforward: "Simply ask Me and I will give you the water of life: My Spirit in your spirit: My life permeating your life: My life flowing through your life to touch and refresh a thousand other lives."

The woman came with her old bucket and worn rope to a tired-out well. She went away with a spring of spiritual water bubbling up inside her.

Up until this momentous hot, sultry morning that Jesus walked into the dusty streets of Sychar, this lovely Samaritan woman had peculiar notions about God. She was very much like most of us. She naively assumed that God was someone remote. If He was to be worshiped, one either had to go up into the nearby mountain, or else away down to Jerusalem to do it.

The idea or concept that He was as close as the very atmosphere that enveloped her was totally foreign to her thinking. It is a mark of the magnanimous generosity of Jesus that He would take time to sit there gently and with patience expounding to this plain peasant girl one of the most profound secrets of true spirituality.

In simple syllables He put it to her thus: It is not a question of having to encounter God our Father either by going to some great mountain or visiting some pretentious temple in Jerusalem. Rather it is a case of communing with Him in Spirit and truth.

The error common to humanity is that God is "near" or "far" in terms of space, that it takes time to cross that space. Some even think of God being far up above us, while we are way down "below." But all this is a distorted, false view produced by our finite minds conditioned by earth's little sphere.

"No, no," Jesus patiently explained. "God is a spirit. He is truth. Not all of the created universe can contain Him. He contains the universe. He is everywhere present. He is as near as the very breath of air within My being or that which enfolds My body. In Him I move and live and have My very being, whether or not I recognize the fact."

Being "near" or "far" from Him is a question not of space but of spirit. Am I in accord with His Spirit? Is my spirit in harmony with His? Am I attuned to His will and wishes? Are His purposes my purposes, His desires my desires? Is my life knit with His life? If so, then we are very "close." He is very near to me. I sense His presence and I worship Him in awe, wonder, and gratitude. I live aware—O God, my Father—You are here!

That remarkable day that woman at the well saw this and understood. Indeed her visitor was none other than very God, the Christ. It was more than the great scholar and scribe Nicodemus ever saw.

CHAPTER FOURTEEN

The First Healing

When our Lord continued His trek northward across Samaria, He again returned to the little village of Cana in Galilee. It was the same town in which He had performed His first miracle of turning water into wine at the wedding. Now the village was to have the double honor of being the place where Jesus performed His first act of healing.

Because of the basic, indisputable fact that Jesus was none other than God in human form moving across the world's stage, it was inevitable that He should minister to the whole man. No matter in which area of life an individual suffered, He was capable of correcting the unfortunate condition. Irrespective of whether people were ill in body, deranged in their minds and emotions, or sick in spirit, He could heal them. This simply had to be so. Had it been otherwise He would have been less than God.

The Gospel narrative makes it abundantly clear that when He came out of obscurity into public life, He moved mightily in the Spirit of God. He came as a man, the Son of man, in human form and guise. But He came also as God, the Son of God, in Spirit and truth. The outcome was, whatever life He touched, there followed transformation. It had to be that way. When men and women responded to Him in quiet, simple confidence, they were cured. If they were skeptics, double-dealers, playing their little phony games with God, He quickly unmasked them and they went away worse than before. With Jesus, people were continually polarized. Either they became His ardent admirers or entrenched enemies.

Either they learned to love Him with intense loyalty, or they came
to despise Him with violent hatred.

Yet always, ever, His intentions toward everyone were good.
His fondest hopes were for their healing. His great heart of compassion yearned to make men and women, families and homes,
whole and wholesome. His utter, absolute holiness was made apparent in His own utter wholesomeness. And wherever He was
accepted in simple faith by simple men, He did His wondrous
work.

Approaching the village of Cana, Jesus was met by a nobleman,
a courtier of the king's court, a member of society's upper crust.
The man had come in search of Christ. His son was very sick, in
fact at the point of death. He was sure Jesus could heal his boy!

With the advantage of our hindsight this may not seem surprising. From the historical record, we know Jesus could heal the sick.
But from this man's perspective, his action represented enormous
faith. For up to this time Jesus had healed no one. He had performed no cure on any case. His only miracle had been to turn
water into wine.

Yet this unnamed nobleman, with quiet confidence and absolute
assurance, decided to find Jesus. He was sure that He could resolve his dilemma and relieve the distress of the boy's disease.

With some caution and reticence Jesus questioned him. Was he
just looking for some wondrous display? Would he only really
believe *after* he saw a mighty miracle? The *intent* of a person was
always of paramount importance to Jesus. He was always concerned about the inner attitudes of an individual. Whenever He
saw honesty and sincerity in a searching soul, He responded at
once in positive power.

The nobleman, with enormous respect and regard for Jesus, assured Him he was sure if He just came to his home in Capernaum
the lad would live. In other words, what he indicated was his
complete confidence in Christ's ability to cure his boy.

This was no small thing. After all, here he was a nobleman, a rich
man of great resources. He had access to the best doctors in
Capernaum. And Capernaum was famous for its medical men. It
was a renowned health resort where sick people came from all over
the Middle East. There they bathed in the mineral springs and

basked in the warm, balmy sunshine beside the blue lake. All of the latest in medications and health prescriptions were available to the nobleman's family.

Instead of relying on any of these for a cure, he had set off across country to find this still rather obscure prophet or sadhu—Jesus, the carpenter from Nazareth. Somehow, deep down, with a sure instinct of spirit, he knew Christ could help and heal.

Jesus knew this. Jesus felt the man's faith in action. Jesus saw the simple evidence of total trust. The man's confidence reposed in Him. And He responded at once to that attitude.

Quietly, gently, graciously He assured the father: "Go home; your boy is well." It was that direct, that straightforward, that demanding.

The nobleman's response to Christ's command was further proof of his forthright faith in Jesus. He simply did what he was asked to do. He took the Master at His word and went back to Capernaum. On the way his servants came hurrying to meet him with the joyous good news that his boy had been healed. When questioned closely, they confirmed that the cure had occurred at the very hour Jesus had spoken the word of assurance to his trusting spirit.

It is significant the courtier did not press Jesus for proof that what He said would be so. He did not ask for empirical evidence to reassure himself that Christ could be counted on to deliver. He did not deviate from forthright faith in Jesus. He did not allow himself to depend on his feelings or five senses for confirmation that Jesus would justify Himself.

What this nobleman did, in going home, was identical to what the servants had done at the wedding in filling the great stone jars with water. They had all done just exactly what they were told to do. This is the faith of obedience. It is the positive response to the command of Christ. This is faith in action. Faith, living faith in God, is having complete confidence in His character. It is an absolute assurance that because of His wholesome (holy) character and impeccable conduct He is totally trustworthy. It is knowing that because He is utterly reliable, one's response to His requests can always be positive. He is ever faithful, ever dependable. So when an individual complies and cooperates quietly with Him in calm assurance, all is well.

The nobleman did just this. He went down to his home in Capernaum to find his son restored. His own spirit had been touched and made alive by his encounter with Jesus. And because of his faith, his entire family came to have implicit confidence in Christ. *Faith can be contagious!*

The next healing Jesus was to perform was not physical. It involved a serious spiritual condition that affected the entire person. In His day it was known as "having an evil spirit." It implied that a person was possessed and dominated by a sinister being from outside himself. In the Scriptures various names are used to describe these spirits: They are called evil spirits, unclean spirits, demons, devils, rulers of darkness, powers and principalities of wickedness in high places.

When these evil spirits invaded an individual they tended to dominate the entire person. They controlled the mind, moved the emotions, and directed the will of the one possessed. By this means they could compel that person to speak profanities, rail at God, froth at the mouth, grovel on the ground, behave like a beast, and abuse himself in terrible torment. Some were even stricken deaf, dumb and well-nigh insane by the influence of evil spirits. The result was some were shackled and manacled with iron chains to restrict their movements and thus prevent them from injuring others.

Such cases were fairly common where I grew up as a boy in Africa. One of the tribes close to where we lived practiced the worship of evil spirits. The type of behavior recorded in the Gospels of people plagued with demons was to be seen in the natives around us. In fact, one night a shackled man broke his way into our home. The sound of his clanking chains and maniacal laugh as he prowled around the house was enough to chill one's spine. Fortunately he could not get in where we slept. At daybreak his relatives were called to come and haul him away with strong ropes. He raved and ranted, struggling violently to break his bonds.

When Jesus came to Capernaum for the first time He was to encounter a demon-possessed man. Of all things, it was in the synagogue where Jesus had gone to read the Scriptures and teach the attentive crowds which came to hear Him.

True to their usual deceptive manner, this particular evil spirit posed first as a *group* of demons. He used plural pronouns, as he screamed out violently: "Leave *us* alone. What have *we* got to do with You, Jesus of Nazareth? Have You come to destroy *us?*" Then, giving himself away in his duplicity, he screamed, "I know You, who You are—the Holy One of God."

The Scriptures make it very clear that these evil spirits know very well who Jesus is. They believe in God and tremble in terror at His power and righteousness.

Promptly and swiftly the Master rebuked the evil spirit. In a frenzy of fury he flung the man he had possessed to the floor of the synagogue, then departed. Happily the man was not injured. When the onlookers in the synagogue saw him so instantly released they marveled at the authority and command of Christ. Here, surely, was the power of God vested in their visitor, Jesus of Nazareth.

The fame and notoriety of this initial incident fanned out across the countryside. Up until now there had been no known cure for such a condition. Chains and shackles of steel were the only remedy. But it was to those so bound by evil that Jesus came and with a word of command set the prisoner free. Little wonder that later in His ministry many such hopeless cases would be brought to Him, who alone could give them release, restoring them to their right minds.

The latter part of the twentieth century has seen a remarkable resurgence of similar evil forces across the earth. The presence of evil spirits in human beings, especially in the Western world, has become fairly common. Increasingly it is developing into one of the pronounced aspects of evil with which God's people must do battle. The occult, witchcraft, Satan worship, spiritism and seances are all a part of the contemporary scene, just as they were in Jesus' day. Yet we are not to be intimidated. They and their instigator, Satan, are a subdued force.

God's Word makes it clear to us that any true child of God who is led by God's Spirit, who abides in Christ's presence, cannot be touched by the Evil One (1 John 5). Nor will our heavenly Father even permit any such evil to impinge upon our lives except by His permissive will and for our ultimate benefit and advantage. In this assurance His people can know rest and release.

CHAPTER FIFTEEN

The Call of Christ to Men

Returning to Galilee from Judea ought to have been a happy homecoming for Jesus the Christ. He was coming back no longer an unknown figure. The mighty events at the Jordan when His messiahship had been declared by the flaming desert prophet John; the tempestuous days in the temple that set all Jerusalem abuzz; the miracles of turning water into wine and healing the nobleman's son; the in-depth discussions of divine truth with Nicodemus, the woman at the well, and His own intimate friends—all had become current news of great interest to the entire country.

Already Jesus moved in a certain early aura of awe and respect that began to draw public attention. He was generally regarded as much more than just another one of the many *sadhus* (holy men) who wandered across the countryside. For many He was their "Promised One." But not for all, unhappily.

One day He decided to drop back into Nazareth. This was His hometown. It was where He had spent about twenty-eight years of His life. He knew its streets, its shops, its homes, and its citizens. He had known many of its people as His friends, neighbors, and customers in the business of a carpenter.

It happened to be the Sabbath day. So, as was His habit, He quietly walked over to the synagogue. He came this time not as a student but as a teacher—for it was very likely in this same building that He had received most of His schooling under an old, tired, second-rate rabbi. He stood up to read, which was His privilege, and there was handed to Him the scroll of the ancient prophet Isaiah.

Deftly, surely, Jesus unrolled it to the sixty-first chapter: "The Spirit of the Lord is upon *Me,* because He hath anointed *Me* to preach the Gospel to the poor: He hath sent *Me* to heal the brokenhearted, to preach deliverance to the captives and recovering of sight to the blind, to set at liberty them that are bruised. To preach the acceptable year of the Lord . . . ."

As He read the passage with great power and pathos a hush descended on the assembled congregation. Every eye was fastened on Him. Seldom if ever did anyone read the prophets with such power or impact. The great promise of God—their God, Jehovah—came from Jesus like a clarion call. It stirred their spirits, stimulated their hopes.

He sat down quietly, after rolling up the scroll with careful deliberation, then handed it back to the rabbi. Every face was turned toward Him intently. Every heart hammered, hoping He would say something special. Every eye watched the expression of strength and dignity in His rugged features. Then He spoke.

The next nine words were a trumpet call from the council chambers of eternity—a public proclamation and challenge to His own community, people, and nation:

"This day is this Scripture fulfilled in your ears!"

The Christ had come! He was here! The long-promised, long-awaited Messiah was amongst them! The Saviour of Israel was none other than He Himself, Jesus of Nazareth!

The crowd's first response was commendation and wonder. Never man spake like this man! No words, few as they were, were ever spoken with greater sincerity or such sweet assurance! What a ring of authority and absolute truth they bore.

But—but—wasn't this man Jesus, the son of Joseph?

The piercing question—like a dark shaft of black doubt—stabbed their spirits with searing skepticism.

He couldn't possibly be the "Promised One"! How could *He* be the Messiah? He was only a carpenter! He was surely a charlatan, an impostor, a pretender to power.

Jesus did not endeavor to defend Himself from their abuse. His reply implied "*No* prophet is accepted in his own country! I have

come unto My own and My own would not have Me! I call to you,
but you will not come! You simply don't believe in Me! In a word:
you have no confidence, no faith!''

With the unpredictable conduct so characteristic of human behavior the crowd turned from an attitude of respect and reverence
to doubt, then flaming fury. Their rage and anger boiled up into
violent action.

In a body they jumped to their feet and mobbed Him. He was
shoved out of the synagogue. The mob milled about Him shouting
angrily. They shoved and pushed Him up the narrow, crowded,
dirty streets of Nazareth. He was being hustled to the crest of a
craggy hill. There they hoped to hurl Him over the edge to break
His neck on the boulders below.

No doubt as Jesus was being jostled and jabbed by the angry
mob a thousand memories of His boyhood days and manhood
years swept through His memory. In retrospect, in swift succession He saw the times He had scrambled up to this lofty ledge as a
lad to look out across the long vistas of this lovely land. He recalled
the evenings when He sat up there alone in quiet contemplation
watching the sun set in splendor out over the western horizon. He
remembered the fragance of new-mown hay wafted to Him on the
breeze, of spring flowers blooming amongst the rocks, of the sweet
aroma of fresh rain on newly plowed ground.

It was in the gentle interlude of those long quiet years here in
Nazareth that there had come to Him the sure knowledge and
positive assurance that not only was He the Son of man, able to
appreciate all the beauty of His Father's world—He was also the
Son of God, come to call men to Himself, to righteousness.

And as the mob of Nazareth shouted and swore at Him on the
hill, as they cursed and kicked Him, He knew His hour of demise
had not yet come. There was still much greater work for Him to do.
There were other multitudes to call, other lives to touch, other
hearts to mend, other bodies to heal—and at the end, a cross to
bear for the sins of His people.

Empowered and inspired, Jesus strode suddenly in great
strength and dignity through the mass of milling men around Him.
They fell back like jackals from a kill when the great lion monarch
stretches himself strongly. The Lion of Judah was amongst them!

He left Nazareth—never to return again. She had her call and had rejected it!

Though Jesus often addressed Himself to large audiences which gathered round Him, it is impressive how interested He was in individual men and women. It is touching to see the very special attention He gave to any man or woman who showed the least inclination toward Him. And His enormous patience with such people warms our hearts and stirs our spirits. It endorses what we ourselves have found to be true of Him. He loves us with an everlasting love. He draws us with tender understanding if we respond to His overtures of affection. Ultimately the decision rests with us. He will not override our wills. He will not force Himself upon us. He calls. We either come or turn to go our own way.

Jesus turned from the hill country of Nazareth to drop down into the valley of the Jordan. There nestled between the stark brown hills of the valley walls lay the silver sheet of shining water known as the Lake of Galilee. It was a resplendent sight. The lake could turn to blue, gray, or almost black, depending on the weather that swept over it.

The countryside around the lake, in Jesus' day, was a lush, rich area referred to as The Garden of the Gods. Terraced hillsides and rich farm fields produced a wide array of crops. Busy towns encircled its shoreline. And hundreds of hardy fishermen combed its productive waters for the famous tilapia, a fish of delicious flavor.

Bethsaida and Capernaum were twin towns on the shore. Here was where most of Jesus' great miracles would be performed. Nearby was the little retirement village of Emmaus. There was a spa which attracted the aged and the sick who came from all over the country to soak in its mineral waters. This explains why there were so often crowds of people around Jesus, many of whom were infirm and ill with all sorts of diseases.

In course of time Capernaum became somewhat of a home base for the Master. Though He never owned a proper home of His own, He drew a number of His most intimate disciples from this district. After He had called them to follow Him, their homes had become His home, and their families had become His friends.

Despite the fact that men, young men like Peter, Andrew, James, and John, had met Jesus earlier down along the Jordan where John the Baptist baptized, they had not stayed with Him. They recognized Him as the Christ. They knew somehow He was their Messiah. But until His authority was established they felt inclined to stick with their fishing. So they had gone back to their boats and nets and the lovely lake that was so dear to them.

One warm, balmy morning Jesus was strolling along the shore when He came across Simon (Peter) and his brother Andrew casting for fish with hand nets. This was a very ancient art. It took sharp eyes to detect the slight movement of the fish below the surface. It took swift reflexes to cast the net quickly. It took artistic skill to have the net drop in a precise circle around the fleeing fish. The weighted edge of the fine-mesh net, when thrown by an expert, fanned out into a graceful arch of shimmering skeins that dropped into the sea with a swift splash. Quickly the lines were drawn, and if one was fortunate there would be silver bodies struggling in the mesh. It was an exciting game. Amongst primitive people, all over the world, it still goes on.

Peter and Andrew just loved it.

Jesus watched them for a little while.

Then He gave them a call. "Fellows, come along with Me. I'll make you fishers of men."

Their immediate response was a measure of their deep respect for Jesus. They simply packed away their nets and promptly followed. The two lads probably left their gear in Peter's home.

Down the beach a bit farther Jesus bumped into another pair of brothers, James and John, sitting in their boat with their father, Zebedee. The fishermen must have had a rough night on the lake. Their nets were badly torn and tangled. Sitting in the gentle morning sun, the young men kidded each other as they worked at repairing the damaged nets.

In the same way, Jesus invited them to come with Him. Apparently without hesitation, they dropped the nets, climbed out of the boat, and left the startled Zebedee sitting alone to finish the job.

The prompt response of the four young fishermen has often been thought to represent a deep and decisive commitment to the Christ. It was really not that way. It simply was not a once-for-all abandonment of their old familiar way of life. Again and again they returned to the beloved boats, the lovely lake, and the former fascination of fishing with their friends.

This is very much the pattern of behavior common to those whom Christ calls. It has ever been thus with human beings. God speaks. His voice elicits a warm response within the human spirit. The will is set to follow and serve Him. But by and by the old allurements of life, the former friendships, the familiar fun and attractions, the old desires, drives, and delights draw men back irresistibly. Gradually men return to do their own thing, go their own way, live their own lives.

Yet, in spite of such perverseness the Master comes again to call. He is patient. He is persistent. He is present in our lives even though our own preoccupations take us far from Him.

It was some considerable time after this initial call to His favorite disciples that Jesus again came to the lake. By now He was well known. He was, at least in Galilee, a popular hero. He was widely acclaimed not only as the great healer but also the mighty teacher, the miracle man. Crowds thronged around Him. He was virtually caught in the crush of humanity that surged about Him.

To provide Himself with a little respite from these pressures, Jesus loved to walk alone along the lake. There He would commune quietly with His Father in heaven. But it would not be long before He was discovered, and again masses of people would congregate around Him.

Meanwhile His young companions had returned to fishing. Jesus saw them out in their boats on the lake one day and appealed to them for help. If they would put Him in Peter's boat and push out from shore a bit, He could speak to the multitudes massed on the beach without being smothered. The boys responded promptly. So Jesus, using Peter's boat as a platform, and depending on the amplifying effect of the lake, lectured to the crowd at a comfortable distance.

The arrangement worked well. And before too long the crowd, fully satisfied by His discourse from the lake, dispersed and headed for their homes. In typical fashion Jesus now turned His attention to the tired young fisher boys. They had been out all night, rowing their heavy boats, hauling heavy nets in and out of the dark waters, without any luck. All of them had been skunked. So they were weary, discouraged, and ready to go home to catch up on sleep.

Jesus spoke to the eldest, Peter: "Shove off into deep water. Just drop your nets. There will be a great haul!"

If Peter was skeptical he did not show it. He reminded Jesus that they had already fished all night without success, so daytime fishing would likely be even less productive. "But whatever You say, Master, I'll do it!"

It is a measure of Peter's forthright faith in Christ that he would even consent to try fishing during daylight. Quite easily and on good grounds he could have protested, if not audibly at least to himself, "What does the Master know about fishing anyway? He's a carpenter, whose life has been spent confined to a shop."

But Peter and his friends pushed off into deep water. They dropped their nets exactly where they had been told. And the result was they encircled a huge school of fish. So tremendous was the weight of thrashing tilapia enclosed by their nets that the skeins began to tear under the strain.

Tremendously excited, Peter waved frantically to the other fellows, James and John, in the other boat to come out and give them a hand. The upshot was such an enormous haul that both boats were filled to capacity. Gradually, as the huge catch was brought in, the boats well-nigh sank before they got back to the beach.

In all his years of fishing, Peter had never had such a haul. The sight of both boats loaded to the gunwales with shimmering silvery fish literally overwhelmed him. There were enough fish there to give him and his companions a glittering grubstake. He finally had it made.

In that moment Peter saw himself as he really was, a crude, coarse, limited man. And he saw Jesus in a new light: as the Son of God—as Lord not only of heaven but of Peter's lake.

In contrition of spirit—deeply conscious of his own selfish inclinations, always eager to make his pile—he saw the Master had come to him still once more in compassion. It broke Peter's tough, rough exterior. In utter contrition, he collapsed in the sand before Jesus and asked forgiveness.

Jesus was quick to pick Peter up. In gentle, strong, reassuring tones He spoke those gracious words that ever come from God to man—a man in repentance, a man in remorse, in contrition: *"Fear not."*

Then as though to doubly reassure him He added, "From now on you will take men for Me—not just fish from this lake." The statement had an electrifying effect on not only Peter but all four of the young men.

Without hesitation they all left the huge catch—left this veritable fortune in fish—and followed the Master. Where once before they had been prepared to leave their nets, leave their fathers, leave their boats, now they were leaving the very business of fishing itself, which was the backbone of their lives.

On the surface it seemed like the final step. It would appear that at last Jesus had their complete loyalty. But time, and subsequent events, showed it to be otherwise. For one thing still remained: they all still loved this lake. They loved fishing. In fact it was the great love in their lives.

After all the great miracles, after all the healings, after feeding the multitudes, after cleansing lepers and raising the dead, after Calvary, after several years of the most intimate companionship with Christ—Peter went back again to fishing. It seemed the only safe, sure, sane thing left to him and his friends, despite all they had seen Jesus do.

One dawn several years later, in His resurrection form, Jesus again walked on the beach beside this silver sheet of water. The eastern sky lightened softly. There on the sandy shore He prepared a fire and placed upon it a frugal fisherman's breakfast of wheat cakes and fresh fish.

Out on the lake His young friends had fished all night, and, as before, so long ago, without success. Again they were weary and worn.

Across the water Jesus called to them: "Fellows, have you caught anything?" Of course He knew they hadn't.

"Shoot your nets to the other side of the boat," He called. "There's a school there!"

Somehow they recognized the old familiar voice. It had that familiar ring of authority. They were used to doing what He said. And the nets were dropped once more. As the lines were drawn it was obvious they had an incredible haul.

It was a repeat performance.

How slow they were to learn.

It could be none other than the Lord who stood on land.

Beside himself with emotion, Peter dived into the lake and went thrashing to shore. This would be the third time the Master met him at the beach. It would be the third time he was encountered in the midst of his fishing. It would be the third time he would be called to leave the life he loved to follow Christ.

Graciously, with enormous empathy, Jesus prepared a hearty breakfast for His friends. They were too overwhelmed by their huge catch of 153 large fish to indulge in idle banter or empty bravado. They sat in silence, munching the crisp toasted cakes of wheat flour and delicious white flesh of the baked tilapia.

The sun rising over the desert hills to the east began to warm their bodies bared to its warmth. The world was not such a bleak, dark place after all. With their appetites satisfied and their tired bones relaxing in the sun, a poor fisherman's life seemed pretty sublime just at that point.

It was then Jesus turned to Peter and asked, "Peter, do you love Me more than all of these—these nets, these boats, these waters, these fish, these fellow fishermen?"

It was a sobering, searching, stabbing question. Three times it came. Each time with greater intensity. Peter's response was always positive: "Of course, Master, of course I love You more!"

"Then leave it all, Peter—all of it, even your love of it—and embark on a brand-new life for Me and others. Go and care for others; care for My people. No longer live for yourself."

From that day on these four men did just that. Never again would they look back. They had become true disciples, faithful followers.

What had really happened to the four young men who were to follow Christ to death itself? What was it that transformed not only dear, rough, tough, impulsive, powerful Peter, but also Andrew, James, and John from fishermen of Galilee to Shepherds in Israel—Shepherds in the early Church, ultimately; in due time, Shepherds to all men everywhere?

It was a new love.

It was a new flame of affection.

It was the expulsive energy of a new life center.

No longer were the nets, the boats, the fish, the gay camaraderie, the business of fishing, nor their love of the lake the center about which their lives revolved. At last, at long last, all of these had been left behind. And now their vision, their outlook, their absolute priority was centered in Christ, the Lord. He was their motivation. He was their power. He was the One who would enable them to go out and turn the world upside down. He was the One who would help them unhinge the might of Rome.

Of course they never realized this that warm, gentle day by the lake in Galilee when He first called them from their nets and from their boats. In their wildest dreams they had no idea such great events could spring eventually from such small beginnings.

It all seemed so very ordinary. It all appeared to be so very matter of course. Just Jesus of Nazareth quietly coming alongside His young friends, inviting them to follow Him. What could be more natural? There was no great publicity attached to it. There was no pomp and ceremony. There were no spectacular arrangements that would impress and sway the onlooking crowds.

This is so often God's gracious way of getting things done. He simply comes alongside us gently. We sense the call of His Spirit to our spirits. It is such a gentle invitation. He does not impose upon us. He is never harsh or rude or pushy. Yet He eagerly awaits our response. Patiently and with enormous love He comes again and again. Even when we turn away. Then one day, at last, our little spirits catch fire from His flame of love.

Then it is that little is much when God is in it!

CHAPTER SIXTEEN

The Forgiveness of God

Jesus came to Capernaum one day at the height of His popularity and was well-nigh mobbed. We can only assume it was around Peter's home that the crowds collected—shoving, pushing, yelling, trying every trick to get near Him and get His attention. Eastern people are readily aroused and easily excited. So we may be sure there were youngsters scrambling to climb the pillars of the porch or stretching on tiptoe to see in the windows. For Jesus was in town, healing the sick, cleansing the lepers, and casting evil spirits from those who thronged about Him, as well as teaching.

Amongst those who came that day were several young men carrying their paralytic friend on his pallet. Paralysis was an incurable condition in those times. It had a variety of causes. The most common was the result of venereal disease. And it is assumed this young man, stricken helpless, lying there immobilized on his thin mattress, was paying the high price of his prodigal life. He had been off to some alluring harlot city to squander his strength and savings. There some sloe-eyed beauty with smooth lips and soft words bequeathed him this dread disease which now exacted its terrible toll from his manhood.

The world has always had its share of prodigals and prostitutes. To many of the men and women who pride themselves on being very proper, prodigals and prostitutes are but the scum and offscouring of society. They are the despised, the disdained and the downgraded dregs. Yet, strange to say, often the prodigal is a downright cheerful, good-natured, outgoing, generous individual who has friends. He frequently has a much more desirable disposition than those who condemn him. And though he may sin grievously in his body, his disposition may well be more free of faults than his fellow human who is so quick to criticize.

At any rate, this man's friends were determined to deposit him in front of Jesus. Since they could not persuade the crowd to make way for them to get to Jesus, they decided on a daring move. They would tear some of the tile from the roof and let the poor chap down with ropes in front of the Master.

When the Master saw their scheme executed He was deeply touched. Here were fellows who really cared. Here were men with enormous empathy for their smitten friend. Here were fellows who obviously had enormous confidence in the Christ. They were sure He could cure the paralyzed playboy.

As they lowered the lad and laid him at Jesus' feet, the tempo of excitement increased. The crowd chattered, then fell silent. For Jesus looked down gently at the young man, and enormous understanding filled His features. He didn't need to be told the sleazy story of the boy's past behavior. Jesus had lived in tough, rough, wild Nazareth too long. He had seen lots of loose living in His hometown. He had known gentle young girls lured into selling their innocent, beautiful bodies to brutish men. He had known fine young men to be corrupted and ruined by the sly tactics of the professional prostitutes. And all of it made His blood boil and His righteous anger flame with white heat. No wonder He thundered, "If any man cause one of these little ones to fall, it is better he had a millstone strung round his throat and be drowned for his dastardly deeds."

The Master looked and loved the lad.

His very first word to him was pregnant with pity.

"Son . . . My boy . . . My dear young fellow . . . ."

Then with unbelievable hope, cheer, and encouragement came the strong assurance: "Your sins are forgiven." It was not just healing of muscles, sinews, joints, and bones this young man needed. He needed a healing of spirit, a purging of his soul, so deeply stained. He knew it. Jesus knew it.

The onlookers were taken aback!

The scribes, the scholars in the crowd were scandalized. "Forgive sins?" they gasped in false religiosity. "Who could forgive sins but God only?" With sham shock and horrified glances at each other they tugged their long beards, pretending superpiety at such a sacrilegious statement.

What they did not know was that it was indeed God, very God, who that hour spoke to the depths of this young man's deepest need. What he required at this special point was sure forgiveness. It was the only thing which could cleanse his conscience and erase the awesome guilt that enslaved his spirit.

Jesus not only knew the tumultuous thoughts racing wildly through the paralytic's passionate memory, He could also readily decipher the deep doubts and grievous misgivings chasing through the minds of the scribes.

Men have always had perplexing problems understanding God's generosity. Somehow they assume very wrongly that He moves and acts and behaves as we do. That His character and conduct are infinitely more magnanimous than man's escapes most people. They stumble over God's gentle, greatheartedness. They cannot grasp His selflessness. His enormous concern and compassion for us is beyond their understanding.

So the scribes looked at Jesus and thought to themselves, If He knew anything at all, at least He should know this young hellion was just getting exactly what he deserved. If he has played the fool, he would simply have to pay the penalty for his perverseness.

What they did not realize was that this lad, they themselves, and all of us, have grieved God with our petty pride and selfish self-centeredness. All of us somewhere, sometime, somehow have offended and fallen far short of complying with God's wishes. We have sinned perhaps in the inner privacy of our own thoughts, attitudes, or intentions. Our actions may not have been as open as the obvious sins of this unfortunate fellow at Jesus' feet, but they have been every bit as heinous to a holy God.

Yet in the midst of all our sin and sham and shame God comes to us with the great good news that Jesus gave this lad: "Your sins are forgiven!"

Most of us do not really believe this.

Most men refuse to accept this.

Somehow they feel certain that it is only their own good behavior, their own commendable conduct that will somehow appease God. It never can. It never will. Only the perfect life and the impeccable Person of God in Christ can satisfy the infinitely lofty demands of deity. And He has. He being the infinite, eternal One, ever laying Himself out for us—ever giving Himself on our behalf as demonstrated in His dying for us at Calvary—He completely and utterly satisfied the justice and judgment of God on us sinners.

All men, of all time, stand justified, acquitted, forgiven and accepted before God our Father, not on the basis of our good behavior, but on the grounds of His giving Himself as our substitute in our stead. But the individual must accept this personally.

Jesus, when He looked longingly into the eyes of that boy and said "Son, your sins be forgiven you," already had suffered and died in His stead. Perhaps not in terms of our limited view and restricted concept of human history, but very definitely from the eternal standpoint of an eternal God. For, even before the foundation of the earth, this Christ had tasted death for every man. He had already given His life a ransom for many. He dwelt in the ever enduring, ever-present dimension of the eternal I AM, which ever pays the penalty and endures the suffering that sets us free—forgiven before God.

From man's limited view of history this boy and multitudes of others before him were forgiven of God, in Christ, as they looked ahead to God's Lamb offered on Calvary. Likewise all of us since that epoch hour look back to the cross. But this is because we are locked into a time/space concept conditioned by life on planet earth.

What we all should do, really, is "look up"—as this lad looked up—to find forgiveness. That forgiveness is ever extended to men. It is ever available to all of us. It is ever purchased by the doing and the dying of God in Christ. We cannot purchase, merit, or earn it. We simply accept it in enormous gratitude to God for His generosity and love. It is He who has paid the price for our peace with Himself. And in our acceptance of His provision we find ourselves at peace with Him. We are reconciled. We are forgiven. We are accepted into His family and affection. We are indeed—as Jesus called this lad—a *son*.

All of this was beyond the scribes. They were cynics. They were skeptics. Like their ecclesiastical contemporaries, the Sadducees and Pharisees, they never would grasp that Jesus was God, very God. Always they would regard Him as a threat. They would treat Him as a charlatan, an impostor or pretender. He had come unto His own, but His own—except for the publicans, sinners, and a few fishermen—received Him not.

But to those who did receive Him, like the paralyzed lad, He gave the capacity to become the "sons of God."

Even though Jesus could not convince the scribes that He was indeed God, able to forgive sins, He would demonstrate that He was God, able to cure the incurable. No one had ever seen a paralytic restored to health. For at that time paralysis was a terminal disease without hope of recovery.

Jesus addressed Himself directly to the young man: "I say unto you *arise!* Take up your pallet and go home!" And he did just that, to the utter amazement of all the onlookers. A hush of awe swept through the bystanders. Never had they witnessed such a recovery before. This could only be a divine act of God.

It is important to pause here just a moment. The events reported here in the Gospel account have, across the years, become rather commonplace to us. But for the crowds milling around Peter's little house that day they were momentous: Not only was there a great prophet come to Israel. Not only was there a great teacher amongst them. Not only was there a man of God endowed with ability to heal moving across the country. Not only was there a gifted "seer" with enormous spiritual power who could cast out evil spirits at work in their world. But more, much more, than all of these: God, Jehovah—the One who alone could forgive sins—had come.

It took a lot of faith to believe that.

Quite obviously the boy had such confidence.

At Christ's command, he neither argued nor debated that it might be possible for him to get up and walk. He just did what he was told to do. And in that instant there was transmitted to him the life of God that enabled him to get up and go home.

We hear no more about him or his four companions who brought him to Jesus. Often I have longed for further information about the folks whose lives Jesus transformed. Someday, of course, we shall know more, much more, when we meet in person.

Of one thing I do feel quite sure. It was with this young man in mind, and perhaps others like him, that Jesus later gave His winsome, wonderful story of the prodigal son.

CHAPTER SEVENTEEN

Matthew the Man

As the months moved along, Jesus, now known as the Master by His young associates, gradually gathered up a following. We are given very few details about most of these men. At one stage there were well over eighty who showed some sort of allegiance to the Messiah. But, as is so often the case, most of these found the demands of dedicated discipleship too tough to stay with it. For one reason and another they dropped out and turned back to their former way of life. It is this which prompted Jesus to say: "Any man who sets his hand to the plow, then turns back, is not fit for service." And on another occasion He asked His closest intimates if they, too, were going to desert Him. Peter promptly protested that they couldn't, since no one else had the words of truth and life which they had found with Him.

Of the twelve who remained most faithful, Matthew was perhaps one of the most unlikely to succeed. In fact he was also one of the most unlikely that could be imagined ever to be invited to join this select circle. That the other eleven would even tolerate Matthew is somewhat of a minor miracle.

Matthew was a publican, a public servant in the despised service of the hated Romans. He was a collector of taxes for the foreign power. He was one of a group of citizenry that was regarded with utmost contempt by his countrymen. To them tax collectors were equated with traitors: fifth columnists and agents of the detested

Romans. Anyone who lowered himself to levy taxes on his fellow Jews was looked upon as the lowest of the low.

This was doubly so because of the greed, graft, and corruption that attended the extraction of taxes from the common people. Any amount of money over and above that demanded by the Roman officials that the tax collectors could wring from the populace by extortion went to line their own silk pockets. By threats, blackmail, deceit, and outright corruption, the tax collectors became blackguards who managed to satisfy Rome's demands while becoming enormously wealthy themselves at the expense of those they taxed. This is why John the Baptist thundered at them not to extort more than was due from the poor.

Taxes at this point were well-nigh intolerable to bear. They were a burden about to break the back of the poor taxpayer. There were personal taxes, property taxes, poll taxes, road taxes, trade taxes, temple taxes, besides other dues of one sort or another that were in truth also taxes.

Jesus and His other disciples had been exposed to these taxes. For their homes, for their families, for their businesses as fishermen, carpenters, or farmers, for their travel, there always had to be found money to meet the insatiable demands of a despotic government. So taxes and tax collectors were equally hated, equally resented by the Jews. It was what ground them down in subjection to Rome's iron might.

It is not surprising that one day Jesus was accosted openly about taxes. People wanted to know His position on this explosive issue. "Did one really have to pay taxes to an evil emperor like Caesar?" In quiet simplicity Jesus responded by asking for a coin. Probably He didn't have one in His own pocket. "Pay to Caesar the things that are Caesar's," He replied, turning over the rough two-sided coin between His fingers, "and give to God the things that are God's!" It was that simple.

Another time Peter and some of the other fellows had been accosted by the tax collectors in their travels. Even if they were only transients, the tax had to be paid. In protest they came to the Master. Their kitty was empty and there simply wasn't anything at hand to discharge the debt to Caesar. Jesus did not try to dodge or evade the tax. "Simply go down to the lake, Peter, and catch a fish!'' Happily, by this time Peter knew enough to just comply with a simple command. When the fish was caught, Peter found a coin in its mouth of sufficient worth to pay the tax collector.

So when the day came that Jesus decided to call Matthew to His side, it was a startling event. It was similar to inviting the enemy to join the ranks. If the other disciples had deep reservations about Matthew, Jesus did not. No doubt Jesus had passed Matthew's post a good many times. Something about the Messiah appealed to the tough-minded young man. Perhaps he had dared to ask one or two questions that revealed there was that within his tough exterior which would respond one day to the Christ.

Fortunately for Matthew, when Jesus looked at him He did not see just a tough tax collector, a perverted publican. What the Master saw was *a man*—a man of latent possibilities, a man whose life could be completely changed in character and direction, a man who would no longer live for the love of money but for the love of God. And looking on this man, the Master loved him and called him to be His follower.

How marvelous that this man responded to the quiet, compelling overtures of the Christ. Because of his response all the world has been enriched. Because of Matthew's coming, millions upon millions of men and women have been given a glimpse into the splendor and majesty of Jesus the Christ as the Messiah—the King of Israel, God's Anointed. In Matthew's account there is recorded the majestic Sermon on the Mount, itself the loftiest standard for human conduct ever presented on the planet. It is Matthew who stirs our spirits with the awareness that in the coming of the Christ the Old Testament prophets were fulfilled and vindicated. And it is Matthew who has given us the magnificent insights into the future plans of God for His people, recorded so splendidly in the Olivet discourse.

If ever our flagging spirits need to be rejuvenated, if ever our heavy hearts, burdened by our own limitations, need to be lifted, a heartening exercise is to remind ourselves of what the Lord made of Levi (Matthew). If Jesus could take a tough tax man and turn him into a loyal ambassador for the Most High God, He can do mighty deeds with any one of us—if we but respond and become totally available to His tender touch.

Matthew's response represented a much greater sacrifice than any of the other disciples'. He was a man who had it made. He was a man who had a secure position and power. He was a man who had already amassed wealth. To leave all this was much more demanding than to abandon some old nets, some crude boats, or the unpredictable profession of fishing that might or might not pay off.

For Matthew to follow Jesus into abject poverty, privation, and years of wandering across the then-known world was a tremendous step to take.

To celebrate his going, Matthew threw a farewell party. The dinner guests were a motley crowd. Most of them were Matthew's old cronies, other publicans like himself, who had more or less banded together as common outcasts ostracized by a belligerent society. Matthew made no bones about it, he was changing course in life. He was not about to become a secret follower of the Christ; he had made up his mind whom he would serve. It was he who later reported what Jesus taught so clearly: "You cannot serve God and money. You cannot have two masters. Either you love one and hate the other or vice versa. You can't play both ends of the field."

Some of the other company that came to celebrate this special occasion were the town toughs—the ruffians employed by the publicans to extract the taxes from the more recalcitrant residents. And of course in their train were the so-called sinners, scum of society—prostitutes, pimps, and profligates.

Surprising as it sounds to us and shocking as it was to the Pharisees, Jesus and His other disciples joined this dinner party. It is always well to remind ourselves that by attending affairs of this sort the Master was in no way condoning the character or conduct of His associates. What He was doing was reaching down to touch and transform those who up until this hour had never heard a word from heaven. These were the offscourings of society. These were the dregs of the community. These were the lost sheep. These were the men and women on whom no eye had ever looked in pity, on whom no hand had ever rested to rescue them.

And then Jesus came along.

When accused of misconduct and improper behavior by the very "proper" religious people, His reply was simple: "I—God—insist on mercy, on justice, on compassion for fallen, despised men. This is more important than any temple ritual or solemn sacrifice. I am come to call not self-righteous snobs but poor sinners.''

That day Matthew, a black sheep, a lost sheep, was called. That day that wayward, wicked man turned to follow Christ. That day he took his first steps on a long, torturous, blessed journey that eventually led him to be the great apostle who would bring the good news to Ethiopia and other northern regions of Africa.

CHAPTER EIGHTEEN

Jesus Deals With Death

Jairus was a prominent person in the town of Capernaum. His position as one of the directors of the local synagogue gave him considerable prestige. He was wealthy enough that he was regarded as one of the local celebrities who did not fraternize with common folk. In fact most of them would tip their heads slightly as a sign of humble respect when he passed. Some would even call out *shalom*—peace be to you—when he proudly walked by them.

The day Jesus had cast the evil spirit from the man who railed at Him in the synagogue, Jairus was there. He had no doubt been deeply impressed by this amazing act. But even more, Jesus' familiarity with the Scriptures and His ability to teach from them with enormous authority had left an indelible mark on Jairus. Something within his spirit responded to the young prophet and miracle worker from Nazareth. Jairus recognized that here was no ordinary Galilean—but rather, *a Master come from God.*

Then one day it happened. Death—man's implacable enemy—stood on the doorstep of Jairus' home. Death—the ancient reaper of men's souls—knocked loudly on his door. Death—with its grim foreboding—laid its icy fingers on the frail little life of his fair, lovely daughter.

In that frightening hour Jairus discovered that death reduces all men to the same level. Death is the common denominator that makes no distinction between weak and strong, rich and poor, famous and obscure, prince and peasant, good and evil. And in that discovery he saw that when death is on the doorstep, men and money and resources of earthly sort have little to contribute. It is then a man must seek support and strength from some spiritual source outside himself.

So while the little maid lay prostrate on her bed at the point of death, her father hurried off to find Jesus. There he prostrated himself at those roughshod, sandaled feet of the One who above all others could help him in his dark hour. Jairus in this crisis forgot his pride, forgot his prestige, forgot his prominence. Death had stripped him of any false facade.

In this humbling, faith sprang to life. He had complete confidence the Master had but to lay His hands upon his little girl and she would be restored. He did not hesitate to say so loudly and clearly. In his prostrate position there was no one else who could help, no one else who could heal.

"I beg You, Master," he pleaded earnestly with upturned eyes, "come, lay Your hands on her. She will be healed. She will live!"

It was a forthright, pragmatic declaration. This was bold, brave faith in God. And Jesus responded positively. He started off at once toward Jairus' home.

Those of us who have faced death close at hand in our own homes or families have found God always responds promptly to our pleas. The calm comfort and quiet courage He imparts to us far transcends any support that might come from men or women. It is at such times that we find in Him a comrade in arms, the One who stands beside us and goes with us through the ordeal.

Jesus set off with Jairus, but His pathway was jammed with mobs of men and women who crowded around. It was slow going. And as the time slipped away, Jairus became impatient with the interminable interruptions and delays. If they didn't hurry, his daughter would be dead.

Suddenly Jesus stopped. Someone with an unusually severe disease had touched Him. In that instant, strength and vitality had drained away from Him. He sensed the life-giving stamina flow swiftly from Himself.

"Who touched My clothes?" He turned to look over the sea of faces crushing in around Him. His disciples were surprised He

would ask such a question. Scores of people, different people of all
sorts, were constantly crowding around Him, brushing against
Him, touching Him on every side. Why would He ask such an
absurd question? But for one weak, sick little woman in that crowd it was a crucial
question. With commingled relief, joy, and fear at being found out,
she came out of the crowd and crouched at Jesus' feet. She was
made whole. Her fears were laid to rest. And she went away in
peace.

But all of this had taken time. Precious minutes had passed by
and Jairus wondered if it was too late.

Yes, yes. It was too late!

For at that very instant some excited servants from his house
shoved and pushed their panting way through the milling masses.
With dilated eyes and sweat-streaked faces they searched for
Jairus in the crowd. When they found him they blurted out the
dreadful news.

"Your daughter has died! No use expecting the Master to help
now! It's too late!"

Happily, Jesus overheard the conversation. He always does,
even though we may not realize it. He turned to Jairus and in calm,
even tones reassured his fear-gripped heart: "Be not afraid—just
believe."

It is one thing to be told to do this; it is quite another thing to
comply with the instructions. Always, ever, the initial word of God
that invariably comes to us is "Fear not. Peace be to you. Believe
in Me." This is always Christ's approach to us troubled, trembling
men. With our hearts pounding, our minds racing, our anxieties
seething with turmoil, He puts His hand upon us and speaks peace
to our spirits and strength to our souls.

"Jairus, don't be troubled."

"Jairus, just have confidence in Me."

It is a mark of the man's faith that he persisted in having Jesus
come to his home. In spite of the protests of those who had brought
the bad news, he would just carry on. Jesus' response was prompt
and moving. Firmly He forbade the crowd to crush them anymore.
Then swiftly, with only His three favorite disciples in attendance,
they hurried off to Jairus' house.

In typical Eastern fashion, a tremendous tumult was going on because of the bereaved. Women were wailing, screaming, and beating their breasts. Men moaned through their beards, chanted groaning lamentations, and held their heads in despair. Alone and apart from God most men and women are distraught in the face of death. There is something terribly final and terrifyingly dreadful in death. To those who do not know the One who has vanquished death, it is a horrifying thing.

But for those who know Christ, death is but a doorway into a magnificent new dimension of life.

Christ is the One who lived on the other side so long before coming to dwell on our side. He is the One, as the old former slave once put it on his deathbed, who "owns the land on both sides of the river." He it is who is familiar with both "here" and "there."

Without being facetious, Jesus called to the disconsolate crowd of weeping, wailing mourners, "Why all this ado? Why all this grief? Why all this mourning?" (They were startled and shocked. Was He mad? Didn't He understand?) "The little girl is not dead—just asleep!"

Now their shock and incredulity turned to scorn. He must be out of His mind. With derision and contempt they jeered and laughed at Him.

Isn't it amazing how volatile human nature can be? Here were people who one moment mourned and wept with tear-stained cheeks, then the next burst into lurid laughter. People are utterly unpredictable, totally unreliable, completely contrary to what might be expected.

Jesus did not delay. He did not waste words in pointless debate. Death was something beyond men's ability to manage. He alone could cope with it. He would have to show Jairus—who alone had confidence in His control—how He would handle it.

With firm but quiet authority Jesus cleared the house of the skeptics and cynics. Then, alone with the child's parents and His three disciples, Peter, James, and John, as witnesses, He entered gently into the child's sickroom.

In His usual tender way, with enormous compassion He stooped down and took her tiny hand. It was so small lying there in the strong grasp of His big hand. Then He spoke softly—"Little girl, get up!" It was all so simple, so unostentatious. It was just like Jesus. Clean. Clear. Strong. Sure. Sublime.

Immediately the little lass rose from her bed and walked quickly to her parents. Eyes large with wonderment, joy, and relief, they were utterly astonished.

"Tell no one!" He said gently, smiling on them as they hugged each other. "But see that she gets something to eat."

Then He was gone.

For our Lord, this was to be the first of three direct encounters with death. The second time He restored the son of the widow of Nain. The boy was already on the bier, being borne away to the burial ground. The third was His friend Lazarus, brother to Martha and Mary. Here again, because of delay, death had come, and the corpse had been interred for four days. In each succeeding case the impact of death was more prolonged, yet the Master was able to restore them to the earth scene, reuniting them with their sorrowing families.

Jesus found no particular pleasure in reversing the natural processes of death by His supernatural power. He, better than anyone else, knew, loved, and delighted in the freedom and joys of eternal life. To Him the exciting ecstasy of life with God beyond the grave was a sublime dimension of living. It far, far transcended the tears, trial, torment, and turmoil of life on this planet. And for anyone who had tasted of its delight, to return here would be sad retrogression.

This is why He wept at Lazarus' grave. It was not remorse for Martha or Mary in their distress, but agony of spirit for Lazarus. It was akin to a bird set free in the field, at liberty to fly with free abandon only to be recaptured and returned to its confining cage again.

But Jesus raised these three people from death because of enormous compassion for the bereaved ones left behind. He restored them in response to the living faith of the loved ones. He sensed that Jairus and his wife longed for this precious little girl who had so gladdened their lives. He knew that the widow of Nain, alone without a husband, needed a strong son to provide for her care. He could see that Mary and Martha would pine for the sweet companionship and strong support that only Lazarus could give them.

This is one of the truly thrilling things about God. He does know. He does feel. He does understand. He does come to men and women in distress, disease, and death to give us that which is best suited to our individual needs.

In that we rejoice and in that we find consolation.

CHAPTER NINETEEN

Commissioned Out of Compassion

It is sometimes thought, erroneously, that Jesus was always a despised and somewhat scorned figure. At the end of His first year of public ministry He was easily the most popular person in Palestine. He had won the love and loyalty of thousands. His healing touch had attracted masses to Him, many of whom would be eternally grateful. He had delivered those possessed by devils from their dungeons of despair. He had taught about God as His Father and our Father in a way no other man had ever dared to do. It had electrified the crowds. They were attracted by teaching that touched their hearts, that moved their hopes toward heaven, and set their spirits singing.

In fact, so much was He in favor with the general populace, especially of Galilee, that His implacable enemies, the priests, Pharisees, Sadducees, and scribes dared not lay hands on Him in public. Always they planned their strategy of trying to trap Him with special regard to how the whole country might react. They were extremely afraid that if He were ever seized openly it would precipitate a riot. The upshot would be to endanger their own position of privilege with the Roman authorities.

So for the first year of His public life and well on into the second, Jesus moved freely across the countryside. He was anxious to visit as many villages, towns, and hamlets as the short span of time allotted to Him would permit. There is no question at all that Jesus knew with a deep, divine intuition that His time as an itinerant minister would be brief. At best it could not be more than a small fraction of that He spent in the carpenter shop.

The Gospel report of this period is likewise brief and pointed: "He went about doing good."

What a record!

The difficult thing for us to bear in mind about Jesus, when thinking about His earthly life, is that He was more than a man. He was also God, clothed in the clay of common humanity.

When He touched lives, it was God touching men and women.
When He taught the Scriptures, it was God transmitting truth.
When He healed the sick, it was God's hand of restoration.
When He preached the Gospel, it was God's good news firsthand.
When He looked on the masses, He saw them as God does.

Unless we grasp this concept, we are bound to conclude that Jesus of Nazareth was no more than a very superior man. And we end up compressing Him into the very limited role of a mere man. He was much, much more.

When He looked out over the multitudes which thronged Him day after day, week in, week out, He was not moved to conceit or self-adulation. Instead He was moved to tears. The fact that men hung on His words did not pander to His ego. Rather, He realized He was amongst multitudes of hopelessly lost souls. Like sheep without a shepherd, they were dazed, bewildered and destitute. He knew this even better than they did themselves, because He understood mankind better than they understood themselves.

But even beyond all of this, being God, He saw not only the masses milling about Him with His physical eyes but also the millions already born up to that hour—and, besides, the multiplied billions yet to be born. Planet earth would, across the long centuries of human history, bear men and women as plenteous as grains of sand upon the shore, as countless as the stars that populate the enormous immensity of outer space.

And it was for all these multiplied millions upon millions that He had come. It was to redeem, restore, and reconcile them that He now ministered amongst them. Yet steadily He moved toward the great climactic events of Calvary, His Resurrection and His Ascension.

Looking out across the crowds, He called His disciples to Him. His eyes were misty with tears. His voice was low, broken with sobs. His deepest emotions were overwhelmed with empathy. His whole big, strong frame shook. The young, rough, tough Twelve had never seen the Master in this state before. It was a bit embarrassing for the boys. They were abashed and turned to look away. As far as they were concerned, the eternal crowds were a bit of a pain. People were so unpredictable, so fault finding, so complaining, so stupid, and so often very ungrateful. No matter how much the Master did, someone always demanded more. They were never really satisfied. Why not send them home?

And yet here was the Master, all broken up over these people. How He cared. What enormous compassion He displayed for the sons of men.

"Boys," He said, pointing His arms out over the multitudes, "there are millions of lost sheep, but precious few pet lambs to bring them home."

He turned and looked at the young fellows intently. "Start to pray that the Lord, the Great Shepherd, will send out some bellwethers to bring back the wayward wanderers."

The disciples, none of whom was a shepherd boy, nevertheless knew exactly what Jesus was talking about. They had all seen local shepherds gathering up sheep. They did not use dogs to do this job, the way shepherds in the Western countries do. Their scrawny, mangy dogs were kept just to guard their homes and sheepfold from marauders.

When an Eastern shepherd wanted to bring home lost and wayward sheep he took his pet lamb along with him into the wild pastures. These bellwethers would then gently follow the shepherd back home, bringing the strays and stragglers in their footsteps. It was a delightful ancient practice that worked to perfection.

The disciples must have complied promptly with the Master's unusual request, for their prayers were answered immediately in a most unusual way: Jesus turned to them and said, "You are the ones I shall send out. You are My pet lambs. You have become very attached to Me as the Shepherd of the sheep. I am sending you out now to the lost sheep of Israel. You will be as sheep among wolves. But don't be afraid; I am with you."

It was quite a commissioning.

The disciples had never imagined before that the Master would so soon send them out in service. After all, they really didn't know Him all that well yet. In fact several of the last to join Him were pretty raw recruits.

Happily for them, Jesus made it very clear that they were being sent out under His authority. They would go in His name. He gave them amazing ability to heal the sick. They were endowed with immense power to cast out evil spirits. They were enabled to speak and teach and preach with great effectiveness. In short, what He Himself had done, they could do. What He had been attempting single-handed would now be multiplied at least twelve times over . . . perhaps many, many times over as He commissioned further disciples.

It was an excited and stimulated group of young men who set out in pairs on the first great missionary thrust of the Christian era. So often it is assumed that the early Church did not begin until the first Pentecost after Christ's Ascension. The first deep plowing and first planting of the seed that later was to grow into a great Church was done by these twelve young fellows up in Galilee, about two years before Pentecost.

And before that there had been John the Baptist's mighty mission to millions.

Without any financial support, without gold or silver or even brass coins in their purses, they were to go. God Himself would supply support. They were not to have any prearranged itinerary, no blueprint of planned procedure. The Spirit of God would be their guide. No extra clothing or provision for overnight stops was to be taken along. The hospitality of prepared hearts and prepared homes along the way would take care of that.

It was a tough, challenging assignment. Especially for a man like Matthew who had enjoyed luxury, comfort, and security, this would be a dreadfully demanding ordeal. He gives us all the precise details of what was actually entailed in this commissioning.

The Master made it abundantly clear what their responsibilities were. It wasn't just a happy holiday. It wasn't just a lark for the lads. It wasn't just a far-out adventure. Here were His instructions: "Don't go to the gentiles or Samaritans at this point. Just go to the lost sheep of Israel. Preach the Gospel of God's kingdom. It's here. Heal the sick. Cleanse lepers. Raise the dead. Cast out devils. Give away and share whatever you have been given. Be as wise as serpents, harmless as gentle doves. Don't be afraid! For whatever you need to say in any situation will be told you by God's Spirit."

What a fantastic assignment for these rough fellows.

Just to carry out one part is all most men want today. On the mission field a man is considered either a teacher, an evangelist, a doctor, a social worker, an agriculturist, or some other single profession. Here were twelve youths entrusted by Christ to fulfill the entire full-orbed responsibilities of ministering completely to the entire person—*body, soul, and spirit.*

Incredible as it seems, they did just that—*in His power.*

In my view, this ranks with the greatest and most marvelous of all Jesus' miracles. It especially thrills and captivates my spirit because it demonstrates what Christ can do with anyone who is available to Him. We have to remind ourselves that in this group of twelve, who went out with such confidence, were men with enormous imperfections and failings. Amongst them were hotheaded fiery fellows like James and John, the Sons of Thunder, who wanted to call down fire from heaven to burn up a community. There was impatient Peter, utterly unpredictable, a tough, coarse fisherman who could swear a blue streak of profanity. There was Judas, a grafter and schemer, greedy for gain and quick to steal.

Despite all their defects, despite all of their peculiar idiosyncrasies, Jesus did not discard nor jettison one of these fellows. He simply sent them out to do a job just as He found them.

The secret in the whole enterprise escapes most people. The reason they succeeded so well and later returned to Him with such jubilant reports has not registered with many of God's people. It is this: It was Christ Himself by His Spirit within them who achieved the results.

It was He who taught; it was He who healed; it was He who cleansed the lepers; it was He who cast out evil spirits; it was He who brought the good news of the kingdom.

What the boys learned during those trailblazing events was the basic fact that the Master could be relied on, even when He was not there in person, that He is just as real, just as powerful, just as effective by His Spirit as He was in person.

It was a lesson that they would soon forget. For after all, they were just fallible men like you and me. We too forget.

CHAPTER TWENTY

The Fragrance of Gratitude

While the disciples were off on their exciting mission, Jesus Himself moved about steadily from city to city, village to village. In one town a prominent Pharisee named Simon prevailed on the Master to come and dine with him. Strange as it might seem at first, Jesus agreed to go, even though He knew Pharisees despised Him. Obviously He was as willing to eat with Pharisees as He was to associate with publicans and sinners. No doubt He would be less comfortable in the company of those who condemned Him; it is, however, a mark of His magnanimous character that He gave Himself to whoever asked of Him.

Subsequent events would lead us to believe that the Christ knew full well what excitement would be generated by His visit to this home. It was to be a memorable day for both Him and His host, Simon, and an uninvited stranger who came stumbling in off the streets.

She was what the Gospel record refers to as a "sinner," which in modern parlance means a prostitute or call girl. It is commonly thought that this woman was none other than Mary Magdalene, out of whom Jesus had cast seven evil spirits: the girl who was set free from those dreaded demonic forces to become one of His most adoring and ardent followers. She was the very first to have an intimate encounter with Him after His death and Resurrection.

On this particular day, as Jesus and Simon, along with other notable guests, reclined on soft cushions, eating a sumptuous meal, the beautiful girl stepped into the room. Softly, swiftly she slipped over behind Jesus. She stood behind Him sobbing. Great hot, uncontrollable tears trickled down over her smooth flushed cheeks to fall on His feet. His feet were dusty, soiled with long miles on the hot road. That was surprising, because normally a guest was given water to wash his feet. But this host had such contempt for Jesus that He was denied this simple courtesy.

The gorgeous girl, her whole frame shaken with sobs, stooped down and let her long raven locks fall about His feet. The tears flowed freely, bathing His skin, washing away the dust. Gently she dried those feet with her lustrous, lovely hair. Then she kissed them in tender, moving contrition.

It was an act not of erotic infatuation but of the most profound homage. Louder and clearer than anything she might have said, it proclaimed to all present "I am Your lifelong slave! I am Yours and Yours alone, forever."

In a moving gesture of the utmost gratitude she broke open a jar of costly perfume and poured it over those dear feet. Its sweet, pungent fragrance enfolded the Master's feet. Those dear feet that had brought Him to her town, brought Him into her life, brought Him to this house. Now the pungent perfume pervaded the whole place. To Jesus, the Christ, it came as a sweet incense of gratitude. To Simon it came as a scurrilous scandal.

How people saw Jesus in His day depended, even as it does now, on the point of view from which they looked at Him.

From Simon's standpoint Jesus was just an object of curiosity. He had heard about this famous wonder-working mendicant teacher from Nazareth. He would have Him to his house to display Him to his friends. It would put him up a notch on the social ladder to say that he had entertained such a celebrity, even though at heart he was sure Jesus was a charlatan of the lowest order. But one could be very phony as a Pharisee—not only in word but also in action.

This is why, pretending to be terribly humiliated by the girl's presence in his home, he was at the same time saying to himself, "If this man were a genuine prophet, a true man of God, He would have known what kind of awful sinner had touched Him. But quite obviously He doesn't, because He even allows her to bathe and perfume His body."

What Simon did not know was that Jesus knew this young woman well. He also knew Simon well and could see right through his phony facade. In fact they all knew one another very well. It was no mere coincidence that this attractive girl felt so free to enter this Pharisee's house with such nonchalance. She had been there before. She knew it well. The pious old pretender had been one of her most frequent clients. His only possible cover-up now was to playact the part of a man scandalized by her sudden appearance. How phony could one be?

But before all this—before the banquet, before the breaking of the expensive alabaster box—Jesus and the woman had met. That meeting was an event destined to redirect the whole of the girl's life. For when she met Jesus she met true love for the first time in her stormy life. The love she met in Christ was not erotic love based on physical attraction or masculine magnetism. It was not filial love, in which he sensed a friendly sympathy for her lowly position in society. It was the love of God.

This love, spoken of so often and frequently by the Master, was a selfless, self-giving love. For the first time she had run into a man who did not exploit her, who did not take her for the selfish self-satisfaction he could get from her, who did not use her to gratify and indulge his own private ego.

The encounter had an enormous impact on the call girl with her lovely face and lithe form. Here was a man who loved her for her own sake. Here was a man who saw through her tough exterior to her heart that asked for love. Here was a man who set her free from the dreadful dungeon of her old life-style of selfish self-centeredness. For she too had exploited others as they had exploited her. Here was a man who had given her a glimpse of what God was like, of His generous forgiveness, and of what He could make of her. Here was a man who was, in fact, *God*.

Her encounter with Christ had been the great crisis in her life. She would never, could never, be the same again. She had been transformed, remade, reborn. Her virginity had been restored to her. She was now a girl chaste in body, pure in mind, sublime in spirit. For her life and spirit had been touched and cleansed and redirected by the loving Spirit of the Saviour.

The tears that flowed from her that day were tears of joy, tears of known forgiveness, tears of gratitude. Her humble gestures of washing the Master's feet and drying them with her own shining, scented hair were gestures of utter adoration, utter wonder, utter appreciation. Her extravagant outpouring of the perfume on His person was a declaration of her devotion, love, and allegiance to the One who had become the Lord of her life.

From the account given to us we must conclude that she never spoke a single sentence or uttered a single word the whole time she was in the Pharisee's house. But what she did spoke volumes in tones more clear and penetrating than anything she might have said.

Out of an enormous sense of her soul's emancipation her whole being expressed thanks. Out of the depths of total forgiveness for her polluted past her spirit spoke gratitude to God. Out of the delight of deliverance from her bodily passions she gave praise with the fragrance of her perfume. That which previously she would have expended upon herself to become more attractive, now she poured out lavishly with total abandon upon her Lord and Saviour.

It is not surprising that Jesus turned around and looked full into the girl's flushed face and shining eyes. What He saw was not remorse. It was radiant expectancy. His words were to her leaping spirit a stimulating fragrance more refreshing, more potent than any man-made perfume: "You are forgiven! You are remade. Go in peace!"

For Simon this was a most difficult day. He had no idea he would get himself into such deep water simply by trying to satisfy his curiosity about Jesus. What had started out as just another trifling little social affair had suddenly become a most painful spiritual interlude. He had never dreamed a man like Jesus could see clear through him. He had been able to run a bluff on most of his friends for years. He had successfully pulled the wool over most people's eyes all his life. But now he found suddenly that he just couldn't play games with this One—this teacher who called Himself the Son of man but whom others declared fiercely to be the Son of God.

Though Jesus had kept His gaze fastened on the girl, He had kept His remarks directed to Simon. And what He had to say was like a knife cutting away the man's mask.

"Do you really see this woman, Simon? Do you really see her as she is now? Do you see her as a sinner, or do you see her as a saint? Do you, Simon, vaguely understand the spiritual transaction that has taken place? You are a Pharisee, one of those supposedly learned in matters spiritual—you ought to be able to comprehend!"

But evidently Simon did not. Like his contemporary Nicodemus, and like so many students of Scripture who are steeped in deep teaching about spiritual things, these were men who knew all about God, but who really never knew God. There is a world of difference. Simon's abused and humiliated guest that day was God—but he did not, could not, recognize Him.

"Simon, I, God very God, came into your home today as an invited guest. You never even offered Me a basin of cool water in which to refresh My tired, aching feet. That is the very least courtesy extended to a stranger. But intentionally you tried to snub Me. Your omission was more than made up for by the tender tears of a contrite, gorgeous girl."

To him that knoweth to do good and doeth it not—it is sin.

"Simon, you had no towel at hand for My feet. For you to even hand Me one, let alone dry My toes, would be asking too much of a proud Pharisee. You would never lower yourself to such a menial task. But this beauty has taken the crowning glory of her own gorgeous hair and wiped away the dust and dirt and sweat."

Let him that would be greatest amongst you be a servant.

"Simon, you could not condescend to kiss My cheek in greeting as I crossed the threshold of your home. It would be too humiliating for you to be seen by your associates extending this welcome to a wanderer off the dusty roads of your town. You just save your kisses for your very special friends and family who can always return the compliment. But My feet have been caressed by the sweet, soft lips of this lovely lady who at long last has found true love."

Be careful to entertain strangers. For some unwittingly have entertained angels unawares—yes, and even God.

"Simon, you could not find it within yourself to share a little ordinary olive oil with Me. Just a few drops to refresh My face and hair would have been enough. It would have shown you cared a little for a common man. But that would have been debasing for a proud, rich ruler like you. Meanwhile this woman, this unusual woman, in glad abandon has anointed My feet with the most expensive of perfumes. Its fragrance envelops My whole body. It permeates the whole house. It even enfolds your selfish, shriveled soul."

Freely she is forgiven, and freely she has given. Her gratitude makes it so apparent she knows God.

That momentous day Simon had to search his own soul as it had never been searched before. In the blazing light of the love of God he would have to discover what motivated him. Where was he going? Could he, like the woman, go on in peace?

CHAPTER TWENTY-ONE

The Story of Two Storms

Jesus' increasing popularity and national prominence drew ever larger crowds around Him. The personal pressures from hordes of people mounted. There were days when by eventide it seemed He could scarcely take another step or speak another syllable, so weary was He. The incessant demands of those in need drained strength, love, and vitality from Him like streams of life flowing from a fountain. He was in fact, in truth, the eternal fountain of divine vitality, but He was also a man, with the limitations of our common humanity imposed upon Him.

The result was that there were times when He simply had to slip away softly from the thronging multitudes. He had to be alone for spiritual communion with His Father. He had to find islands of privacy, intervals of peace, when the pressures were off and His total person—body, soul and spirit—could be restored and refreshed.

It is worthy of note that the Christ never found either His satisfaction or fulfillment in popularity. Though at this period of His public life the entire world was more or less at His feet, He desired no sense of personal gratification from the applause of the masses. Even His detractors conceded that "the whole world has gone after Him." Yet Christ's one and only satisfaction was to be one with His Father. By that is not meant some supernatural spiritual union beyond boundaries of our understanding. That such a oneness did exist is not denied. But the union of which I speak and the satisfaction to which I now refer is one we can all understand. His one motivation, His one purpose for being, His one satisfaction—in short, His *oneness*—was to do His Father's will. It was to fulfill His Father's wishes. To be exactly what His Father intended.

And in order that this might be so, He repeatedly detached Himself from the never-ending demands of humanity to be alone with His Father.

There in quiet, gentle, private intercourse He would be restored fully in order to serve fully. There He would be energized to enter the arena of sin and death, disease and despair that make up our disordered world of distraught men and women. And whenever He returned, it was to bring light into darkness, life into death, love into distress and despair.

One of our Lord's favorite retreats was across the Lake of Galilee, away from the crowded towns of Capernaum and Bethsaida. The eastern shores and slopes above the lake were a desert region. It was a country of stark khaki-colored hills, burned gray brown with the desert sun. Here only scattered thorns and dwarf scrub brush survived. A few wild asses and tough-tongued Bedouin goats managed to thrive on the sparse herbage. And at night the plaintive cries of the wild jackals and yapping of foxes echoed across the starlit wasteland. This was a region shunned by men. In its solitude and great empty spaces, under sweeping desert skies, the Master communed deeply with His Father. There His spirit soared to sublime heights far transcending the lower levels at which most men grope.

He requested His young companions, so familiar with the lake, to take Him across one day. They agreed. It was always a thrill for fellows like Andrew and Peter, James and John to feel the sun-warmed planks of a boat beneath their bare feet again. It was ever a solace to their souls to hear the wind singing in the rigging, to hear the splash of the bow wave, to smell the freshness of the moist lake air in their nostrils. It was a break from mobs of jostling, tiresome, impatient people.

Just as they were ready to push off, a young would-be follower came running up to Jesus. Could he come along? The Master reminded him gently, "Foxes have holes, birds have nests, but I have no place to put My head at night that can really be called home.'' All too well He knew that His pillow that night might well be the iron-hard gunwale of a boat; the next, an equally hard granite boulder in the desert.

The boat was just being pushed from the beach when a second devotee rushed up breathlessly. He would like to go along, too, but first he had to attend to his father's funeral. ''Let the dead bury the dead, My boy,'' Jesus replied with quiet compassion. ''But you, if you are truly alive, will leave the dead to the dead, and follow Me!''

What the response was from the two young men, Matthew never told us. Perhaps it was not positive as his own had been when the Master called him from his tax office.

Then the gang, in light heart, hoisted their sail, dipped the oars to clear the shore, and set off across the lake. Hardly were they out of earshot from the beach when Jesus settled Himself in a corner of the stern and fell fast asleep. So deep was His dreamless slumber that the rising sound of the wind and increasing splash of waves against the sides did not disturb Him.

This little lake, cupped between high hot hills, is subject to sudden squalls and frightening storms. The harsh winds often come rushing down across it in angry gusts. Its surface can be churned into foaming fury in a few minutes. Raging, white-capped waves roll across its tossing turbulence threatening to capsize or swamp any boat caught in its caldron of raging wind. At such times it is a veritable cockpit of terror to fishermen, who flee for shore.

And now the boys were suddenly taken unawares in just such a storm. In a matter of moments the threatening clouds had blocked out the sun. The lake turned from bright blue to steel gray then ominous black. The rising wind screamed through the shrouds. Water started to hiss around the heaving hull and wash in over the wallowing sides. The waves flung in more water than could be bailed out. The ship began to sink. The men were terrified. They had never fought such a storm.

But the Master slept on in utter serenity.

At last, in panic, they pocketed their pride. All their old skills and tricks and experience as fishermen were unavailing in this gale.

They would wake the Master. Though He had always been just a carpenter, a landlubber, perhaps He could somehow still the storm or save their souls someway.

They shook Him brusquely. They shouted in His ear. "Lord, save us; we perish!"

Still lying prone in the stern, rubbing His tired eyes open, Jesus replied drowsily, unperturbed, "Why are you afraid? Where is your faith?"

Obviously their faith had been in the boat. Now it was sinking beneath their feet. Their faith had been in their old cunning skill and ability to beat the storms. Now a tempest had them in its deathgrip and they all were bound to drown. Their faith had been in their knowledge of wind and weather and how to read the sky. Now all of that was naught and they faced sure disaster.

Quietly Christ stretched Himself, stood up calmly and faced the raging wind tearing at His hair, beard, and rain-drenched clothing. Firmly, with low, strong, well-modulated tones He addressed the winds and waves. "Peace, be still!" It was an explicit command from the One, who Himself had brought sea and land, sun and stars, wind and air into being. There was an immediate lull in the storm.

The wind died.

The atmosphere was dead calm.

The whole world was still.

The frightened crew stood silent, awed, stunned.

Each in his own inner spirit asked, "What sort of person is this Master of ours? Even the wind and sea obey Him!"

He was God—yes, in truth God. But somehow it was so very hard to really believe it.

We are inclined to lift our eyebrows in disdain. We are apt to wonder how men could be so slow to recognize really who Jesus was. Had He not turned water into wine? cured the incurable? restored sight to the blind? raised the dead? How much more evidence did they need to be sure their companion was not only divinely endowed but deity Himself? Could they have utter confidence in Him now? Was He worthy of their implicit faith?

To be fair to the disciples, we must remember that up to this point almost everything their Leader had done had been done for others in distress, not for them personally. This was the first time they themselves were in a real jam, and His presence and power had extricated them from sure disaster. For the first time it was they themselves who had to be delivered. For the first time it was they who were not the onlookers but the leading characters in the life-and-death drama enacted before their own eyes. For the first time—if they were to be saved in this hopeless situation—they had to exercise viable faith of their own in Christ. For the first time they had to pocket their pride as a group, come implicitly to the Master, expecting help and finding Him faithful to provide it.

He was there in the storm with them. They knew it. Happily, they were humble enough, sensible enough, and sincere enough to seek salvation from the One who could deliver them. And He did.

God, in Christ, by His Spirit, is in all the storms of His followers' lives. It is when we give up battling them in our own ability and turn to Him that we find relief and rest.

This storm on the lake that dreadful day was no crisis for Christ. He had known it would come up. He was not taken by surprise. God never is! He knew how the storm would be stilled. He always does! He was not frightened or fearful. He cannot be! He is always in control. This is His strength, His splendor, the grandeur of His character.

The crisis that stormy day was in the mind and emotions of the disciples. All the crises in a Christian's life are in the realm of his mind (imagination) or emotions. When he has Christ's mind, there are no crises.

The second storm on this same lake was, if anything, even more dramatic than the first. This time, however, the setting was different, because the disciples did not have the Master aboard. He had gone up into His favorite wilderness haunt to pray, after dispersing a large crowd. The disciples, meanwhile, had left to cross the lake alone, sailing by night after sunset. It proved to be an exciting crossing that would get them into a situation such as they had never faced before. But they had been willing to go because it was Jesus' request that they do so.

The little voyage became a terrible contest with both wind and waves. The crude sail was no help. The young men took to the long, heavy oars hoping to beat their way against the gale. Hour after hour they struggled and sweated and strained in the darkness. Unless they kept headed into the wind it was sure to drive them onto the rocks in the dark. Nine hours of rowing yielded only three miles.

As they fought for their very lives out on the lake, Christ was up on the hills, crying out to His Father on their behalf. He is always interceding for His own that their faith and strength do not fail in the storms and conflicts of life. As the night passed and dawn drew near, Jesus left the hills and went down to join His friends in their struggle with the elements. He knew what they were confronted with. He would be their comrade and companion in the battle with wind and water.

They were in this dilemma not because they had gone their own willful way, nor because of any selfish desire; they were there because it was where Christ had sent them.

So often people have the strange notion that when things turn out contrarily in life and storms of adversity blow up, they must be out of God's will. Not so. Some storms and tough times are allowed to strengthen our faith, to show us that even though we may not actually feel or think Christ is there, He is there nonetheless.

The straining fishermen peered through the darkness of the stormy night. Their eyes caught a glimpse of what seemed a ghostlike figure moving toward them. Tired, tense, their nerves taut, it was easy for their imaginations to run wild. What was this—an apparition? Their fantasies gave way to fear. In terror the tough fishermen shouted out loud in alarm. It was like a small boy whistling in the dark to bolster his own flagging courage. Perhaps if they yelled hard enough the form would disappear.

Instead Jesus drew near . . . walking on the water.

Then He spoke—spoke those same strong words He always speaks to sinking hearts: "Be of good cheer! Be not afraid! It is I." A more accurate phrasing of these last three words is *I AM*—the eternal I AM was in the storm with His friends, even though they had not known or recognized His presence.

Peter, boisterous Peter, beyond himself with relief and excitement, at the Master's invitation, climbed over the side of the rocking boat. In sheer confidence he began to cross over the waves to Christ. It was a daring deed—but short lived. Jesus' outstretched hand saved the big brawny fellow from going down. Moments later they were both back in the boat.

It was a subdued Peter who clambered over the side. The Master had checked him for his lack of confidence. If he could take two steps without doubting, why not twenty or a thousand?

Peter was plagued with the same degree of doubt common to most of us. Today we can trust. Tomorrow our faith fails when the going gets rough. We get our eyes off God and focus our attention on the turmoil around us. Then we go down in despair.

As soon as Jesus got on board, the storm abated.

It was the second time it had happened.

Surely now they knew who He was! He was indeed the Son of God. He was worthy of their adulation. He did deserve their undivided loyalty.

CHAPTER TWENTY-TWO

Ministering to the Whole Man

The events which took place in the life of Christ at the height of His fame were so numerous and followed one on another with such rapidity that to record them all in exact chronological order would be nearly impossible. In fact John at the conclusion of his record states that if they had all been reported, the then-known world could not contain them properly.

By this sweeping statement he no doubt alluded to all that Jesus both said and did with His disciples. The reports left in the four Gospels represent but the highlights of that wondrous life which changed the whole direction of human history. Other authors have gone to great lengths and taken endless pains to paint as precise a picture as possible of our Lord's life in exact sequence. That is neither attempted, nor intended, here. Rather the desire is to depict Christ as He appears to a simple layman, both in His conduct and in His character.

It must be noted that from time to time in this volume, events of a similar nature are grouped together. This compresses the narrative and reduces the number of scenes to a more manageable size. Very often the same lessons or principles can be drawn from similar settings. This dispenses with the need for repetition which might prove tedious to the reader.

For example: There were several storms on the Lake of Galilee; there were a number of times Jesus restored sight to the blind; there were several resurrections from the dead; there were numerous healings of the sick; there were innumerable sermons preached and parables given; and on at least two different occasions He undertook to feed enormous crowds of people with bread and fish.

In all of this it is noteworthy to observe that the Master was very much concerned with the whole man: He brought serenity to men's spirits; He gave purpose to men's wills; He restored stability to men's minds and emotions; He came with healing for physical ailments in abused bodies; He provided food for those in want and hunger.

This concept of ministering to the whole man seems to elude us at times. It was the beautiful balance always so apparent in the Christ. Yet it is often in this area that we human beings fail miserably. In fact some people even fight over the question of which is the more important—the evangel which ministers to men's spirits or the social services which minister to his body. It is as though the messenger of the Gospel, bringing good news from God, was obliged to limit himself to one aspect or the other.

There was none of this about our Lord. In fact it is a pure joy to see how He meets man's every need. No matter what problem is presented to Him, He promptly provides the solution and satisfies the situation. If men or women suffered in the spiritual bondage of sin, He set them free and forgave their wrongdoing. If men were possessed of evil spirits, He cast them out and restored them to their right minds. If men and women struggled with divided emotions and distraught hearts, He comforted and refreshed them. If their bodies were tortured by disease and wracked with physical pain, He touched them, bringing them vigor and health. When He saw women, children, and men in hunger, He fed them. And when the crowds craved for truth, He taught them. In short, He ministered always to the whole man.

We who claim to follow in His footsteps do well to remember this. Our responsibility to our generation is to come to them with open, outstretched hands. In the right we bear the word of truth, the great good news of salvation for men in body, soul, and spirit. In the left we carry all the social services needed to minister likewise to body, soul, spirit.

To do this is tremendously demanding. And one day after Jesus and His disciples had all regrouped, following their foray as His first missionaries, He suggested they take a little holiday together. It would be a brief respite from the strain of teaching, healing, traveling, and living in the public eye. They would draw apart for a while and head up into His beloved hill country for a quiet interlude.

After all, one of the great prices to be paid for such a marvelous ministry amongst men was privacy. Just to get a bit of seclusion and solitude was not always easy. And if one were famous, the chances of finding a quiet spot away from the maddening crowds were rather remote. People were bound to beat a well-worn path to one's hideaway.

On this particular occasion Jesus and His companions had crossed the lake, hoping to head into the quiet hills. But by the time they beached the heavy boat on the far shore a huge crowd had already gathered. Guessing where Jesus might be going, they ran around the lake and forestalled the holiday plans.

Like most crowds, the multitudes in Jesus' day were subject to the mob instincts that run with such impulsive force through massed men and women. Most of them, in excitement and frenzy, failed to even think of food. They gave no thought to where they might spend the night. All that mattered was to be within earshot and hear what the Master had to say. Their first and major impulse was simply to see Jesus. He had captured their imaginations. By some He was even looked upon as the most eligible leader and potential potentate that had appeared on their national scene for a long, long time.

Mark tells us that there were so many coming and going, with all of their diverse demands, dreams, and aspirations for the Master, that there was not time for anyone to eat. Perhaps many even came with political motivation, hoping Jesus might be pressed into accepting public office.

No doubt the crowds meant well. Christ was always ready to read the best possible intentions in sincere people. He saw that many were searching for truth and spiritual reality not available to them from the tired old rabbis in the sleepy synagogues. So in His typical unselfish way, He took the time and trouble to teach them many great truths with gentle, plain parables that most people could grasp.

But even this was slow and discouraging work. Again and again He chided them like careless little children in a class. "Eyes you have," He remonstrated, "but you simply don't see. Ears you have," He protested, "but you really don't hear." Spiritual concepts were hard for them to lay hold of, even at the best of times. His own favorite Twelve were often confused and bewildered by what He said. They just could not understand Him. Often they would come to Him privately, after the crowds had dispersed, asking Him to explain His parables.

For Jesus this part of His ministry and lifework must have been by far the most frustrating. What to Him was so clear, to His hearers was frequently obscure. What to Him was so simple to see, to them was utterly confusing. So often they put the wrong interpretation on what He had said. His truth was twisted and distorted beyond recognition. And of course there was always the fringe element of skeptics and cynics who deliberately endeavored to draw Him into pointless debates and disputes for their own ends.

Sometimes His discourses would go on for hours. The sun would move slowly across the sky while still the crowds lingered on. They had never heard spiritual realities taught with such incredible authority. The truth, even though not fully grasped nor completely assimilated, still stirred a response in their spirits. And so the day would gradually wear away. The sun would sink lower over the western hills. Babies whimpered with hunger. Men and women, beginning to feel increasing hunger pangs, wondered if they should look for food. While the disciples hoped desperately they would all pack up and go home.

But it was not to be. At least not on the two occasions that He decided to feed the huge crowds—once five thousand of them, another time more than four thousand.

Instead of dismissing them He turned to the tired Twelve and said softly, "You feed them"! It seemed an impossible demand. Where could they scare up food for such a crowd? Even if they emptied their common kitty, it was certain the two-hundred-odd pennies they could collect would not begin to buy bread enough. Their meager resources simply were not sufficient.

So often, too often, it seems this way with us who follow Him. He seems to ask so much of us. And we in turn appear to have so little to offer. Perhaps it is His gentle way of getting us to see how poor and unprepared we are to meet the needs of those around us. When we discover the paucity of our own personal resources, we finally turn to the One who has unlimited means at His disposal.

Yet the strange and wondrous thing is that He still uses His men to get the job done. Jesus did not brush aside the tired, distraught disciples. He did not, with a wave of His arm, turn the desert boulders into bread. He did not display the might and power at His disposal to dispense food to this famished crowd.

Instead He asked gently, "How many loaves have you got?" Momentarily He smiled upon them. "Go, and see."

God always expects us to use the resources available to us. He asks us to simply take stock of our time, our talents, and our strength. It matters not how great or small they may seem to us, He simply wants them put at His disposal.

The chagrined disciples brought Him five small buns and a couple of tiny fish. "What are these, to feed four thousand hungry mouths?" If they did not say it aloud, at least the question was clearly implied in their doubtful eyes.

Jesus took the five tiny loaves and two tiny fish. Enough!

As always, He was in control of the situation. The tiny handfuls of food were no embarrassment to Him. Little was much when He was in it. His touch could and would transform this little bit into a splendid banquet.

In short order, without chaos or confusion, He had the crowds sit down on the green grass. They were quickly arranged in groups of fifties or hundreds with room to pass between them. From a distance it looked like a field with even patches of crops arranged in orderly array. Suddenly the chattering died away and silence fell across the scene.

The bread and fishes held in His big brown hands, the Master raised His eyes and face toward His Father in heaven. He blessed the food. Then beginning to break it between His great strong fingers, He passed it out to the wondering disciples.

There was bread and bread and bread coming from His hands, and fish and fish and fish passed from His fingers. There was no shortage. All that was required, and more, was supplied in generous, overflowing measure.

The bread was fresh and crisp, the fish delicious. With relish and in happy conversation mountains of food disappeared in the brief twilight before dark. There was to be no waste. Twelve baskets, one for each disciple to carry, were filled with the fragments of crusts and bones and tails that were not consumed. Some nearby Gadarine who kept pigs would use the leftovers to feed his herd. The Master asks us to minister to men. He invites us to turn over our meager resources to Him. Most of us are afraid to do this. We fear He will take away what we have. We think He asks too much of us. All He wants is to bless and multiply it. He returns it to us enhanced, to share with a waiting world. Most of us are reluctant to comply with His request. We try to hoard and save our little store for ourselves.

When placed gladly in His strong hands, He blesses our little bit to the ends of earth's multitudes. That truth the disciples learned that day!

In spite of the apparent delays caused by the huge crowds, Jesus was determined to spend, time alone with His disciples in a brief holiday. It became increasingly clear that this simply could not be achieved in the familiar haunts of His beloved Galilean countryside. Wherever He went He was followed. If not by the general masses, then by the persistent Pharisees and Sadducees: Veritable bloodhounds that would not relent, they trailed and tracked Him everywhere with cruel, crafty cunning.

These deadly intelligentsia were forever demanding, insisting that somehow Jesus should supply them with some "sign" that He was in truth the Son of God, which was the claim made for Him. As with skeptics and cynics of all times, they wanted empirical proof that He was deity. The colossal conceit and audacious impertinence men have in challenging God to submit to their puny tests of divinity are astounding. Proud, perverse, puny men in their appalling ignorance and terrible blindness assume that God will allow Himself to be subjected to their finite, scientific examination based on their five fallible senses. It is as though somehow He can be apprehended by our physical sight, hearing, smell, taste, or touch.

God is God!

His whole presence permeates the whole universe.

He is everywhere apparent, sustaining and enfolding all the universe. The earth, complex and intricate as it may seem, is but a single minute particle of the enormous whole which He contains within Himself.

It is as if men, like barnacles on a shore stone, were to insist that their little boulder with its colony of marine life encompassed all there was to life—oblivious to the immensity of the gigantic ocean that sustains that life and stretches unlimited distances beyond their tiny horizons.

God, in Christ, refused to be cramped into the confinement of the little ecclesiastical colony of His times. He had condescended to be confined to the dimensions of a single cell at His birth in order to be identified with humanity. But He would not be restricted by mere egotistical, self-centered men into the small scope of their narrow, cramped spirituality. For at best it was a false and phony spirituality, a counterfeit concept of godliness that at best was only a pathetic caricature of truth.

"I refuse to give you a sign," He insisted.

"Even if one were to come back from the dead and preach to you, it would not avail. You would not repent."

Across the centuries men had been appealed to by God. He had spoken to them directly in dreams, visions, and visitations from angelic beings. He had communed with men personally and privately. They had been instructed in detail by great saints like Abraham, Moses, Joshua, Samuel, Elijah, and David. There had been a whole retinue of priests and prophets who cried out to them on God's behalf. Yet always men had turned away to go their own way. They had abused, punished, and put to death those who warned them of their wicked ways.

And now they were doing exactly the same to Him.

It was the same old tragic tale, repeated again by men blinded by their own sin, plagued by their own proud perverseness. There are none so blind as those who deliberately refuse to see, none more deaf than those who willfully refuse to hear.

So Jesus knew it was high time to take His twelve companions apart, not only for a happy holiday but also for in-depth talks about spiritual truth. They simply had to be instructed. For just as He was ever ready to minister to men's physical and soul needs, He was eager to minister to their spirits. And in order that they might be established in spiritual truth, He had to warn them clearly against the falsity of the concepts propagated by the Pharisees, Sadducees, scribes, scholars, and other religious dilettantes of His day.

He decided to take a long trek north to Caesarea Philippi.

In Jesus' time there were two Caesareas. One was a flourishing seaside town on the Mediterranean Sea. This was where Philip the evangelist was later to have his great evangelistic services after Pentecost. It was the town from which he was sent by God's gracious Spirit to minister to the solitary Ethiopian eunuch crossing the desert on his way home to Africa.

But Caesarea Philippi was a remote mountain village that snuggled amid the foothills of Mount Hermon to the north of Galilee. It was a picturesque place, with its hillside orchards, running streams fed by the melting mountain snows, and grassy rolling hills dotted with groves of giant cedars.

Mount Hermon is by far the loftiest, grandest mountain mass in Palestine. Its crest, covered in ice and snow most of the year, can be seen for miles, standing out in regal splendor against the blue sky. Mountain meadows of gentle beauty run up its flanks. Here the wild anemones and blue irises fling their beauty across the high country in multicolored carpets of wild flowers. The mountain winds ripple the long grass in undulating waves of greenery. The native birds wheel against the cliffs and cry out across the wide valleys where streams sparkle silver in the sun.

It was a tranquil setting in which to rest and relax.

But it was also a suitable environment in which the Master could lift the spiritual comprehension of His young friends above the lowlands of their old life.

All of us need interludes of this kind.

It is not that we desire to withdraw completely from the company of common men. It was never intended that God's people be cut off from their contemporaries. But rather it is a refreshing retreat and respite for the restoration of weary men. From here they could return refurbished for the rigors of the workaday world in the common round of living.

Up there—quiet, undisturbed, perhaps in the gentle shade of an outspread cedar of Lebanon—Jesus sat on the grass and asked His disciples a searching question:

"Who do men say that I am?"

Of course He knew very well. But it was a ploy used to see what was going through the minds of His own men.

"Some say You are bound to be John the Baptist, risen from the dead after being beheaded in the black dungeon of Machaerus. Others say You are the grand old giant of old, Elijah the prophet, who flamed like a firebrand across the dark years of Israel's ancient history. Others say You are the noble, fearless Jeremiah, who despite atrocious persecution and endless abuse bravely warned God's people of the awful doom and devastation that Babylon would bring to Israel. While others say You might well be any one of the ancient prophets."

Jesus looked at them longingly, with enormous penetration and deep compassion. There was a long silence. Then came the great test question. The question which ultimately every thinker, every person in search of truth must answer for himself:

"But who do you say that I am?"

In other words, who is this Jesus of Nazareth? Who is this wandering preacher, teacher, healer? Who is this One who reclines on the ground with you, relaxing in the shade of these great outstretched cedar limbs? Who is the One who sleeps out under the stars, wrapped only in His rough tunic; who shares the same bowl with you; drinks from the same cup; breaks the same loaf?

Is He a mere man? Or is He God?

Peter's forthright response "You are the Christ, the Son of the *Living God*" was a spontaneous declaration of His deity.

And it was and is upon the solid granite of that guarantee that all men must stand who would know God. No other foundation would do. "He that hath seen Me hath seen *the Father. The Father and I are One.*"

CHAPTER TWENTY-THREE

Tremendous Truths

During the mountain holiday the Master disclosed deep truths to His disciples. These underlie all that was to take place later on during His last stormy days on earth. And they were the very foundation upon which in the years ahead His Church would be established for all eternity.

One sunny morning as they strolled across the grassy slopes Jesus made it clear that they were now standing at the great divide of His public career. Up until this point He had enjoyed the growing acclaim of a popular hero. But now the time had come for Him to again set His face toward Jerusalem. His feet would trudge the rocky trail that led to that tough city. That it would turn against Him, just as it had turned against all the great men of God before Him, was inevitable. In the end He would be arrested, defamed, mocked, and killed by the combined forces of ecclesiastical and political power. It was a terrifying and unbelievable forecast—not the sort of thing to cheer or hearten His followers.

Somehow they just could not accept it. Especially up here in the sublime serenity of the fragrant, sun-kissed mountain meadows, anything like a cruel murder seemed far, far away indeed. How could they even entertain the idea of scheming rogues trying to rob them of their Messiah? It was abhorrent.

Just the thought of it roused Peter's volcanic temperament. He grabbed hold of Jesus with his big rough hands and began to disabuse Him of such rash ideas. Excitedly he began to shout into Jesus' face.

"You just can't talk that way, Master!" His eyes flamed. "You can't let this happen to You! Never, never!"

Jesus, Himself a big powerful man, whirled out of Peter's grasp. With clear, steady eyes and strong, well-modulated voice He addressed the big, lusty fisherman.

What He said shocked and stunned Peter, so he fell back.

"Get behind Me, Satan!" It seemed an impossible statement, made to a man who just a few days before had been commended by the Master for such deep spiritual insights. "You are an absolute offense to Me. Obviously in this case you do not understand God's viewpoint. All you see is man's outlook."

Poor Peter. Poor blundering boatman. What had he done wrong this time?

Peter's problem is often our problem. Peter had grown up convinced that a man in order to survive, to surpass, had to save himself, push others around—yes, if need be, tramp them down to get ahead. One simply had to preserve himself no matter what. One had to push himself ahead. It was a simple case of survival of the fittest. This was the world's way. It was man's way. But it was the wrong way, as far as God was concerned.

The basic reason it was so very wrong is that it is the way of utter, absolute *selfishness*, of total *self-centeredness*. And this was expressed through unrelenting *self-will*.

When any man or woman expresses this philosophy, this attitude, this way, it is in diametric contradiction to the very nature and life of God. For He is absolutely *selfless*, utterly *self-giving*, totally *self-denying*. That is why Peter's action was so abhorrent.

And what Peter had failed to grasp was the realization that his Master, the Messiah, the Christ, had come to earth to give Himself as ransom to redeem men. He had come to *deny* Himself in death, to die instead of sinners who would otherwise die for their own misconduct. He had come in utter *selflessness* to suffer in our stead that men might go free.

Any attempt made by anyone to deflect Him from that course was seen by Jesus as an affront by His archenemy, Satan. The devil would use every means possible to try to divert Christ from accomplishing His mission to men. He would employ any deceit or resort to any ruse to try to wreck God's rescue operation.

Jesus would have no part of it. His will was set like steel.

When the brief blowup with Peter had subsided, the Master turned to all twelve of His disciples. He did not blame them for being so slow to understand. After all, since early babyhood they had been conditioned, as we all are, to fight for their rights, assert themselves, and push for the top.

His eyes filled with compassion. A winsome look of deep endearment spread across His features. How fond He was of these rough-and-ready fellows.

"Boys," He said, a look of earnest concern stealing over His face, "if any of you or anyone else is going to follow Me, let him give up his rights, daily, and take his cross and come with Me!"

It was a challenge. How many would ever accept it? How few could ever live up to it? It was a tough route for any man to take through this world.

All of us insist that we have certain inalienable rights which no one dare take from us . . . except ourselves. These the Master asks a man to surrender gladly, freely, day after day: Rights to do as I wish: Rights to go my own selfish way: Rights to please myself: Rights to assert myself: Rights to indulge myself: Rights to ride roughshod over others: Rights to *self . . . self . . . self.*

But that is the path not of peace but of conflict.

And if we choose to follow in the footsteps of the Prince of Peace, we take the route of self-denial, daily.

This is not asceticism. This is not morbidity. This is not solemn, glum introspection. This is to set my feet upon the highway of gladly abandoning myself in freewill giving to others and to God.

My time, my strength, my abilities, my talents, my thoughts—in short my life—is poured out, spent, lavished on and for others. This is to take up the cross that denotes death to selfish self-interest, that crosses out the great *I,* the great ego, that dominates my days.

This is to be set free from slavery to myself to run gladly along God's highway.

No doubt as Jesus discussed this in some detail with His men, dark doubts invaded their minds. Worried looks came into their eyes. Deep furrows lined their foreheads. No one, absolutely no one, had ever spoken to them this way about life. And really, was it possible in the rough-and-tumble of a tough world for a man to live like this? Wouldn't it spell absolute disaster? It must be sheer madness!

But Jesus went on, gently but firmly presenting His thoughts to them. This was truth. Either they had to accept it or reject it: "Whoever thinks he can save and secure his life is bound to lose it," He smiled softly—the sentence startled His companions as it startles us—"but whosoever will lose his life for My sake is bound to preserve it."

Somehow it just didn't seem to make sense. Or did it? There was a long silence as the Master let the impact of His statement sink into these rather stony hearts.

Anything a person saves for his own selfish ends is already lost to everyone else. And what is more, there is the eternal worry and anxiety that at any moment it may be snatched from him by some covetous contemporary.

But whatever is shared, whatever is given away, whatever is poured out upon another is in truth ours forever. Because in the giving we are enriched beyond our wildest dreams. It is only through giving that we gain the good of others, the benefit of others, the joy and pleasure of others, the delight and gratitude of others—and most important, the approval of God Himself.

Our *self* giving, our sharing, our losing ourselves in others is exactly in accord with the selflessness of Christ—and it is His selflessness which is *His love* . . . *His care* . . . *His concern.*

That is why He insisted that a man in selfish self-seeking could gain the whole world and end up with an impoverished, shrunken, empty soul that was as good as lost and worth nothing.

What is more, the final standard by which it shall be determined whether or not we share God's eternal bounties depends on our learning to share our own benefits.

These were profound, heavy, weighty truths. It would take a long time for them to be assimilated. In fact they were almost revolutionary in content. And even down to our own day, few are those who have ever found this way. It is bound to repel the majority of men, who dismiss it with a skeptical shrug of the shoulders.

After all, life is for living; let us eat, drink, and be merry, for tomorrow we die—destitute in soul, dead in spirit.

Jesus and His disciples spent about a week in the high country. When they turned away from these lofty alplands it would be to go back into the lowlands of the south country. A region which would see them exposed to enormous pressures and suffering far beyond anything they could anticipate at this point.

But before they left, Christ selected Peter, James, and John to accompany Him up above the snow line on the mountain. There suddenly before their unbelieving eyes, He was remarkably transfigured.

Their vivid recollection of the event was that the Master's face actually outshone the brilliant sun in radiance. His clothing glistened with an intense whiteness that outdazzled the snow sparkling around them under the shimmering sunlight. It was a breathtaking spectacle. In those moments the intense glory and person of God Himself was made manifest through the flesh and form in which He was clothed.

The transfigured Christ communed briefly with Moses and Elijah. Their conversation centered around His coming death, which would spell deliverance and redemption for all men.

Suddenly a bright cloud enveloped them. From it God spoke clearly: *"This is My beloved Son, in whom I am well pleased."* The same approbation conferred on Him at His baptism.

Then the frightened disciples, lying prostrate on the ground, found themselves alone with Jesus. Again those old familiar reassuring words: "Be not afraid!" Not even when God was displayed in all His glory before their wondering eyes need they fear. Nor need we!

CHAPTER TWENTY-FOUR

Back to the Lowlands

Jesus knew full well that His mission to men could never be accomplished in the quiet solitude of Mount Hermon's lovely foothills. As tranquil and beautiful as it was up there in the high country, it was not the place He was intended to stay. The restful holiday interlude had restored Him and His men for the fierce confrontations that would take place in the lowlands of Galilee, Samaria, and Judea.

The remaining months of His life would see this brave little band harassed and attacked mercilessly. His forays into Jerusalem would be repulsed ferociously. Finally His avowed adversaries would carry out their crafty schemes and nail Him to a terrible tree of torture. His ignominious death there would appear at first to be a tragedy of the first magnitude. But in the economy of God it would turn into the greatest triumph of eternity. For out of it love overcame hate; life overcame death; and light overcame darkness.

As soon as the little group of thirteen returned to the valley at the foot of the mountain they were met by a crowd. In the crowd was a man with an only child possessed by an evil spirit. He had once before appealed to some of Jesus' men to heal the lad, who was terribly tormented, screaming, foaming at the mouth, and flung on the ground.

Unhappily, the disciples had found the case too difficult and were unable to help the boy. But the Master, with a single simple command rebuked the demon, had him depart, and healed the suffering son.

The disciples were deeply impressed. Without a trace of bravado or boasting, Jesus reassured them that some very difficult cases like this one did require times of prayer and fasting. Their quiet time on the mountain had been not only for the upbuilding of their own spirits but also for the benefit of struggling souls in the lowlands below.

Slowly but surely, through personal example, the Master was teaching His followers that their lives were to be lived out amongst men. That the intentions of God are that His people should not be hermits, recluses, or religious cranks who opted out of society, but rather be much amid life. As Jesus Himself was to pray later, "Father, I do not ask that You take them out of the world, but that You keep and preserve them in it."

Yet, if they were to live very much in the milieu of their times it was inevitable that they would be subject to the stresses and strains of society. The world, its philosophies, its appeal, its priorities would exert enormous pressures on them. And being young men bursting with energy, enthusiasm, and enterprise, they would be exposed to enormous temptations common to all men.

This became apparent one day when they began to argue and quarrel about which of them would be greatest. This was a touchy point of contention. Whenever it came up, tempers would flame. Pride would rear its ugly head. Self-assertion would grow grim. Jealousy would flare up to flash between them like forked lightning.

Perhaps Judas felt superior because he alone came from Judea. Or Matthew was sure he was superior because of his business background. Maybe Peter was convinced he was the one to command because of his more mature years. James or John, with hot tempers at the flash point, would insist that as Jesus' closest relatives they deserved special recognition. So the rivalry would rage on until they almost came to blows.

For the Christ this was a pretty pathetic, painful business. In the midst of their debates and angry charges He felt ill at ease and very uncomfortable. Finally one day, in despair, He picked up a tiny innocent black-haired boy with enormous brown eyes. He set the wondering shy little lad on His knee.

"Unless you become as a little child—full of awe and genuine wonderment—you cannot enter the kingdom of God."

At first it seemed a paradox. They were puzzled by it.

"Become like a child to become great in God's economy? Why?"

The answer is really quite simple. A man preoccupied with his own pride and selfish self-interest has blocked the inflow of new truth or knowledge from God. Only the docile mind is receptive and open to new revelation. That is why the Master made it clear that even the most accomplished people have to become children to enter the kingdom of heaven. They simply must admit, like children, that God knows much more than they ever will.

It was a hard, coarse crumb for the young fellows to swallow. In fact, right up to the hour of their last supper together they still hammered each other for prestige. It was a painful thing for Christ to cope with this endless contention. The more so since He Himself, creator of all, had so humbled Himself as to become a selfless servant to selfish men.

As they wandered across the countryside all sorts of people came to engage Jesus in conversation. Philosophical and religious disputations are much more a part of Eastern cultures than of the West. Even very ordinary Easterners love the game of arguing about religious beliefs. It is a pastime that appeals to their peculiar philosophy of life. They are not the least embarrassed by talk that turns to God and eternal verities. Whereas in the West many people prefer to quickly change the subject as soon as spiritual issues come into the conversation.

The result was that a great teacher was always under attack. And it was natural that his devotees would endeavor to defend him. Jesus' disciples were no different. Once they tried to forbid another man from casting out demons simply because he was not one of their circle. Jesus replied, "He that is not against us is for us!" They had to be at least a bit charitable to their contemporaries.

On another occasion they tried to make overnight arrangements for Jesus to stop over in Samaria. They were not welcomed as they had hoped they would be. Actually they were told in rather blunt terms to keep moving along. This infuriated the fellows. Their first impulse was to call down fire from above to burn up the countryside in a raging holocaust.

Again Jesus had to be rather severe with His young stallions. "Really, you don't realize what spirit it is that motivates you to do this," He reproached them sternly. "It most certainly is not My spirit. I came into the world not to destroy and annihilate people, but to save them!" It was part and parcel of His whole life pattern—utter selflessness as opposed to angry selfishness.

Further down the road Jesus, despite the unpredictable behavior of His favorite Twelve, decided to select another seventy disciples. Like the first He had sent out, these too were empowered to perform mighty miracles. They too went out to preach the good news, to teach new truths, to heal the sick, to cast out evil spirits. And true to form, in due course they did all this and returned to report their astounding achievements.

Those were electrifying times. In all of its colorful history, Palestine had never seen such a display of divine miracles on every hand. People everywhere talked of the tremendous events that were taking place all over the country. Surely this was a most unusual visitation from God. No longer were miracles performed by just one outstanding person; apparently even His followers were endowed with enormous powers to preach, teach, and heal. The widespread impact of the disciples was felt all over the country. All kinds of people, from beggars to business tycoons, from peasants to haughty Pharisees, were drawn to Christ.

One of these was a brilliant solicitor. He came to inquire of the Master what He considered to be the most important single command of God that entitled him to eternal life. It was a trap.

Jesus was never trapped. He could not be crowded into a corner, even by the most cunning mind. He knew what was in men's minds, even before a thought was expressed. The lawyer's question was facetious. He was merely trying to play games.

Cutting through the crafty questioning like a hot knife slicing through soft cheese, Jesus came quickly to the point: "Your first obligation before God is to love Him with all your strength, your heart, your soul, your mind." This was nothing new; it was the ancient edict declared by Moses away back in the revered book of the law, Deuteronomy. Being a lawyer, he ought to know it.

But then Jesus added an important rider: "And you will love your neighbor as yourself."

With caustic cynicism the lawyer retorted, "Who is my neighbor?"

To make it abundantly clear Jesus then told the world-renowned story of the good Samaritan. It was typical of Jesus that even though so recently the Samaritans would not even let Him stay with them, He would choose a Samaritan to be the great hero in His story.

In spite of the innumerable sermons preached on that account, it impresses me that often the main point has been missed: The good Samaritan is a picture not of good-hearted people but a dramatic picture of Christ Himself. He is the One who always comes alongside the downtrodden, the abused, the beaten men of earth. It is He who picks them up, washes them, feeds them, heals them, pours over them the oil of His presence and blessing.

Then He brings them to the innkeeper. He lays them at his door. He entrusts them to his care. And it is we who are the innkeepers of the world. All sorts of men and women in distress are brought to our doorsteps by divine intervention. Our responsibility is to care for them, tend them, minister to them. It is Christ who initiates the action of relief and restoration. It is we who must complete it in close cooperation with Him.

Christ is our friend, our neighbor. Likewise we should be to those He brings into our lives!

CHAPTER TWENTY-FIVE

Two Lost Sons

In this book no attempt is made to discuss all the discourses or teaching which our Lord shared with His followers. For example, the Sermon on the Mount has had many books written about it. Other volumes have dealt with the parables of Jesus in detail. Here only the highlights are mentioned in order to portray some of the outstanding truths given to men by which they can live. This is essentially a layman's work. And my most profound hope is that from these pages men and women may draw practical insights into the life of Christ which will enable them to live as He wishes us to live amid a confused society.

Of all the stories which Jesus told, perhaps the most intense and poignant is that commonly called "The Prodigal Son." A much more accurate title would be "Two Lost Sons." Both the young prodigal and the elder son were in truth lost to their grieving father. The younger boy had cut himself off by his self-willed actions. The older son had alienated himself by his self-righteous attitudes. Neither of them enjoyed close communion with their father. To all intents and purposes, both were equally lost boys.

No other story told by Jesus gives us such a penetrating insight into the true character of God as does this one. It throws open the doors to His innermost being. From this account we can understand clearly what He is like. And what we see with our limited vision stirs a warm response within our spirits. It arouses the love of our souls. It sets our feet upon the path of righteousness that leads us home to Him who loves us with an everlasting love.

Only occasionally in the Old Testament was God referred to as a Father to His people. The emphatic revelation that He is indeed our Father in truth, who can be known and loved intimately, was uniquely Jesus' great gift to His people, and to us.

The Scriptures portray the relationship between God and His people in three diverse and beautiful pictures. The first is that of a *Father* and His wayward sons. The second is a *Shepherd* and His lost sheep. The third is a *Husband* and His estranged, unfaithful wife. In each case the drama that unfolds is one rich in pathos. God reaches out to reclaim, restore, and reconcile the wanderer to Himself. It is a most moving enterprise designed to touch our spirits, eliciting a powerful response toward truth within our wills.

As Jesus told the story of the younger son, He was depicting exactly what happens to many of us. Here was a lad, dearly loved yet demanding his rights and insisting on pursuing his own selfish self-interests. He cared not a whit what impact his wayward behavior had upon his father. What if he did ruin his reputation, drag his name into the dirt, squander his hard-earned savings, and crush his aching heart with remorse?

The father was no fool. He had lived long enough to know where the boy was. He was well aware of the terrific temptations and slippery companions that could quickly lead his son into abject slavery. The young man might think he was free, that he was at liberty to do his own thing and go his own way—when all the time he was in fact being fettered by his own self-indulgence. He had literally sold himself into slavery to a disinterested pigman.

It was a pathetic picture. Yet it depicts many of us in living colors. We turn our backs on God. Using the generous resources He has put at our disposal we go out to willfully waste and squander our lives. We do our own thing, go our own way, deluded into thinking we are free. Slowly but surely we become shackled by our selfish self-interests. We discover that the way we thought would be so wonderful is the downward path which leads only to despair and desperation. We forfeit our freedom to live like sons of God. We exchange that lofty life for the ignoble game of grubbing about in the mud and muck of materialism and man-made madness. We are trapped and we know it.

It was at this point of utter despair that the prodigal made a profound decision. He decided he would turn around and go back to his dear old dad. This was not an emotional choice, for he was utterly alone with himself when he made it. Nor was it a decision based on pure reason, for logic would have concluded that his chances of being well received at home were remote. Rather it was a straightforward moral act of his will. He said to himself, "I *will* arise and go to my father."

It was definite, direct, and determined.

And its results were dramatic.

Too too often in our dealings with God our decisions are not of this kind. They are far too shallow. Choices or commitments are very frequently made only at an emotional or intellectual level. Either we are influenced or cajoled into making decisions that do not touch the deep mainsprings of our wills. The result is that our actions are weak and sometimes do not comply with our commitments, leaving us crippled and self-condemned before our heavenly Father.

Not so with this boy. He was bound he would go home at any cost. It is touching to see him reciting to himself what he would say to his father. "Father, I have sinned against heaven, and before you. I am no longer worthy to be called your son. Make me just one of your hired servants."

Obviously the lad did not fully know his father. He was estranged and far from him. He saw him as harsh, hard, and very vindictive—just the way so many see God our Father.

What the prodigal did not understand was the compassion, love, and concern of his father. All the time he was away with his back to his father, the dear old gentleman's heart had been drawn out to him. Not once had his father cut him off. Not for a moment was he forgotten. Never was there anything but a longing and yearning toward his son. Even forgiveness was there. He did not know this. He had to come home to discover it.

As human beings we have enormous difficulty grasping the true generosity of God our Father's character. Always, always we tend to equate His conduct with our fallible, fickle human conduct. But He simply is not like us in any way. And the very reason Jesus told this moving story is to help us understand the goodness of God our Father. He deals with us altogether differently from the way in which we deal with each other.

And as this father saw his ragged, mud-stained boy staggering up the road toward home, he rushed out of his home and raced down the dusty road to meet him. Never mind the boy's remonstrations, never mind his remorse. He flung his arms around the disheveled lad. He kissed his besmirched face. He hugged him hard.

Meanwhile the boy blurted out his confession of wrongdoing. He admitted openly he was no longer worthy to be called a son. But his father would not let him say any more.

He was his son.

He was home.

He was forgiven.

He that was lost was found. He that was dead was alive.

In that reception the self-willed, wayward boy found full and complete acceptance. He found his true destiny. He found his purpose for being. He was a son. He was an heir. He was loved. It was never intended that he should be a wanderer, a slave either to himself or someone else, nor even just a servant to his father. He was intended for the noble, lofty role of a son.

So with us. Our Father's intentions toward us are always good. He does not turn His back on us. He does not reject or repudiate us. He does not cut us off. We cut ourselves off from Him. We turn our backs to Him. We reject His overtures. We condemn ourselves.

Yet the instant we turn toward Him, there He is, waiting with open arms, ready to welcome us home. His forgiveness is given. His love is expressed. His acceptance is made evident as He enfolds us in the warmth of His own winsome goodness.

To experience this in our relationship with God is to know something of His wondrous character. Many of the distraught sinners in Jesus' day had this happen to them. After meeting Him they were never the same again. They knew for certain that they had passed from death to life, from darkness to light, from despair to love.

The father, in his great joy at the son's return, instructed his servants to slip a gold ring on his finger, to wrap about him the finest white robe in the home, to put brand-new shoes on his weary feet.

The ring spoke of total acceptance: "You are Mine!" The robe spoke of total righteousness: "You are wrapped in My righteousness!" The shoes spoke of total redirection to life: "You will walk in My ways!"

Those of us who have come home to God our Father are keenly aware of all this. His gracious Spirit bears witness with our spirit that we are His sons: heirs and joint heirs with Christ. We realize we stand freely forgiven in His presence, enfolded in His righteousness, not ours. We desire only to walk in the paths of peace and righteousness that He intends for us, in which He gently guides us by His gracious Spirit.

There was a tremendous celebration in that home that evening. The stall-fattened calf was to be butchered and a regular banquet prepared. There would be gay festivities, music, laughter, and dancing for sheer joy. The boy was back. He had begun a new life. He had been reborn.

In Eastern cultures great festivities always attend the birth of a royal child. Likewise in God's economy enormous celebrations always mark the new birth of one of God's sons.

Most of us somehow have never even thought of God our Father making merry. It seems incongruous to us that God could dance with delight, laugh with joy, and be merry in heart when some poor sinner staggers home to Him. But He does!

And all the myriad angel hosts join with Him.

It was in the midst of such gaiety that the elder son trudged his weary way home from the fields where he had been working so diligently. No doubt this boy was regarded by the local people as a very stalwart, upstanding lad. He was a hard worker. He did not fritter away his strength on wine, women, or song. He could be depended on to do the job. In short, he was a very proper person.

But was he?

From the conversations which took place when he returned from the field, we simply must conclude otherwise.

When the prodigal left home he took with him all that was his share of the estate. This had been given to him in advance by his

father. Because there were two boys, this meant that the younger
took one-third of the property. The remaining two-thirds belonged
to the elder brother. In the Jewish culture the firstborn son always
inherited twice as much of the estate as did his siblings. So after the
prodigal left, all that remained was the rightful inheritance of the
elder brother. The father endorsed this, when he later came out and
reassured his older son, "All I have is yours!"

Why then was the older son so diligent on the farm? For the
simple reason that he knew everything he did was building up and
enhancing his own self-interests. He did not work hard because he
loved his father or was devoted to him. In fact, the way he later
accuses the old man of unfair treatment shows that he held him in
contempt, and that an insurmountable barrier of selfish self-interest
and self-righteousness had been built up over the years between
him and his father. There had been complete alienation, and communion between the two was cut off. Though he worked in the
home fields he was just as far from his father as if he were away off
in a far country the way his brother had been.

Returning home to the sound of lighthearted merriment, music,
and dancing, his dark selfish soul grows black with jealousy. He
refuses to join the celebration. Hate, anger, bitterness darken his
emotions.

Self-pity surges over him. His view of the proceedings grows dim
and dangerously angry. A black mood descends upon him, and like
a small child he goes into a deep sulk.

What made him so mad? Jealousy, burning with hate!

His own selfish self-interest!

How dare his father share his love with the wayward son? How
dare his servants and friends shower their affection on such a wast-
rel? How dare they give a calf—yes, a whole calf, *his* calf, from his
estate—to this prodigal? How dare they throw a party for such a
useless fellow?

No one had ever done anything like this for *him*. How come?

The answer was that because of his intense selfish self-interest it
is more than likely he had few if any friends. Who would ever even
want to celebrate with him? His had been a narrow, jealous, drab
life centered only in himself.

In the outburst of anger and venom his true nature was laid bare.

"Out of the abundance of the heart the mouth speaketh." Jesus had taught this principle repeatedly. Here was a living demonstration of it.

As his passions flamed out he poured contempt on his father. His true character was painted in bold, blazing color. The anger, bitterness, jealousy, criticism, scorn, and selfishness of his shriveled soul spilled out over the whole scene. Like acid spilled from the cells of a battery, it corroded and burned everyone it touched.

He refused even to call his brother a brother. Instead he referred to him sarcastically as "your son"!

In spite of all his father's pleading, the selfish, jealous, angry elder son, consumed with criticism and scorn, would have no part in the celebration.

We are left with the distinct impression that he never did enter the home. He never did experience any of the joy. He remained outside, aloof and alone, black with his own vile behavior.

Through all the pathos of this drama Jesus endeavored to draw for us the clear portrait of God our Father's winsome character.

With both boys his attitude never altered, never faltered. He was always the same. He loved them both. He yearned for them both. He was willing to forgive them both. He was glad to share all he had with both. He wanted only the very best for both.

Both lads had abused their father terribly. Both boys had only their own selfish self-interests at heart. Both boys had treated him only with scorn and contempt. Both boys had grieved and saddened him until it well-nigh broke his heart.

Really the only difference between them was that one had sinned grievously in the higher regions of his disposition, the other in his body. One was self-willed, the other self-righteous.

This in essence is the picture of human beings which the Master endeavored to portray for His disciples that day. "All we like sheep have gone astray, each of us has turned to his own way, and the Lord hath laid on Him the iniquity of us all." Each boy had gone his own way; each of us goes his own way, does his own thing, lives his own life, decides his own destiny. All this places a perennial load of grief and sorrow upon the shoulders of our Saviour.

Yet, in spite of such abuse, God, like this father, comes to us with outstretched arms to welcome us. He reassures us of His love. He extends His gracious forgiveness. He enfolds us with His own righteousness. He embraces us with affection. He puts His best at our disposal. He reassures us that all He has is ours.

What more can God do?

Still, men whom He intends should be His sons, spurn God, feeling at best they can only be but slaves to Him. How sad! He calls us to be members of His household. He welcomes us into His family. Yet many refuse to respond!

CHAPTER TWENTY-SIX

Two Lovely Sisters

Steadily but surely Jesus and His men moved back and forth across the countryside moving gradually southward toward Jerusalem. The Master's teaching took on increasingly solemn tones. It became ever more apparent that He was approaching some enormous climax in His life. The demands made upon those who would befriend and follow Him were mounting. Not all men could or would accept the lofty life of total self-denial set before them.

Some began to turn away from Him.

They went back to their comfortable cottages, their little shops, their family farms.

With winsome eyes Jesus turned to His faithful Twelve and asked gently, "Will you also leave Me?" It was not that He could not bear to be alone, but He wondered if even a dozen could be found who would remain loyal to the end.

Peter's prompt response was: "To whom shall we go, Lord? Only You have the words of life!" It was a brave statement from the big, burly boatman. He had tasted spiritual truth, and anything less was not likely to satisfy his thirsting spirit.

Gradually the little band of wanderers moved down the Jordan Valley toward Jericho. From that busy city that panted in the desert sun beside the Dead Sea, a narrow winding road climbed into the Judean hills. It was a notorious road, not just because Jesus told the well-known story about the good Samaritan on it but because it was an area famous for brigands.

In a distance of about twenty-three miles it climbed nearly four thousand feet from the stifling heat of the valley floor to the cool hills around Jerusalem. Its sharp twists, turns, and tight switchbacks snaked through wild, lunarlike landscape where caves and cliffs gave thieves and robbers every advantage in attacking travelers.

Near the summit of this tortuous road stood the peaceful little village of Bethany. It had a beautiful location on the eastern flank of the upthrust limestone ridge separating it from Jerusalem. From Bethany one had majestic sweeping views out across the wild terrain of the Jordan Valley. And though the tiny hamlet was so close to Jerusalem, it basked in semiseclusion under the warmth of the eastern sun that flooded it with light from earliest dawn.

In this village was a special home. Probably it played the same role in Christ's life down in Judea that Peter's home played for Him in Galilee. It was a spot to which He would return whenever He felt need of refreshment and rest. Since He owned no home of His own, others had opened their homes to Him, and in Bethany was perhaps His favorite of all those He visited.

This home belonged to Martha. She was the eldest of two sisters and a brother. Her younger sister, Mary, lived with her and also Lazarus. As sometimes happens, none of the three had married, rather a rare occurrence in Jewish culture. They were deeply devoted to each other. And in course of time they all became equally attached to the young man of God from Galilee, Jesus of Nazareth.

Their home became Jesus' favorite stopping place. During the last months of His life this home was to become an oasis of peace and refreshment in the midst of the terrible pressures and heat put on Him by His oppressors. Again and again when He was attacked and assailed in Jerusalem by His adversaries it would be to this tranquil spot beneath the overhanging, graceful pepper trees He would retire for repose and refreshment.

Some ancient legends have it that Lazarus was the rich young ruler whom Jesus looked at and loved so dearly—who, though, when told to go and sell all he owned, turned away from Jesus saddened, never to do so. But at least he was generous enough to open his heart and home freely to the Master. We will never know for sure.

It was the Feast of Tabernacles, sometimes called the Feast of Booths, when Jesus climbed the twisting track one day and came to Martha's door. The little booths of green boughs and branches had been constructed in the inner courtyard of the gracious home. They were a reminder to the children of Israel that for forty years after their exodus from Egypt they had lived as wandering nomads in the desert. During all that time Jehovah God, their God, had provided them freely and fully with all they needed to survive in the wilderness. Each morning fresh manna lay on the ground; from time to time quails supplied them with meat; water gushed freely from the rocks, and their shoes and clothes never wore out. It had been an incredible story, and to remind themselves of God's faithfulness to His people they now prepared sumptuous meals, eaten outdoors in the cool shade of the green-boughed booths.

Martha, taking her responsibilities very seriously as host of the home, was busy baking, cooking, and preparing the banquet. It was hot in her little kitchen. The little fire of dry thorn brush and smoldering camel dung added to the heat and discomfort of the smoky room. Yet she was happy to be busy, for there was a special guest to share the food. But her contentment of heart lasted only until she glanced out the kitchen door. She caught a glimpse of her younger sister, Mary, sitting gently in the shade with Jesus.

Mary looked so calm, so cool, so composed, while she herself was so flurried, so hot, so busy with baking and cooking. It was not jealousy that prompted Martha to come to the door and blurt out boldly, "Lord, don't You care that Mary has left me with all the work? Tell her to come and help." Martha did not need to be jealous. She knew she was loved just as much as her sister. She knew Jesus played no special favorites in this family. No, Martha was simply one of those bighearted, fair, generous women who speak their minds and demand fair play.

Jesus' reply to her was not a rebuke as so many imagine. He loved her too much to hurt her. "Martha, Martha . . ."—her name was repeated in great, gentle tenderness; He took her by the hand and looked deep into her dark brown eyes—"you are so thoughtful, so concerned, so careful about every detail!" And a winsome smile crept softly across His strong face. "I appreciate it. But really, Martha, you don't need to bother about so many dishes.

Just one will do!" He paused a few moments, letting the truth sink in quietly to this gracious woman. "Just being with you, just sharing this little interlude the way Mary is—that is really the best part. That is all we need."

The Master's kind remarks took all the strain from Martha. She didn't have to rush around anymore. She didn't have to lay an elaborate table. She didn't have to serve several courses. Just a bowl of lamb broth shared with her favorite guest would be a banquet.

It was characteristic of Christ that in every way He was a wonderfully simple person. His wants were few. His needs were readily met. He asked little from life. His greatest joys were in the simple pleasures that were freely provided by the world of His own creation. He saw beauty in the wild lilies. He saw compassion in the birds that nested overhead. He found refreshment in the company of His Father alone by the lake or high in the hills. He made His friends amongst simple souls with open spirits and trusting hearts. Children adored Him, and common people were His companions. He could sleep under the stars, rolled up in His tunic; He could share the same cup with a despised Samaritan woman; He could eat from the same bowl as a Pharisee, publican, or sinner; He could gather grain or glean fruit from field edges or hedgerow trees to appease His hunger: Always, ever, He was in harmony with His environment.

And in Martha's home He was a man beautifully relaxed, wonderfully at ease, and deeply beloved by three dear people.

It was several months after the Festival of Booths that Lazarus was suddenly stricken with a fatal illness. His condition deteriorated rapidly. Martha and Mary ministered to their brother with utmost tenderness, but all to no avail. He sank lower and lower. Over and over they whispered to each other, "If only the Lord were here. One touch of His hand, one word from His lips, and Lazarus would be well!"

As the days moved on slowly, the sick man showed no signs of recovering. Slowly the cold, clammy grip of fear and foreboding began to fasten itself around the emotions of the two sisters. Something desperate must be done, and done quickly. Could they find the Master? If they could, surely He would hasten to their help.

After all, Lazarus was one of His favorite friends. With urgency they called in their most reliable servant. He was sent off with the urgent message to the Master. The latest news on the local grapevine was that Jesus was somewhere out in the hill country east of the Jordan. After several days of hard travel, following the clues given to him as he went, the sturdy messenger found Jesus in seclusion with His Twelve. "Lord," he said respectfully, "he whom you love, Lazarus, my master, is very ill."

Much to the messenger's surprise, Jesus' very calm reply was: "His illness does not mean the death of the man. You will see both God and His Son honored through this ordeal."

Disappointed that Jesus would not just drop everything and rush off to Bethany, the servant returned alone to Martha and Mary. His only consolation for them was that they were all deeply loved. Somehow, some way, some good would come out of this excruciating experience.

Within a day or two of the servant's return, Lazarus died. His remains were interred in a magnificent mausoleum carved out of the limestone ridge behind their home. The women wept.

Hot tears trickled down across their flushed cheeks. Death is dark enough when there is nothing more that can be done to forestall it. But it is a double anguish when it *seems* the victim could have been easily spared but was not.

The passing of Lazarus left an enormous vacuum in the hearts and home of these two wonderful women. The void that throbbed and ached so fiercely could not be easily filled. And the stabbing anguish that seared their souls and hurt their hearts was sharpened by the agonizing question, Why didn't Jesus come?

Four days after the funeral, word came that Jesus was trudging up the Jericho road in the blazing heat. A little late, it seemed, to do much about this situation. But God is never late. And this was a lesson both Martha and Mary were to learn that day.

Disregarding the numerous guests who had crowded into her home to console them, Martha slipped her slim feet into a pair of sandals and sped off down the hill toward Jesus. She was a lady of action. She was no idle dreamer. Within her breast there still stirred a strong hope that somehow Jesus could help. After all, the servant had said that God, in a wondrous way, would derive great glory from their dilemma. And anyway, who was better able to comfort and reassure her than this One. She loved Him and He loved her. Just to be with Him would lift her spirit and reassure her soul that even out of evil He would bring good. He always did.

"O Lord," Martha sobbed quietly, "if You had just been here my brother would not have died." She took control of her emotions. She was a strong-willed woman. She was also a lady of enormous faith and calm confidence. "But I *know* that even now, whatever You ask of God—even the restoration of my brother's life—He will grant it!"

This was one of the finest declarations of calm, strong confidence in Himself that Christ ever encountered. This was faith in action: *"I know."*

In immediate response to Martha's firm faith, Jesus replied, "Your brother will rise again!"

Momentarily Martha assumed that He referred to the great expectancy and hope of all God's people—resurrection after death, the future bestowal of spiritual, glorified bodies that replace our transient and temporary earth tents.

But the Master seized the moment to share with this lovely lady a truth that up until now had been kept secret to all men: *"I am the resurrection, and the life: he that believeth in Me, though he were dead, yet shall he live: And whosoever liveth and believeth in Me shall never die"* (John 11:25, 26).

It was a truth that throughout the centuries to come would be spoken in gentle reassurance over millions upon millions of graves in scores of languages all across the world. No other single statement would bring such hope, such comfort, such calm assurance to human hearts.

Standing on the dusty, hot Jericho road, sweat stains streaming down across His strong face, Jesus looked deep into Martha's warm brown eyes. "Martha," He inquired tenderly, watching the scalding tears slip softly across her smooth cheeks, "Martha, do you believe what I just said?"

She looked up at Him with inexpressible love. "Yes, Lord, yes, I believe!" Out of the depths of her anguish, out of the depths of her remorse, this gracious woman's strong, steady spirit rose in positive, powerful response to the truth before her. "Lord, You are the Christ. You are God's Anointed One. You are God's Son. You are the One promised. You are the Saviour of the world."

It was enough. Therein lay her trust. In Him was her assurance. He had come. All would be well. She was at peace. A warm glow of calm filled the empty void of her aching heart. He was here.

Eyes shining, she turned and raced up the road to tell Mary.

Not only was Martha a great woman, a gracious lady, but also a supremely generous soul. She did not hug her newfound strength just to her own heart. She would share it at once with Mary. Yes, with Mary who had not always been ready to help in the kitchen or too eager to serve the guests and strangers who came so frequently to visit in their home.

Never mind—Mary must know; Mary must be comforted; Mary must be reassured that the Master had come and was looking for her. Martha sped up the dusty road, little plumes of powder flying up under her soft sandals. Her long dark hair flowed in the air behind her. Her lithe, graceful form moved freely like a fawn in flight.

"Mary, Mary, the Master is down the road waiting for you!" She gasped out the words secretly, her breath coming in rapid pants.

Mary quickly slipped out of the crowded home and down the garden path. The guests assumed she was going to the grave to weep. Instead she was running toward the One she loved.

Mary did not possess the inner strength and quiet stamina of her sister. She was a finely drawn, highly charged, emotional woman. The moment she saw Jesus she was overwhelmed. In overwrought emotion she collapsed at His feet.

"O Lord," she gasped feebly, crying uncontrollably; "If You had just been here, my brother would not have died."

The words were identical with what Martha had said. Syllable for syllable they were the same.

But with Mary there was no affirmation of a faith that He could now still help. Instead, only disconsolate despair. Mary wept and wept. Words were beyond her.

In fact, as the assembled guests gathered around Him, all wailing and weeping, He became troubled in spirit. Was there so little faith here? Was there no confidence in what He could do?

He asked to be led to the sepulcher. Standing there beside the sealed doorway, its great stone in place, He too wept.

The onlookers assumed He was crying out of compassion for Lazarus. They supposed rather naively that He loved Lazarus so much He was sorry to find him dead and buried. Their lack of spiritual understanding even made them doubt if there was anything Jesus could do at this late date, except cry as they were crying.

The reason the Master wept was indeed that He did love Lazarus, and loved him deeply. Knowing that He would raise him up from death and restore him to this troubled earth scene was what really grieved Christ. He hated to do it to His friend! What a retrogression to be brought back from the beauty and ecstasy of life beyond the grave to reenter the remorse and anguish of life on earth with all its turmoil.

What was even more, Jesus knew full well that from now on Lazarus would become a marked man, hated by the scribes and Sadducees especially. The latter did not believe in the resurrection. And because Lazarus could now declare unequivocally from firsthand experience what life was like beyond the grave, he more than any other man would be under bitter attack.

Jesus gave instructions calmly but firmly that the great stone sealing the entrance to the mausoleum be rolled away. He who had raised Jairus' little girl, who had restored the son to the widow of Nain, now stood quietly before a corpse that had undergone decomposition for four long, hot days. Powerful putrefaction had set in to reduce the body to a nauseating mass of corruption.

But this did not dismay the Master. Nothing ever did. He was ever in control of every situation. He whose own body would never see corruption was not daunted by death nor by decay. He had come to break the hold of both upon the human race.

As He called out loudly to Lazarus to come forth—to be set free—it was the clarion call to all men of all time who would likewise be set free from the bonds of death and decay because of their belief and trust in Him. He alone had the power over death and decomposition.

It is deeply significant that the opening of a grave, normally unheard of, was something from which neither Martha nor Mary shrank back. To most people this would have been an impossible request. With quiet confidence in their Friend, they complied with His wishes and rolled the stone away. The result was a resurrection: not only for their brother but also for their own faith in Christ.

Jesus did not focus His attention on the decomposing corpse. He lifted His eyes to His Father in absolute assurance that His petition would be granted. It was. And Lazarus arose to shuffle slowly out of the darkness, bound hand and foot.

This whole drama was an open display for all to witness the response of God to human belief in Him. Jesus had calmly reassured Martha that "if you just believe, you are bound to see the character, the faithfulness (God's glory) of God!" He had not disappointed them in any degree. He never does whenever He finds even the most minute fragment of faith at work in any human heart.

Jesus promptly instructed the astonished bystanders to free Lazarus from the long windings of linen cloth in which he was wrapped. No doubt they were so overcome by Lazarus' reappearance they were too stunned to do him this simple favor without being told.

"Loose him, and let him go!"

Not only had Jesus brought His friend back to life, but also, He wanted him set free. It was typical of our Lord.

Lazarus' death and resurrection, painful as it was for Martha and Mary, resulted in many of their friends coming to believe in Christ. Suffering, in God's economy, always produces positive results. It may seem to us negative and distasteful; in God's hands it can be made to work both for our good and that of others.

This ordeal did not make these two winsome women bitter; instead they became more lovely and beautiful.

CHAPTER TWENTY-SEVEN

One Man Must Die for the People

For Christ, the raising of Lazarus was the pinnacle of His public life. Up to this point the Master had enjoyed enormous popularity amongst the common people. His supernatural power, previously demonstrated in majestic miracles, attained its zenith in the full restoration of a corpse subject to four days of decomposition. His prestige was at its penultimate with the general public of this weary, woebegone nation of Israel.

Ironically, this miracle, which otherwise might have catapulted Jesus of Nazareth to ultimate spiritual leadership for the lay people, actually triggered a chain reaction that led to His death on a cruel instrument of inhuman torture. It was the entrenched, jealous, fear-ridden ecclesiastical hierarchy that would arrange the ghastly end for God's Son.

The resurrection of Lazarus from the darkness of death, from the clutches of decay, from the power of putrefaction to the fullness of life and light and love amid his family and friends, was a burst of bright light around dark, dead, old Jerusalem. Truth, intense, incontestable truth, blazed about our Lord. Here was God, very God, in human guise, overcoming the power of the grave. Here was victory over death. Here was demonstrated the deity which the common, plain people adored—but whom the religious leaders dreaded.

John reported that the polarization resulted in two things. On one hand many, many Jews who up until now may have been skeptical of Christ's credentials believed on Him. But for the chief priests and Pharisees, the time to take council how they might destroy this One had finally come. He was too great a threat to them.

What are we going to do? was the tormenting question that they wrestled with in that formidable council meeting. For at least four hundred years no gathering of the priests had ever been so important, so ponderous, so weighty. On their deliberations and decisions hung the destiny not only of the nation Israel but of the whole then-known world. Yes, and even more, of all mankind for all time.

The priests and Pharisees and scribes were driven by fear, moved by flaming jealousy, and goaded by selfish self-interest. "If we leave Him alone," they whispered apprehensively to one another, "all men will believe on Him."

Of course this was a colossal lie. All men never did nor ever do believe in Christ. He Himself repeatedly warned His listeners that restricted was the entrance and narrow the way to life eternal. Few would ever find it. To find it was to follow Him. And most preferred to reject Him and pursue the wide pleasant route that led to ultimate destruction. No, the numbers who would ultimately believe in Him to the point where they would live for Him would always, ever be a meager minority. It has never been otherwise. Perhaps some 2 percent of the earth's populace at any given point in history give this Jesus their undivided allegiance.

What the priests and Pharisees feared for was their own future. They were jackals and hyenas who gorged themselves on the kill that was made from the temple trade. From that first frightening day when the prophet from Galilee stormed through the temple porches, tossing out the traders and lashing the money changers, they had cringed at His coming. He was The Lion of Judah before whose blazing eyes they fell back in fear. This bold and flaming figure terrified them. If not destroyed, He would destroy them. He would lead a popular revolution that the Romans would suppress and crush under a fist of steel.

Their beloved temple, beloved only for the monetary bounties it bestowed on them, would be razed to the ground. Their rich resources would be lost. Their prestige and prominence would vanish. Their pride would be shattered. They themselves would be reduced to the same abject poverty as the common people whom they now parasitized. No, this would never do. This was worse than death.

Little did they imagine, much less know, that what they would decide to do with Jesus would eventuate actually in the very disasters they hoped to avoid. Men do not break the laws of God with impunity. Those laws break, bruise, and crush men who contravene them. When in the dark hours of that council it was decided to destroy Christ, they were in fact determining their own destruction.

Almost in pompous piety, Caiaphas, the high priest that year, rose to speak. Stroking his flowing beard with smooth fingers and soft hands that had never done a day's work, he began thus: "You know nothing at all!" He drew his flowing robes around his portly, soft body and in feigned piety proceeded: "It is better and more expedient for all of us that one man should die for the people than that the whole nation perish!"

It was all very plausible. To some it may have seemed profound. Certainly it was prophetic. Prophetic in two ways: First, the innocent Christ would indeed die on behalf of not only the nation Israel but all the world! Second, it was prophetic in ushering in an era of unmitigated sorrow and suffering for the Jewish people.

The judgment of God upon Jerusalem for its awful abuse of the Redeemer, who had come to save them, would take place within forty years of this portentous council meeting. That night in deciding on Jesus' death they sealed their own destiny.

In A.D. 70 the grim, angry Roman legions under Titus laid siege to this city of blood: this city that had stoned its prophets and crucified its own Messiah, the Christ. It would literally writhe and agonize in torment and torture as more than a million of its people starved and rotted within its massive walls. Their corpses would pile up outside those ghastly walls to putrefy in the blazing sun, and when at last those walls were breached, the survivors would be bound hand and foot to be laid upon a thousand crosses that formed the world's most ghastly forest around this fierce and wretched city.

Caiaphas—the pretentious, pompous, prophet—spoke better

than he knew. Christ must die. His city must die.

Men do not flout and taunt God with impunity. The kindness, mercy, long-suffering love and patience of our Lord are beyond human comprehension. Yet likewise the justice, righteousness and integrity of His character are inexorable. Men do well if they remember this. For thousands of years He had come and come and come to His own with open, outstretched arms. Always, always, always they had spurned His overtures of love, trampled on His tears, turned their backs upon His precepts in disdain, spat in His face—and now they planned to kill Him.

Yet, in spite of this—because of His very nature, because of His concern and caring love—He would yield Himself deliberately to their devilish designs. It would seem a disastrous end. In God's economy, however, it was the appointed and positive way to ultimate triumph. From death would spring life. From despair would spring love. From darkness would spring light.

Why was this possible? Because it was not a man, not just a mere human being, not just a mortal person whom that august council had decided should die. It was God in man. It was God who was giving Himself on their behalf . . . on our behalf.

There was a great mystery to this coming death. It is a mystery of such majestic magnitude no mortal man can comprehend its dimensions. It was none other, none less, than the infinite God who it was decreed should die. Titanic transactions far surpassing any human understanding would be accomplished at Calvary. The Master knew this. He faced the formidable facts with a will of flint.

Before those final cataclysmic events at the cross were consummated He would share a few insights with His faithful band of young stalwarts. "Even men will deign to die for other good men," He pointed out, and "No greater love hath any man than this—that a man lay down his life for his friends." But His love, that unique and wondrous love of God, enabled Him to lay down His life for His enemies. Yes, even for the cunning priests and crafty Pharisees who in that cruel council contrived His destruction.

Their misdeeds, their selfish motives, their flaming jealousy and proud revenge were not unique to them. They are the common property of all mankind. All of us, if not criminals in action, are no less so in attitude. We all stand indicted before the bar of divine justice, mercy, and righteousness. Who has not sinned, and sinned grievously in the inner sanctum of his soul and spirit? Who has not thought cruel thoughts, entertained evil emotions, made dreadful decisions deep within the privacy of his own person, unknown to others yet fully known to God?

So it was, so it is, that for all of us who are guilty, this innocent One, the Christ, had to die. In Him the judgment of God would be exhausted and His justice exonerated. In Him the penalty for sin would be paid and His love demonstrated. And because He was the infinite God, it would suffice for all finite men of all time, everywhere.

But from that day of the council meeting, Jesus walked no more openly. He was a man pursued relentlessly by the bloodhounds of Jerusalem.

It seems almost unbelievable that from this point on in His earthly life the Master would live like a fugitive. No longer was He free to preach and teach openly. No longer would the multitudes crowd around Him, hanging on His words of comfort and cheer. His movements would be restricted, almost secretive. Slowly and inexorably, hostile forces were closing in around Him. He was virtually being driven underground. He who had gone about doing good, healing the sick, feeding the hungry, curing the blind, forgiving the sinners, and raising the dead, now moved furtively like a pursued criminal. The irony of it all overwhelms the heart.

Only once more, the week before the Passover, would He display Himself boldly in the temple of His people.

The Passover feast, that great celebration commemorating God's deliverance of Israel out of Egypt some fifteen hundred years before, was approaching. It was the highlight of the entire Jewish year. And Jesus was determined He and His men would celebrate it in Jerusalem. He alone then recognized its ultimate significance. His followers did not. He alone knew at this point in history that He, the Lamb of God, was also to be the Passover Lamb offered on behalf of all men as a substitute for their sins. Later the disciples would discover this great truth, but not now.

Just as the blood of the Passover lambs, sprinkled on the doorposts and lintels of their homes, had preserved them from the death angel in Egypt, so His blood, sprinkled upon men's consciences and lives, would deliver them from the destruction of their own misdeeds.

It was a deep principle still a bit beyond the grasp of His rough, tough young comrades.

Significantly, the symbolism of God's Lamb lingers until the present day. When an international banquet is served at the United Nations, the only meat dish which can be freely partaken of by all, is lamb. It is no accident our Lord was called God's Lamb.

Here He was, the Lamb of God, now purposing to go up to Jerusalem, there to deliberately offer Himself as God's Passover Lamb.

CHAPTER TWENTY-EIGHT

Men Along the Way

For a short time Jesus hid out in the desert hills across the Jordan. It was a wilderness area familiar to Him but little known by His antagonists. We are not sure of its exact location but assume it was in the same barren, rocky wasteland where He first endured such severe temptation from Satan.

It was no easy thing for one who had known the acclaim and adulation of the crowds to hide in the hills like a noble hart hunted by the hounds. The picture is well-nigh incongruous—that God, whose Spirit pursues men in mercy, as the Hound of Heaven, should here in turn be pursued and hounded by hostile men determined to destroy Him.

The agony of soul which was His during those dreadful days has never been disclosed. He who came to save men was driven to hide from the very ones He wished to reclaim and reconcile to Himself. He came to His own, but His own received Him not. But to as many as did receive Him, He imparted the great honor of becoming His people.

One day the stress of secretive living ended. With bold determination the Master turned His strong face toward the south and set out for Jerusalem. It was the last time His strong feet would carry Him across the rough hills and valleys of Samaria and Judea. Never again after this would He set foot on the hot, dusty roads of the Jordan Valley or climb the torturous trails that wound up the dry dongas between Jericho and Jerusalem.

He would celebrate the great Passover feast with His loyal band of younger men in the great metropolis. It would be His last banquet with the boys. He was bound to make this His final great assault on Jerusalem, no matter if it meant His certain death. Traveling southward through Samaria, Jesus met ten lepers on the outskirts of a small village. Being lepers, they were not allowed within the town proper. Wherever they went they cried out in awesome warning, "Unclean . . . unclean . . . unclean . . . ." Lepers were the offscouring of society. Unwanted, rejected, dreaded, and disdained, they drifted about the countryside begging for handouts or scrounging scraps of refuse. Barely able to find enough to survive, they lived like furtive animals in the tenuous twilight of semistarvation.

Many lepers were grotesque and repulsive in appearance. The despicable disease they suffered literally ate them alive. By degrees, sections of their emaciated, scrawny frames would be eaten away by decay. The extremities especially were subject to horrible disfiguration. Fingers and toes, hands and feet, noses and ears would be consumed in rotting flesh, leaving the leper maimed and deformed. Sometimes they dragged themselves about in the dirt, unable to walk erect or care for themselves as proper human beings. The disease reduced them eventually to a subhuman level of life. As if this were not torture enough, they suffered the soul-searing agony of total segregation from society. Ostracized outcasts, they lived out their desperate days in solitude and lonely agony of soul. The only consolation they ever knew was the miserable company of other sufferers like themselves.

Ten such men saw Jesus coming at a great distance. Unable to approach Him closely, they shouted at Him from afar, "Master, have mercy on us!"

It was a desperate cry coming from desperate men. It attracted Jesus' attention. He and only He could meet their need in mercy. Anyone less would have turned from them rather than toward them. Seeing their dreadful condition, moved with compassion, constrained by overpowering love and concern, His majestic life went out to them in healing and wholesomeness.

"Go, show yourselves to the priests." Any leper who presented himself to a priest did so for only one purpose. It was to be declared cured and freed from this awful affliction. In the ancient laws of Moses very explicit and carefully detailed instructions were given for priests in dealing with lepers. Our Lord was thoroughly familiar with those precepts. He demonstrated that He endorsed them by sending these ten men to the priests for absolution.

There were two remarkable aspects to this brief encounter between Jesus and the lepers. The first was the amazing faith all ten men displayed in starting out to find the priest even before they were cured, for their complete cleansing occurred only after they were well on their way.

It is worthy of note that of the ten healed, only the Samaritan came back to express his deep gratitude to the Master. In part this was probably due to the forgotten fact that only he of the ten would not be allowed to see the priest. Jews and Samaritans, except at the level of lepers, had no dealings with one another. On the lofty level of religious rituals this poor fellow would remain an outcast forever. But he was healed and he knew it. He was made whole and he was glad. He had been touched and transformed by the life of God, and he came back to give God the glory and honor that welled up from within his body, soul, and spirit, now made well.

The second noteworthy aspect to this event was that only 10 percent of those delivered from their dread condition cared enough to come back and thank their benefactor. Was it gross ingratitude? We shall never fully know. Perhaps they were so terribly excited over their cleansing they could not wait to rush off and find the first priest available. He it was who would declare them clean. It was his word that would return them once more to the company of their community. It was he who alone could allow them to be reunited with their families and friends.

Perhaps most of us are a bit that way. We have great regard for the form and rituals of our church or religion, while sometimes forgetting it is God Himself who has done the great work in our lives. We are preoccupied with the tangible trappings of our faith, while forgetting the source of our healing lies in the invisible power and presence of our God.

In any case, all ten men were cleansed. All ten men went out to live new lives. All ten men were never the same again. But for the Samaritan leper especially, Christ had a special word of commendation: "Arise, bestir yourself, go your way into a brand-new dimension of living. Your confidence invested in Me has made you whole."

Somehow our Lord always had a soft spot in His affections for the underdog Samaritans. When He told His classic story to demonstrate our obligations to others, He chose as the hero the well-known "good Samaritan." When He disclosed the deep truths about His being Himself the "water of life," it was to a despised Samaritan woman at the well. And here again, He singles out a Samaritan leper as a lesson for all men, to teach what it means to have faith and gratitude in God.

This lowly, distraught, devoid member of society stands for all time as a symbol of a balanced believer. He was one who called out to Christ in unshakable confidence. And when that faith was vindicated by the Master, he returned quickly to render Him the appropriate praise and appreciation He deserved. It is not enough only to pray and petition God in faith. To be fully rounded, beautifully balanced beings, we need also to come again and again in gratitude and praise to God for all the wonders He performs on our behalf. This the Samaritan did, and he was deeply blessed. Not only was he made whole in body, he was also completely restored in soul and spirit.

From Samaria, Jesus and His men moved down the fiery, burning Jordan Valley toward Jericho.

Outside Jericho, that city of a thousand palms standing still beneath the blazing desert sun, Jesus met a short little man named Zacchaeus. He was a notorious man in the town. He was rich and he was a scoundrel, made rich by extortion of taxes from his compatriots. He was a man hated by other of his townsmen both for his pride and his parasitism.

Yet in some peculiar and profound way the coming of the Master had made a powerful impact on Zacchaeus. In contrast to himself, Jesus was a poor person. He was one who had never deprived anyone of his property. He had many friends amongst the common folk. And those riches which He possessed were of the spirit, not the purse.

So strong was the magnetism of the Master that the little shyster decided somehow he would have to see Him. He was a determined little character and he would let nothing stop him. But there was more than mere human determination at work within this hardheaded man. The Spirit of God had also touched this hard heart. It was starting to soften under His impact. And the old fierce pride was being displaced with downright humility.

Proof of this lay in Zacchaeus' making a public spectacle of himself. There were such mobs of men and women crowding and crushing around Jesus that the little short man, even if he stood on tiptoe, could not even get a glimpse of Him. So he decided to scramble and scratch his way up into the shrubby growth of a sycamine tree.

These bushy, dwarflike trees were not the big, broad-limbed trees so often depicted in Bible storybooks. They were the scraggly little scrub trees that grew along ditches, canals, and farmers' fields. They were the wayside trees whose bitter, puckery fruit was eaten only by the birds, beggars, and lepers.

In the tradition of the times anyone who even touched a sycamine tree was identified with the lowest level of society. It was akin to being an outcast—the lowest of the low. For only those driven to desperation, like lepers or beggars, would even eat this awful fruit.

Zacchaeus knew all about this. And it is a measure of the man that casting all his pride and prestige to the winds, he boldly, yet humbly and contritely, climbed as high as he could in one of these tortured little trees. It was a pathetic sight. A little shriveled man swaying about in a shriveled little tree just a few feet above the ground, hoping somehow, some way, to get a glimpse of Christ.

And when Jesus saw him there He knew at once that here was a person in whose life a profound work had already been done by the Spirit of God. Here was a man who had humbled himself. Here was a man who cared not what the crowd thought just as long as he could come to Christ.

It is no wonder the Master invited him to come down and take Him to his own home for a meal. God always draws near to those who draw near to Him. He ever deigns to enter any heart and home where a man or woman in open honesty and sincere humility gives Him opportunity.

The meeting between these two was a joyous occasion. For Zacchaeus it was the turning point in the tangled trail of his untidy life. No longer would he cheat and chisel and defraud others. No longer was he bent on satisfying only his own selfish ends and indulging his own selfish self-interest. From here on he would share his property and prosperity with the poor all around him. Anything not truly his would be properly restored and repaid in generous measure, four times over, to the rightful owners.

This was what we call the conversion of a crook. It is what can happen when a man encounters Christ in open honesty. The event jolted Jericho almost as much as when its walls were flattened by Joshua's army 1480 years before, under the hand of God.

CHAPTER TWENTY-NINE

A Pound of Precious Perfume

The winding, twisting, serpentine road from Jericho to Jerusalem clawed its tortuous way through the hot hills. In twelve tough miles the Master and His men climbed roughly thirty-eight hundred feet from the scorching valley of the Jordan to the cooler heights of Jerusalem. The road was dusty and it was dangerous. Roving bands of brigands raided travelers who took this route. They hid out amongst the caves and rocky outcrops to come swooping down on unwary victims like fierce falcons stooping to a kill.

This was always a hard hike even for young stalwarts. So when Jesus and His companions, with tired legs and sweating brows, broke over the last hot ridge, it was always a double delight to come to Bethany. This contented little hamlet of gleaming white houses stood facing the rising sun on the eastern slopes, about two miles from tired old Jerusalem.

Best of all, Bethany was a very special spot to our Lord. It was His second home, so to speak, during His public travels. Peter's home, up by the Lake of Galilee, had become His headquarters in the north. Lazarus' home had become His headquarters in the south. He loved to drop in there to visit with His three very special friends Mary, Martha, and Lazarus.

This home with its gentle people and kindly, warm welcome was like an oasis for the Master in hostile Judea. Judea with its barren hills, its rigid legalism, its entrenched ecclesiastical hierarchy, was ever antagonistic to the Christ. Whenever He came to the capital city it was akin to a military commander making an assault upon a well-guarded fortress. The priests, scribes, Pharisees, and Sadducees were set for siege and retaliated violently. This would be the last time our Lord would be dropping in for a few days with His friends. He knew it and they knew it. Perhaps in private conversations He had shared the secret of His nearing end with His friends. Ever since Lazarus had been raised to life, a most intimate and intense bond of spiritual affection and understanding entwined these four people. There were things Jesus could disclose to His friends that even His disciples did not fully grasp.

The evening of their arrival, just six days prior to the Passover, Martha arranged a magnificent dinner banquet in honor of her favorite friend. This really was her home, shared by her brother and sister. And in her womanly way she gave full expression to her affectionate esteem for her Lord in serving a magnificent meal. Lazarus, Mary, Jesus, the twelve disciples, as well as other distinguished guests, crowded the ornate home to pay honor to Jesus.

It was a prestigious gathering.

Martha had spared no pains or expense to prepare the finest food. It was really like a farewell feast, a going-away party. For the Master's departure was imminent.

At the height of the celebration, Mary, a gift parcel in hand, slipped over quietly and kneeled before Jesus. He, like His friends, reclined on colorful cushions scattered around the room.

As Mary undid the wrappings of elaborate embroidery around the jar of perfume in her hand, a hush fell over the house. Every eye was fastened on the kneeling woman. Her hands trembled a little and her fingers fumbled slightly as she softly removed the cover from the ornate container.

Jesus looked directly into her adoring eyes. And those eyes spoke louder than anything she might have said in words. They spoke of total, complete, unequivocal adoration and self-abandonment to the Lord of Glory before her.

With glad, unabashed abandon she began to pour the costly perfume over those tired feet, those beautiful feet, those strong feet that had borne this One to her home. It was a demonstration in real life of that grand old theme from the ancient Scriptures: "How beautiful upon the mountains are the feet of him that bringeth good tidings . . ." (Isaiah 52:7).

Normally the host in a Jewish home bathed the guest's feet with water as a sign of hospitality. Mary used precious, precious perfume to bestow the highest honor she could upon her Messiah—the Anointed One.

There was no need for her to anoint Jesus' head. This had already been done of God the Father when, in the form of a dove, God the Holy Spirit descended upon Him at His baptism. That was His divine anointing for His lifework. Now Mary anointed Him for His death.

As she continued to pour the perfume over His weary feet, its fragrance filled the whole house. The delicious bouquet that lingered on the warm evening air surpassed that of even the hibiscus and plumeria that bloomed in the garden outside the doors.

Taking her long, lustrous, lovely dark hair, Mary stooped to the very floor and gently wiped the Master's feet. The perfume made her blue-black tresses glisten brightly in the flickering lamplight. Gently, reverently, yet extravagantly, Mary demonstrated her undivided allegiance to her Lord. Her action was one of total submission, utter self-giving to the Lord of Glory.

A hush fell over the assembled guests. This was a scene that solemnized one's soul. Seldom did one see such an uninhibited demonstration of devotion to divinity. It stilled the spirit and quickened the soul.

The perfume had been brought hundreds of miles across blazing deserts in the camel saddles of some foreign merchant. It was worth at least three hundred pence. Now in those days an average working man's wage for a day was one penny. So the value of the precious ointment was at least equivalent to a year's income for the laborer. In modern-day terms that would be roughly ten or twelve thousand dollars. It is not every day one hears of such lavish love. It is no wonder this woman's outpoured generosity should have come down to us with enormous impact across twenty centuries of history.

But as the roomful of guests sat hushed and awed, softly enveloped by fragrance, touched deeply by the tender scene before them, there was suddenly a discordant note struck.

It was Judas Iscariot's hard, metallic, rasping voice.

His words were brittle, cruel, caustic.

They shattered the silence, jarred the guests, and injected discord into the delicate scene:

"Why wasn't this perfume sold for 300 pence and the proceeds given to the poor?"

Judas' hard, cold, cramped, selfish soul was totally insensitive to what had transpired. It completely escaped him that anyone could care so much for the Master.

The outpouring of selfless love he had just witnessed was utterly lost on him. He had no reciprocal reaction of empathy or even endorsement for what Mary had done. Instead his caustic soul spilled out its burning acid of contempt and bitterness upon an act of enormous generosity and sweet understanding.

Here stood two hearts in bold contrast, stripped of all pretense.

A woman totally committed, totally giving all she had.

A man withholding, begrudging, perverting even what was not his.

Judas, for me at least, remains ever a man of mystery in the Scriptures. His actions and reactions are beyond understanding.

He was a man who for nearly three years had shared fully and intimately the life of our Lord. Yet, instead of being touched and transformed by that wondrous life he seems only to have grown tougher in personality and more tortured in spirit. He was polarized into passionate dislike.

On at least two occasions when he and the other eleven men had faced certain death by drowning, Jesus had rescued him from the storms. Still not a syllable of gratitude was spoken. He knew the Master and His men were poor, impoverished. Jesus did not have even an extra change of clothing. When taxes had to be paid the money was not in hand. It had to be retrieved from the mouth of a fish caught by Peter, when so instructed, because the kitty was empty.

And though Judas was entrusted with keeping the purse for the small band of penniless men, he habitually stole from it. It was dastardly conduct of the most selfish sort. The others knew and somehow still put up with his crafty knavery.

Jesus had never taken Judas to task over the personal affronts and petty thieving perpetrated against Him. But when this cruel man lashed out in venom against this gracious, generous, innocent woman, things were different.

In hot, flaming, soul-shriveling syllables, the Master silenced Judas:

"*Leave her alone!*" He warned, fastening His eyes firmly on the crafty one. His tones were low and level but fraught with enormous authority.

"Mary has done Me this high honor in preparation for my death." The Saviour's eyes searched and seared Judas' soul. The delinquent could not return the gaze fastened on him. He dropped his eyes to the floor.

Then Jesus went on softly: "You will always have the poor in society to whom men can minister. As for Me, I will soon be gone."

It had been a brief exchange. Judas was cut to the quick. Anger, hatred, and venom boiled up within him. Revenge burned in his very bones. He would not rest, he would not relent until he betrayed this One who had so humiliated him at this banquet.

There was a tremendous principle of godly conduct involved in this event. Namely, our Lord demonstrated that a person is fully entitled to defend vigorously any innocent victim who is being wronged. He would never attempt to avenge Himself for the abuse heaped on Him by His contemporaries. But when He saw another being exploited, His anger flamed in white-hot heat. This is to be angry and yet not sin.

The other tremendous truth made clear through the contrasting conduct of Mary and Judas has to do with stewardship. For a very long time Judas had been deliberately entrusted with the meager funds his friends shared in common. Yet he had repeatedly betrayed that trust. He stole from the others, proving positively that he was not trustworthy. If a man cannot be faithful in small responsibilities, he should never expect that he will be given greater matters to attend.

Basically this was the principle Christ endeavored to show in the parable of the three stewards. Two of the men, entrusted with two pounds and five pounds respectively, went out to trade vigorously and enhance what had been given to him. The third servant simply buried his responsibility, thus abusing and betraying the trust put in him as a person. Little wonder he was stripped of his small sum only to have it handed to someone who would and could be relied on to use it well and be faithful.

By betraying the tiny trust given him to carry the little moneybag, Judas showed he was capable of betraying a much greater trust, that of his Master's very life. "As bends the twig, so grows the tree!" And a few days later he did just that.

Mary, in contrast, though a wealthy woman from a very, very rich family, showed that she was utterly trustworthy. Instead of using her means for selfish ends, she showered them upon the poor: the poor Man of Galilee—and His poor disciples who followed Him.

She demonstrated that she had done what she could and what she should. The precious perfume might have been used on her own person. Instead its fragrance carries across the centuries, a sweet symbol of selflessness.

CHAPTER THIRTY

The Coming of the King

O Jerusalem, Jerusalem, city of cruel passions and raging hatreds; city of cunning and crafty schemers; city doomed to repeated devastation and destruction; city that killed its prophets, stoned its seers and now will crucify its Christ—once more you are visited from God on high. And true to form, you will torture and reject royalty from heaven.

Our Lord knew all this. But He never flinched.

Jesus knew He had only a few days of freedom. Yet in those days He would deliver a mighty warning to this people.

The Christ knew that He came now to this city for a last assault. He would not be crowned, but crucified.

But before that cataclysmic event, He and His men would once again electrify the masses surging through the city streets for the Passover festival. They would see the Messiah mount the temple steps one last time to fling out the false traders in doves and stock. Their blood would race in heightened expectation at the burning words that flowed from the Master's lips, the fiery gaze that flamed from His flashing eyes.

Many were positive that more than a prophet was amongst them. They were sure that their Sovereign, their Promised One, their Messiah, their Deliverer, their King had come at last to redeem them from the Romans.

And the Master also knew all this.

Never before, in all of the 1050 years of its horrendous history, had the temple precincts so pulsed with portents of such magnitude. God, very God, in human form and human flesh was visiting His Holy Hill. Some were absolutely excruciatingly aware of this. They were ecstatic with electrifying excitement. But others doubted. They were sullen, angry, fearful and dark within. He had to be neutralized. He had to be liquidated.

It was in the full knowledge of all these conflicting, counteracting crosscurrents of public opinion that the Master and His men quietly left Bethany to enter Jerusalem.

Gently they climbed the long, low limestone ridge that separated Bethany from the seething metropolis. Over a million visitors from all parts of the Mediterranean world swarmed like eager ants through its choked and crowded streets. The low hum and ominous throb of the city's pulsing life hung on the air that drifted up to the Mount of Olives.

In the clear morning sun falling full upon Jerusalem, Jesus paused to gaze softly at this metropolis that had stirred the emotions and gripped the hopes of His people for over a thousand years. No other city in all the world possessed such a peculiar fascination for its people. Nor had any capital ever been so terribly devastated and destroyed again and again. Repeatedly it had been the scene of awful cruelty and revolting carnage.

Standing there on the Mount of Olives, despite His mighty manhood, glistening tears welled up in His magnificent eyes. They trickled down over His tanned face to drop on His rough tunic. "O Jerusalem, Jerusalem! How often I would have gathered you up in My arms." He stretched His strong arms out toward the city in anguish of heartache. "But you would not have it!"

It was from this mount that He would begin His final entry into the city that despised Him. It was from this spot that He would foretell Jerusalem's awful fall and total destruction. It was in the Garden of Gethsemane, on this mount, that He would undergo such anguish of spirit. And, at last, it would be from this mount His disciples would see Him ascend before their wondering eyes, to return to the Glory whence He had come.

And now He picked two of His men and sent them off down the hill to fetch an unbroken donkey that He knew was waiting for Him in the village below.

Sure enough, just exactly as He had predicted, the young ass was tied with its dam outside the owner's house. Of course he protested at their presumption in untying the frisky animal without even asking permission. "What are you doing anyway?" he objected heatedly. "Oh, the Master needs him," was their calm rejoinder, as if strangers borrowed unbroken beasts every day.

At this the owner understood. Even though a Judean, he was sympathetic to the Prophet from Galilee, and agreed quickly to let the two disciples lead his donkey away. The Master could certainly do the untamed colt no harm. In fact, with His gentle spirit He might do it a world of good.

Even though the two men seemed to take all this in their strides without outward excitement, inwardly they were astonished. Though they had seen the Master perform so many miracles, here was something new. First finding the colt exactly as they had been told, then finding the owner so cooperative, was a bit breathtaking. Jews normally didn't just part with their goods that readily. At least there would be a charge for this service. But there was not.

Jesus might have chosen to ride in splendor into the great capital. He could have come in a chariot drawn by handsome horses. He could have elected to sweep in on the swaying saddle of a caravan camel, as the magi had done. Or He might even have ridden in borne proudly upon the shoulders of His zealous followers.

But instead He rode in on a colt.

The ass was ever a symbol of two great aspects of life amongst the people of Israel. First, the ass stood for suffering service. And our Lord saw Himself always as the Son of man—the suffering servant of the Most High—who had come to save His people from their sins.

The ass was secondly a symbol of judgment. Always of old, the judges of Israel and their sons had come riding upon asses. And here the Judge of all the earth, in human guise, rode this day into this capital for final judgment.

But over and beyond all of this, our Lord's choice of a colt was in complete accord with the ancient prediction made by the prophet Zechariah 520 years previously: "Rejoice . . . Jerusalem: behold, thy King cometh unto thee: he is just, and having salvation; lowly, and riding upon an ass, and upon a colt the foal of an ass" (Zechariah 9:9).

To the utter astonishment of the onlookers, when the disciples flung their tunics over the frisky colt's bare back he never flinched. Normally an unbroken beast would toss his head, kick up his heels and toss the tantalizing garments to the ground.

Calmly, quietly, in complete control, as He was in every situation, the Master mounted the colt. It stood steady as a rock. Then urging it ahead softly, Jesus started gently down the slope into the expectant city.

A gasp of amazement went up from the bystanders. Quickly it gathered volume. They began to shout and gesticulate. It was an emotional thing. Several of the men, swept up in the spontaneous excitement, tore off their tunics and tossed them on the trail. It was like laying out the red carpet of royal welcome for their conquering hero.

In typical human behavior when the mob instinct grips a crowd, others became even more demonstrative. They began to shout and clap their hands. Others scrambled up nearby trees, wrenching off branches and limbs. These they tossed on the ground like garlands of greenery to prepare the path for their marching monarch.

Seeing all this the disciples could not contain themselves. In unison they began to chant. "Blessed be the King that cometh in the name of the Lord." Then they would clap their hands in ecstasy. "Peace in heaven, and glory in the highest."

This was heady stuff. It electrified the gathering crowds. En masse they began to shout and sing. "Hosanna to the son of David!" The cry echoed and reechoed across the city. "Hosanna in the highest." The King had come—but for whom, and how long?

This dramatic spectacle of spontaneous adulation sprang from the masses unplanned and unrehearsed. It was not an idea spawned by Jesus or masterminded by the Master's men. The very artlessness of it made it all the more incredible. It was intoxicating stuff for the common people, who for so long had struggled and suffered under the oppression of Rome's mailed fist. At last, hope that the power of the oppressor might be broken lifted their spirits and set them to singing "Hosanna, hosanna to the son of David."

Even little children, with shrill voices and flashing dark eyes, ran along beside the colt, screaming ecstatically. Some waved branches and others waved sticks. It was an incredible scene that gathered ever-greater throngs in its train as they moved towards the temple.

Amid all the commotion the little colt never shied, never became skittish, never missed a step. Surefooted and steady under the

Master's strong hand, it moved sedately through the crowded streets.

"Peace in heaven! Glory in the highest!" the multitudes cried out. But on earth there could be no peace. He who had come to Bethlehem as a babe was ushered in with the ringing phrases "Peace on earth, goodwill toward men!"

But His coming had brought a sword. It was the sword of truth, the sword of deity, the sword of separation that set one man against another. Jesus Himself had said this would be so: "I come not to bring peace, but a sword!"

And this day, amid this tremendous display, that sword was already dividing loyalties. Not all in the city would give this One their allegiance. Some there were amongst the Master's old antagonists who protested angrily, "Why don't You bid the crowds be silent? Why do You accept such adulations?"

How could He do otherwise? To be true to Himself He could do naught else but accept the homage which was rightfully His. He, the Christ, was none other than the long-promised Messiah for whom His people had waited so wearily. As Isaiah the prophet had foretold 775 years before: "Unto us a child is born, unto us a son is given: and the government shall be upon his shoulder: and his name shall be called Wonderful, Counsellor, The mighty God, The everlasting Father, The Prince of Peace" (Isaiah 9:6).

To have silenced the shouts of "Hosanna," to still the songs of praise to the Most High, to quiet the crowds would have been to deny His deity.

"Why, if these were to hold their peace," He replied sternly to His detractors, "then even the very rocks of these rocky hills would burst forth into praise." The King had come, and the time for earth to recognize her royalty was here. No man would deprive this Monarch of His rightful majesty.

It was not with any ostentation or personal ambition that our Lord accepted the acclaim. The wild enthusiasm was simply a symbol of His inherent sovereignty that He could not disclaim. To have done otherwise would have been to abdicate His role as heaven's royalty. So with quiet dignity and gentle strength He accepted the accolades heaped upon Him that day.

The very fact that He endorsed what was done, thus establishing His kingship, would prove to be the cornerstone in the charges to be laid against Him a few days later in Pilate's hall. "Are You indeed the king of the Jews?" the Roman governor would ask Him.

And, when at last, the bugling bloodhounds of this dreadful city brought Him to bay, nailed to a rough-cut cross, over His noble, bleeding brow, there would be fastened His true title: KING OF THE JEWS.

He was a *King in Glory* . . . *King in birth* . . . *King in life* . . . *King in death* . . . *King of kings* . . . yet, a *King incognito.*

He had come unto His own, but His own would not receive Him as royalty. "We have no king but Caesar!" was the cry this same fickle crowd would scream a few days later.

The unpredictable character of human beings remains an eternal enigma. Men and women are as variable as the wind. One moment they blow hot, the next instant cold. There is nothing so totally untrustworthy as the fickle favor of the unregenerate masses. The Master knew all this. He knew the makeup of man. He never entrusted Himself to their infamous natural forces. Only to those whose entire lives had undergone a complete about-face could He come and give Himself in open, honest generosity. From such He never did, nor will He ever, withhold Himself.

"For, to as many as received Him as royalty, to them He gives the enormous honor and privilege of becoming sons of God."

For the last time Jesus, the Christ, the Anointed One of the Most High, came to Jerusalem. It was a mixed reception He received. He came a last time offering Israel her greatest hour of opportunity to become great. Instead of embracing Him, she ended up rejecting Him. He was to be thrust from her in anger, venom, and disdain.

"O Jerusalem, Jerusalem, if only you really knew who was here: If only you were aware of the awful portents for your future: If only you would repent!" His eyes were dimmed with hot tears. His throat was choked with great sobs of grief. "This is your hour—but you have missed it."

Looking ahead down the long, dark, agonizing corridors of the centuries to come, the Master groaned within Himself. It would be almost 1880 years, after Jerusalem was pulverized by the relentless military might of Rome, before the Jews would return again to kiss the Wailing Wall where He now stood and wailed for His people. It was Jerusalem's death as well as His own that was decided that day.

CHAPTER THIRTY-ONE

Events Preceding the Passover

Had there been the least inclination on the part of our Lord to establish an earthly empire, now would have been the opportune moment. The masses of pilgrims thronging Jerusalem fell under His spell. Though they came from all over the great Roman Empire, they were bound together in one common hope—a Coming King.

It mattered not whether their homes were in Italy, Greece, Asia Minor, Arabia, or even Africa; the scattered sons of Israel clung tenaciously to their ancient national dream of earthly power. Anyone who appeared on the horizon to stir their hopes and inflame their aspirations found an ardent following amongst these forlorn offspring of Abraham. Jesus was no exception. Even children chanted His praises and sent their shrill shouts of "Hosanna, hosanna" ringing through the great temple colonnades.

But Christ had not come to initiate a new national scheme. He had not entered human history to found a world system. The kingdom of God of which He spoke so frequently and fervently was the spiritual regency of God within human spirits. It was the establishment of God's government in men's hearts. It was the allegiance of men's spirits to the ultimate control of Christ. It was the sum total of all those lives in which the gracious Spirit of God Himself became supremely sovereign.

Even the Master's own men, carefully instructed as they had been in spiritual truth, did not fully grasp this concept. Certainly the common people in the throngs that milled around the Master did not understand. And, perhaps most tragic of all, the religious leaders of the era, steeped as they were in the ancient Scriptures, had failed to interpret their teachings aright. They were terrified at the possible prospect of losing their power, prestige, and positions of prominence. It was like a terrible nightmare that haunted them. In hate and fear they reacted violently against this upsetting "Man of Galilee."

They had concluded that there was only one course of action open to them. They simply had to destroy Jesus. They were not exactly sure how to proceed. If it could not be done legitimately through the law, then politics would have to be brought into play. And if both of these failed, then they were not above resorting to contemptible criminal tactics. It mattered not so long as He was silenced without arousing the general antagonism of the masses.

He was kept under constant surveillance. Every move He made was under scrutiny. They observed where He went by day, where He spent His nights. They hired unscrupulous scoundrels to trail Him secretly. They engaged brilliant cynical minds to challenge Him in His public discourses in the temple, where He spent most of His daylight hours speaking to the crowds who gathered to hear Him. The masses had never heard anyone at home speak with such simplicity or such authority. His words were sweet to their taste and stimulating to their spirits.

So for six days the Master commuted back and forth between Jerusalem and the little town of Bethany. If He did not sleep at Lazarus' home, He and His men would bed down beneath the gnarled old olive trees on the Mount of Olives. They would prepare their frugal fare over a small campfire of dead twigs while the stars came out to shine through the overhanging branches. It was better to sleep out under the open starlit skies than in some hostelry in the city where they could be easily trapped by their antagonists.

Food must have been both scarce and fairly expensive around Jerusalem. One morning, not having had a proper breakfast, they were walking back into the city, hungry for a meal. Along the way Jesus saw a flourishing fig tree. Hoping it might provide them with fresh fruit they searched beneath its great green leaves for figs. But there were none. The tree was barren.

Standing before the tree that had yielded no fruit, the Master commanded in quiet authority that its life should be suspended. If it could not produce fruit, it would have to come to an end.

Some of the disciples were astonished to see this tough, hardy, drought-resistant tree dry up from the roots. Normally a tree dies down from its branch tips. Seeing the natural order reversed they were doubly amazed.

This was not an act of impetuous impatience. It was not a childish outburst of vindictive hostility against a hapless tree. Nor was it an empty display of divine power exercised in pique just because of unsatisfied hunger pangs. Christ did not vent His disappointment on a wayside tree.

No, there was inherent in this act a lesson of enormous import for His men. That lesson was to be the very central theme and core of His conflict with the Jewish religious leaders in the next few days: "There must be fruit! Only by their fruit shall they be known! Ultimately a man must be judged on the basis of what his life produces—there is no point in professing much in talk but yielding nothing in action. Religious display and pomp were pointless if no practical benefits resulted. Pretense, pretext, and a phony show simply would not endure—they had to end."

The fig tree appeared so promising, but it was barren.

So many religious pretenders were destitute of divine life. Under the searching examination of God they would not endure. They could not last.

This was an idea bound up with repentance. Men simply had to see themselves undone before God. In contrition and deep repentance they had to turn from their old phony way of life. They had to be turned around, indwelt by God and started on a new life-style. The positive proof this had happened was fruit in the life. Fruit of new priorities, new values, new aims, new behavior.

It was what John the Baptist shouted: Men must repent and bring forth fruit indicative of repentance and a new life within.

Jesus, later in the temple, told various parables to illustrate this principle. These parables of the kingdom were not easy to understand. He told about the man with two sons who owned a vineyard. Both boys were instructed to go and work amongst the vines. One objected then later relented and went. The second readily agreed to go but never did comply with his father's wishes.

He told about the wealthy landowner who rented out his property to unscrupulous operators. When he endeavored to collect his proceeds, the tenants abused his servants whom he sent for fruit. In fact they went so far as to murder the man's own son when he came to collect his rightful share of the crop.

At first parables of this sort appeared to puzzle the audience to whom they were addressed. But amongst that multitude of onlookers were Pharisees, scribes, elders, chief priests and Sadducees. And little by little the painful, penetrating truth came winging home to them that it was they against whom these terrifying thrusts were directed. Nothing can be so devastating as divine truth thrust like a sword into the proud spirit of stubborn men.

With increased fury and hostility they sought some way of taking Christ forcibly. Seething with inner rage, they would have lynched Him in broad daylight. They burned with hatred. Humiliated and castigated before the crowds, they were also fearful of the crowds because of Jesus' popularity. This alone kept them back from an outright physical attack.

As one day slowly supplanted another, the Master intensified His attack on the ecclesiastical hierarchy. He pressed them at every point.

These thrusts all made an enormous impact on His hearers. The common people of the streets loved them. The disciples were so impressed they never forgot them, while the religious leaders fumed in frenzy. Somehow they would fix Him!

To retaliate they set three traps for Him. If they could not yet actually kidnap Him physically, at least they could try to snare Him in His speech.

The first was a political ploy: "Is it lawful to give tribute to Caesar, or not?"

Without hesitation the Master asked for a coin. It is noteworthy that He had no money of His own to use. "Whose image is it on this penny?" He turned it over with contempt between His strong fingers. "Render to Caesar the things that are Caesar's, and to God the things that are God's."

It was a brilliant rebuttal. His questioners withdrew amazed.

The second snare was set by the Sadducees. They had seen the Pharisees so clearly outmaneuvered they decided to try a more spiritual approach.

Dragging out one of their tired old jokes, they asked what would become of a woman who married seven times and was widowed seven times? In the resurrection life, to which of the seven husbands would she belong? It was a double absurdity to even ask this. For one thing, Sadducees did not even believe in a resurrection. And as the Master pointed out, not only were they ignorant of what God does to restore His own after death, they were also grossly ignorant of the fact that in that new dimension of life, marriage alliances no longer hold.

It was a swift, sure retort that silenced the Sadducees.

The third snare was a legal and moral issue. It was posed by a brilliant solicitor: "What is the greatest commandment?"

For Jesus, who knew the Mosaic Law so well, this was a pushover: "Thou shalt love the Lord thy God with all thy heart, and with all thy soul, and with all thy mind.

"This is the first and great commandment. And the second is like unto it: Thou shalt love thy neighbor as thyself."

With three brilliant strokes He had routed His opponents. It was a tremendous strategy triumph.

Quick to capitalize on His advantage, Jesus now turned the tables and asked them a difficult question. It was a masterpiece of perception.

"What do you think of Christ?" He looked at them searchingly. It was the ultimate question. "Whose Son is He?"

Their prompt response was, "He is the son of David."

"If that be the case," replied Jesus, a slight smile playing on His strong, handsome face, "how then, in spirit, did David call this One, the Christ, Lord?" As if to press the attack even further, He went on positively: "If David called Him Lord, how then can He also be his son?"

It was a bit beyond them to reply.

They knew within the deep instincts of their spirits that they had been thoroughly routed. This One whom they had set out to trap had in turn trapped them irrevocably. It was a complete checkmate. There was no place to turn. Their game was up.

From that day on no one ever challenged the Master again. From that day on He held the field of popular attention all to Himself. From that day on no one even dared to ask Him another question.

He had established complete supremacy over His adversaries. His final assault on Jerusalem and its superficial religious leaders had now turned into a total rout for His foes. It was a complete conquest in which right had triumphed over wrong; truth had triumphed over falsehood; integrity and sincerity had triumphed over duplicity.

But Jesus, the Christ, the Lion of Judah, was not prepared to just leave His adversaries running in retreat. With one ultimate awesome attack He was determined to demolish their last defenses of phony pretense and hypocritical pretexts. It would be a warning to all men of all time against the sin of insincerity.

Turning to His disciples and the throngs jamming the temple porches, He warned them against the corruption of the scribes and Pharisees. "These have been entrusted with the oracles and precepts of Almighty God!" He thundered. "Obey them, and observe the laws of God, but do not comply with the conduct of these hypocrites." His face was fierce with intensity. "They say one thing, but do another. They are utterly inconsistent. They load and bend men's backs with grievous and heavy burdens. They make a mockery of serving God. They pretend to be so pious, when at heart they are utter scoundrels."

This was a devastating denunciation. It was literally a salvo of heavy fire exploding against the battlements of the religious hierarchy. The impact was shattering.

Then in rapid succession, without letup, the Master let loose eight tremendous outbursts of imprecations. They reduced all the defenses of phony pretense and blatant hypocrisy of His adversaries to rubble and ruin. Never had formal false religion come under such horrendous attack. Its last vestiges of vanity were blown into oblivion. The rushing hurricane wind of God's Spirit swept across the devastation in blazing fury. Never, never had Christ's men seen His eyes burn with such fire. His words rose and roared around them like molten lava erupting from an exploding volcano.

Eight terrible titanic woes of divine judgment were uttered.

Never before had such dreadful denunciations been spoken. Under their blast the battle was decided:

Woe, scribes and Pharisees, hypocrites! You dogs in the manger.

You close the kingdom of heaven to others, and yet you will not even go in yourselves.

Woe, scribes and Pharisees, hypocrites! You exploit the widows and underprivileged. Yet you pretend to be so pious. For this you damn yourselves doubly.

Woe, scribes and Pharisees, hypocrites! You leave no stone unturned to turn others into phonies like yourselves. And the upshot is they live in utter hell for it.

Woe, scribes and Pharisees, hypocrites! You are utterly blind to spiritual truth. Yet in your blindness and folly you lead others down into the ditch of despair.

Woe, scribes and Pharisees, hypocrites! You are so particular about your picayune tithes. Yet you are utterly devoid of justice, mercy, and love, either to God or men.

Woe, scribes and Pharisees, hypocrites! You are forever so fastidious about your outward appearance. Still inwardly you are corrupt in spirit and rottenly sensuous in soul.

Woe, scribes and Pharisees, hypocrites! You love to look like glistening mausoleums shining in the sun. But within, you reek with wickedness and utter hypocrisy.

Woe, scribes and Pharisees, hypocrites! You snakes who say you would never harm the prophets of God. Yet this very hour you are plotting the death of the very Son of God!

It was all over! No one had ever dreamed that such immense imprecations could come from the gentle Galilean. The judgments of divine justice were torn from Him in a torrent that overwhelmed His hearers.

Turning quietly now, He looked out over this cruel city. "O Jerusalem, Jerusalem! How often I would have gathered your children together, even as a hen gathers her chicks under her—*but you would not!* Behold, your house is left unto you desolate."

They were the last words He ever spoke in the mighty temple.

Slowly He walked out, down the great stairs, never to return again.

Jesus, sensing that the men who were with Him needed to be preserved, withdrew from Jerusalem. Himself He could not, would not, try to save. His hour of being offered as a sin offering for all men was now only about seventy-two hours away.

How best could He use the precious time that remained?

Retiring to His beloved Mount of Olives, He there gave His disciples some final solemn warnings.

The first of these dealt with a wide spectrum of forthcoming events. Again He foretold the fall of Jerusalem. He related the intense persecution that would come upon His followers. He warned of the cataclysmic portents that would precede the end times.

And always the ultimate conclusion reached was, *Watch . . . be ready . . . be alert, prepared, waiting.*

The pertinent point which the Master endeavored to make with His men was simply this: His followers simply did not know when or how their final hour would come. No one could be sure when the call to "come home" would be made. It might be with the mighty trumpet blast of the archangel. It might just as surely be from a quiet bed of illness where the last breath is drawn.

Condensed into its most essential ingredients, this "watching," this "being ready," had two parts to it:

The first was that our relationship to God Himself might be open, honest, and free, that there should be the presence of His life in us and us in Him. He Himself had emulated this all through His earthly sojourn. The unity and oneness betwixt Him and His Father had been beautiful to observe. Always there was the sense of being in His Father's presence—performing His Father's will and wishes, doing His work and expressing His words in a hostile world.

Yet amid all of this His whole life was one of anticipating going home, ready to return to the splendor and glory of the unseen world. And for Christ, this was to *watch*, to *be ready*.

To illustrate this concept in story form He told the winsome parable of the ten young maids waiting for the wedding. All ten had made some preparation for the coming of the groom. But only five had made absolutely sure that everything was in order. The others were taken unawares. Only five really *watched*.

Secondly, our Lord, in His unique way, made it very clear that there was a sense in which men were to *watch* and *be ready* in their relationship to other people. All of us are entrusted with talents, abilities, time, possessions, and personalities which we hold as stewards. These are not given to us to be squandered selfishly upon ourselves. There is the principle of stewardship, in which it is expected that my life shall be wisely invested on behalf of others. This is a trust given to me of God for the benefit of my fellow human beings. An account must be given of how that trust has been discharged.

To demonstrate this concept He recounted the story of the three servants. One was given five talents, another two, and a third one talent. The first two wisely invested that entrusted to them. The third simply buried his.

In the light of this parable He then went on to point out that we are continually surrounded with those in whom we can invest the talents given us. There are the blind, the naked, the poor, the ill, the destitute, those imprisoned. We live in a weary world. On every side are those in desperate despair. Men and women languish in the sickness, poverty, and imprisonment of spirit, soul, and body. The question is, Have I done anything to alleviate the woes of the world?

The degree to which I do it is the degree to which I have done it for His sake and on His behalf.

To live this way is *to watch,* it is *to be ready*—for my call "home" may come at any moment.

CHAPTER THIRTY-TWO

Treason

Only two days remained until the Passover. There would be no more public appearances, no more open discourses, no more clashes with the religious leaders in the temple. From here on Jesus moved furtively with His men. A place to celebrate the festival dinner would have to be found, then the final details arranged.

The Master was in a quiet, reserved, pensive mood. "The Son of man"—His favorite expression for Himself—"will be betrayed to be crucified." He knew full well. For Him it was all foreknown. He faced the appalling prospect without fear or flinching.

With God there are no crises! He simply is not taken unawares. He is not a victim of circumstances! And we do well to remind ourselves of this always.

He knew the priests were plotting His end. Or, as they thought, His end. He knew the fierce, dark temptations engulfing the soul of Judas. He was aware of the brooding blackness seething in that shriveled spirit where Satan would gain a beachhead. Yet amid such mounting tensions He moved in constrained strength and serenity.

It was no surprise to our Lord that His very person and presence alienated His antagonists. Evil cannot tolerate good. Dishonesty recoils from honesty. Impurity reviles purity. Brutality abhors beauty. The contemptible scorns the noble. And hell itself is set against heaven.

Here the sinless, stainless, superb Son of God was being plotted against by all the arraigned forces of darkness. Not because He had done any evil, but because the intense brightness of His integrity and the incandescence of His utterly impeccable character exposed the shame of His adversaries. In ghastly fury they gnashed their teeth against Him.

Yet their anger did not faze Him. Their hostility did not deter Him. Their bitter hatred did not shake His settled soul.

Only the perfect could atone for the imperfect.

Only the pure could compensate for the impure.

Only the virtuous could make up for the vile.

Only the sinless could be a substitute for the sinner.

Though He was now surrounded with those bent on His blood, still there were some who saw, and knew, He was heaven's royalty in human guise.

One of these was an unnamed, unknown woman who just two days before His crucifixion found Him in the home of Simon the leper.

Unlike the sinning call girl who had first anointed His feet in the home of Simon the Pharisee long months before, this one would anoint His head and His body.

It was the third recorded occasion on which the Christ—God's own Anointed—allowed Himself to be honored in this way, anointed by a woman. The second time had been just four days previously, when Mary, Lazarus' sister, had lavished her adoration on Him in her sister Martha's home.

Again in an overwhelming self-abandonment of total giving, this anonymous woman poured out her precious perfume over her Lord. The alabaster box was emptied of its rich contents in a deliberate act of homage to the King of Glory.

The delicious fragrance ran down over His shining hair and thick beard. It enfolded His body with its delightful aroma. Even His tunic and flowing undergarment were drenched with its enduring pungency. Wherever He moved during the ensuing forty-eight hours, the perfume would go with Him: Into the Passover: into the Garden of Gethsemane: into the high priest's home: into Herod's hall: into Pilate's praetorium: into the crude hands of those who cast lots for His clothing at the foot of the cross.

This special rite of perfuming the head and body was a rare ritual reserved only for royalty. It was the most lofty honor that could be bestowed by a common person. Jesus recognized this and so did those around Him. It was a significant moment of momentous meaning.

But its magnificence was marred by a murmur from His men. It was not just Judas who gibed this time. All twelve of His disciples protested in unison. Here, now, a second time in less than a week, women had apparently wasted huge sums of money on the Master. Once was surely enough, but twice was too much! At least too much for young fellows who would have been glad for a few more nights in proper lodgings rather than sleeping under the stars or even a few more square meals instead of scrounging for figs off barren trees or eating raw wheat gathered from the edges of farmers' fields. Perhaps they were all a bit fed up with being poor followers of a poor preacher.

Whatever led to their general protest over the apparently wasted perfume, at least they expressed it openly: "What good purpose does this waste serve?" Perhaps Judas had already done his underhanded work well. His wrong attitude to his Master was a contagion that had spread invidiously to the others. Hatred, bitterness, and vengeance grew like weeds in the fertile fields of faultfinding minds.

For not only did the disciples protest, they were downright angry. In fact they were all furious. Furious with the woman; furious with the Master; furious with the apparent waste; furious at the futility and frustration. Men could live on bread and meat but not on the fragrance of perfume. "The poor"—poor fellows like themselves—could do with more than sweet aromas.

In His typical fashion our Lord did not try to defend Himself. But He did rise to the woman's defense: "Why do you attack her?" His voice was low but penetrating. "What she has done is appropriate. It is for my burial!"

It was a bold rebuff to the boys. It would not sit easily with them. And as for Judas, it was the second direct jolt he had received from Jesus in the week. That was all he would take. In vengeance he went out to find the chief priests. He would soon work out a deal to deal with the One who had twice humiliated him.

The Scriptures are replete with dramatic contrasts. The scenes shift swiftly from triumph to tragedy, from light to darkness then back again.

And here we are taken from seeing the Sovereign Saviour of the world honored by a humble woman, to the dark depths of a devilish design.

Even by extending our imaginations to their extremity it is difficult to understand Judas' dreadful deed. Obviously it was perpetrated first in a mind boiling with belligerence. It was spawned in a soul seething with resentment. It was a volitional act determined and decided in a desperately degenerate will. There is no limit to the depths of depravity to which human nature will descend in its downward path from *hurt . . . to hostility . . . to hate . . . to hell.*

Judas was not alone in descending this stairway to destruction. It is a possibility for any person who allows himself to be perverted by pride or selfish self-pity.

Jesus and Judas had been intimate friends for nearly three years. They had shared the same life, tramped the same trails, eaten from the same bowls, drunk from the same wells, slept under the same trees, seen the same sunrises, shared in the same tragedies and triumphs, talked about the same truths, lived the same rugged way.

But Judas had been hurt. His pride had been pricked. His self-pity had been indulged. His hostility had been inflamed. Now he was at dagger points with his best friend. He was determined to destroy Him. Love had turned to hate.

In the darkened council room of the high priest, Judas asked an incredible question: "What will you give me for Him?" His shifting, furtive, angry eyes moved quickly from one crafty face to the other in the crowd of assembled priests. "How much is it worth to you for me to betray Him into your hands?"

Momentarily there was a hush. The long-bearded, needle-eyed assassins who had so long plotted Jesus' death could scarcely believe their ears. What a fantastic turn of events! One of the Master's own men had turned traitor. It clean took their breath away. But they were too cunning to display their delight. Gladly they would have paid a thousand talents—yes, even ten thousand pieces of silver—to bring this Jesus to bay. They were bugling for His blood and any price would have been paid instantly from the overflowing coffers of the rich temple trade to silence this One. He was a thorn in their sides. He was a threat to their power. He was a terror to their darkened souls. Away with Him!

"Oh, did you ask how much it is worth to us?" They stroked their long beards with cunning hands. They half winked to each other in crafty knavery. Obviously they were dealing with a dumb lout who had no idea what his Master was worth. He would take anything to commit treason. The poor ignorant fool! Maybe he'd be loutish enough to sell his Sovereign for the paltry price of a slave. Try him, anyway.

With feigned sincerity the high priest furrowed his brow. Quizzically he tilted his head. Then forcing a phony half smile that bared his old yellow rotting teeth, he offered hesitantly, as though it really were too much, "Thirty pieces of silver!" It was backed by the flash of silver that he drew from the deep folds of his flowing gown.

Judas' eyes fastened on the glinting handful. It was enough. Reaching out, he took the blood money. It was cold in his hot hands.

Tucking the silver pieces away in the hidden pockets of his tunic, Judas assured the priests he would keep in touch with them. The actual Passover feast day would not be an appropriate time for the betrayal. It was bound to create a public furor amongst the crowds. And all of them knew Jesus was still so popular with the common people that the whole city would be engulfed in civil disorder. No, that would never do. It would have to be something much more crafty, executed under cover of darkness. If possible, the whole trial and execution should be over before the general populace were even awake to know what had happened.

Secrecy—swiftness and sure death were of the essence.

Judas nodded in agreement. He would see to it at the first opportunity.

With head hung low and shoulders hunched he slipped out of the council chambers. He was starting on the most lonely, terrible, torturous trail ever trod by a man.

Inside the great stern stone walls of the council chambers the priests rubbed their hands in glee. Soon He would be in their hands. They would finally have the last word. It was but a step now to silencing this enemy.

Judas had dealt in deity. He had sold an innocent soul. He had bartered the blood of his "love slave" for a few miserable chunks of silver. He had traded the Sovereign of his soul for a few scraps of metal. He had sold himself.

The reason for all of this still lies somewhat shrouded in mystery. It still escapes us even though we endeavor to unravel its tangled strands.

One thing is sure: This man's dark, black soul was a suitable beachhead from which Satan attempted a major assault against the Saviour of the world.

The record given of those horrendous hours is couched in awesome language: "Satan entered into Judas."

CHAPTER THIRTY-THREE

The Passover

All of Jerusalem was abuzz on the exciting festival day. Men and women scurried hither and thither in frantic preparation. There were lambs to purchase and butcher. Firewood had to be found for the roasting. Wild bitter herbs had to be gathered or bought from the street vendors. Unleavened bread was baked in a hundred thousand places. Along with the roast lamb, bitter herbs, and blood-red wine, it would be broken and eaten before midnight stole over the city.

The little wandering band of disciples must have felt the Master was leaving things to the last minute. Finally on that momentous morning they asked Him bluntly, "Where are we to celebrate this feast?" Without an instant's hesitation He chose John and Peter, sending them off into Jerusalem with precise instructions: "You will find a man bearing a water pitcher. Follow him. He will lead you to the appointed place! There make ready the banquet for us!"

It may all have seemed very simple. But it wasn't. For one thing, it was a complete departure for Jesus to decide on spending the evening in Jerusalem. It was to invite arrest by the authorities who shadowed His every move. What was more, men bearing water pots were rare indeed. This was woman's work. And to find one such man amid the milling masses of over a million souls crowding the capital was a bit like finding the proverbial needle in a haystack.

But the young fellows were past asking questions in cases of this kind. Instead they simply sped away excitedly on their errand.

Sure enough, just as an unbroken colt had been found a few days before for the Master, now they came across the man with the stone jar on his shoulder.

It was probably one of the servants from John Mark's home. John Mark's father was a wealthy householder in the city. The home was large and spacious. Big enough that the family could enjoy their feast downstairs while the group of thirteen men from out of town could celebrate their banquet in a spacious upper room. There everything necessary for the occasion had been already provided for them.

It must have startled Peter and John to find themselves in such sumptuous surroundings. The room was arranged with cushions and pillows. The various ingredients for the meal were on a side table. And downstairs, tied by a frayed rope, was a little lamb bleating beside the back door. Within a few hours its blood would be spattered on the door posts and lintel to reenact the great exodus from Egypt.

On that horrendous night, some 1524 years previously, the pride and power of Egypt had been shattered. God's destroying angel had swept across the Land of the Nile. In every home where there was no blood of a sacrificed lamb splattered over the door, He swept in to bring death to the firstborn.

Only the substitutionary death and sacrifice of an innocent, spotless lamb could obviate the drastic judgment and stay the sword of sacrifice. If it was not a firstborn lamb, then it had to be a firstborn son. This was an ancient rite. No greater sacrifice could anyone offer than his firstborn son, the offspring of his own strength, the seed of his own loins.

And on this auspicious night, in this very room, God's own firstborn Son, the only begotten of the Father, would declare Himself to be that supreme sacrifice: God's spotless Passover Lamb— the Lamb slain from before the foundation of the world, the only Lamb which was appropriately capable of bearing away all the sins of all men for all time. Only He was able to be a suitable substitute for all of us.

The Master intimated this fact that very day. But no doubt the statement was lost on His men. He said point-blank, *"My time has come."* But amid the excitement of the preparations even John and

Peter did not get the point. The hour, the horrendous hour when divine blood would be shed and that divine body broken on behalf of bungling humanity, was upon them. Yet they knew it not.

Toward evening Jesus and His men strode into the city and headed straight for John Mark's home. John Mark was only a young teenager then. He had been attracted and sympathetic to the prophet from Galilee. He even considered becoming a disciple. Later that very night when the ruffian band with Judas came beating on the door of his home, expecting to arrest Jesus there, he fled off into the dark. Like a young gazelle he sped away toward the Mount of Olives to alert Jesus that His enemies were coming. And when they did appear, once more he managed to escape their clutches only by a hairbreadth, streaking off into the dark stark naked, leaving his clothes in their grasping hands. He reports this intimate incident in his own concise Gospel record.

In the upper room, meanwhile, the thirteen men arranged themselves comfortably around the walls, relaxing on the colorful cushions provided by their host. A low murmur of contented chatter filled the room. The rich aroma of freshly baked bread commingled with the sweet fragrance of roast lamb permeated the whole place. It whetted their appetites. Eagerly they broke the crisp, flat cakes of unleavened bread and dipped the pieces into the steaming dishes of hot bitter herbs. With gusto they picked up pieces of the roasted flesh and tore fragments of meat from the bones with their strong white teeth. The simple fare was washed down with great gulps of delicious wine that sparkled red in the flickering candlelight.

It was a festive scene. Good-natured banter and wit flowed back and forth among the young companions. They were close knit.

Suddenly a spark of contention was ignited amongst them. They began to quarrel and argue about who should have the most prominent place. Tempers began to flare. Sharp remarks were made. And in short order hostility mounted amongst them. Angry looks crisscrossed the room. Scowls creased their faces. And the atmosphere became electric with animosity. A look of anguish and despair stole across the Master's face.

Always, always God has to cope with the resurgence of our rotten old human nature. And here, despite all His teaching and example, His men were at one another's throat again.

In a gesture of overwhelming generosity and goodwill He swept off His tunic and mantle. With a simple swish He wrapped a towel around Himself. Then taking up a basin of water He began to go from man to man. Kneeling on the floor before each prone figure, He gently washed their rough, dusty feet, then dried them with the towel.

It is beyond belief that upon this rough group of garrulous young stalwarts should depend all of God's plans for propagating the good news of His redemption for the race. Jesus sensed the solemnity of the moment. They did not. It was these very feet He was washing that would bear the Gospel of His salvation, first to this cruel city, then to Judea, then to Samaria, and finally to the outmost outposts of the world. Some of those feet would wander as far as Rome, Africa, Asia Minor, and even India to proclaim that God's Passover Lamb had been offered for all men everywhere.

This simple, humble action of washing His friends' feet embarrassed them deeply. It was probably the most humiliating lesson they had ever learned. "Let him that would be greatest amongst you be your servant!" It was one thing to hear those words; it was another to see them enacted. Here was the Master—their Lord, the Messiah, God's Anointed One, the King of Glory—cleaning dust and dirt and caked mud from their calloused, rough feet.

This was the role of a servant slave—or, if in a home where there was no servant, that of the father and host, who did his guests this great honor. Jesus at this point played the part of both—servant and father. He came as a servant. He came also as a father to those who would receive Him. Yet here He was, too poor to possess any property or own any home of His own. Still He did what was necessary, even in a friend's abode.

A quiet hush fell over the room. The angry young spirits were stilled. The hot flaming words were ended. The flashing eyes fell to the bowed form of their Master kneeling before them. Embarrassed, flushed cheeks replaced the fierce looks and cutting glances that had shot across the room. "The first shall be last and the last first."

It was one of the most powerful sermons Jesus ever preached. It was a message almost without words, yet replete and pregnant with pathos. "Do this to one another."

Peter, as always, protested. Probably he was one who had precipitated the dispute earlier in the evening. He was never short on words or slow to act. He must have been a painful person to live with. "No!" the big burly fisherman objected, "You don't wash my feet." He waved his hands excitedly and drew his big gnarled feet up beneath him.

Jesus looked at him in commingled affection and reproach. "If you don't allow Me to do this then you really have no part in My plans!"

Peter really didn't understand. How could he? First flushed with anger, then embarrassed, excited, and now rebuked sternly, he was overwhelmed with wave upon wave of emotion flooding over him. At best he was a highly charged emotional man. He lived and moved under the impulse of Peter's emotions. Not yet had he come under Christ's control.

"All right then," he thundered. "If You must wash me, wash all of me, from head to foot!" It was typical of the highly animated man. He swung radically from one extreme to the other. Just as later that night he would blatantly disclose that he would even die for the Master, yet an hour or so further on deny Him thrice over in the presence of a little servant girl.

"No, no," Jesus replied. "You have already been washed, renewed, refreshed." He looked at Peter knowingly. "Only your feet need doing."

It was the continuous, repeated contact of contamination that had to be dealt with. It was true of all men. All needed daily cleansing.

Jesus did not even hesitate to wash Judas' feet. Those feet that before the night was out would take him to betray this One who now washed him. What incredible condescension! The magnanimous generosity of God in Christ transcends anything we can possibly imagine.

The washing over, Jesus slipped into His clothes again and returned to recline on the cushions He had vacated.

A winsome, mellow mood hung over the room. The unforgettable gesture of goodwill had knit the little band of young stalwarts

into a close kinship. Really, they had all become such good friends.
They had shared such intimate moments and exciting experiences.
The three years of adventuring together had bound them together
with bands of steel—except for one man. And he was a point of
sadness.

John, in a spontaneous act of endearment, drew himself over
close to the Master. He put his rough suntanned arm around His
shoulder and laid his head against His chest. They were so fond of
each other—this tough young Son of Thunder and the strong Son of
God.

Jesus began to speak again now in low, solemn tones. His words
were weighty—heavy with foreboding:

"One of you will betray Me!"

It seemed like a thunderclap of condemnation.

How could it be? He had just washed each of them. How could
any of them be so cruel, so ungrateful?

In turn each, including Judas, asked, "Is it I?"

At that very moment Judas had the blood money wrapped
tightly, silently, in a secret money belt strapped to his body. It
must have branded him like a burning iron. It took colossal gall to
have this ghastly sum on his very person while innocently pretending he was not guilty. The audacity of it all is shocking. It seems
impossible that a man could sink to such depths of cunning bestiality. But he did.

The problem with Judas was that the central citadel of his will
had never come under Christ's control. He had never fully capitu-
lated to his Lord. The Saviour, by His Spirit, had never been
received as royalty nor recognized as sovereign by this man. It was
really that basic. And it explains why he or any of us can descend
to behave as brute beasts.

As each man asked if he was indeed to be the culprit, the Master
with sad eyes replied simply and candidly, "It is one of you who
has been dipping in the dish of herbs with Me."

The herbs were bitter. They were a bitter reminder of the bitter
bondage Israel had suffered in Egypt. They were a bitter symbol of
any soul in bondage to sin or self or Satan. They were a bitter token
of a bitter man in bondage to the hate, anger, and revenge he
entertained against his Master. A bitter Judas was tasting the bitter

dregs of his bitter life in that bitter night.

The tension and strain of the moment were explosive.

Furtive glances darted back and forth across the room from one man to another. "Who could it be?" was the searching, searing question that burned in the mind of each man—except for Judas. He knew. He had prepared. He was playacting. He was phony and pretending to the last.

Had Jesus chosen to turn the tables in that electric atmosphere, He could have disclosed in one stabbing sentence who the traitor was. He knew. All He needed to do was point an accusing finger at the nervous man from Judea. Just with one gesture Jesus could have betrayed Judas to His rough, tough young Galilean comrades. In a storm of rage they would have torn the traitor arm from arm, limb from limb, into a writhing, dying mass of flesh.

They were already armed with two swords. The air was charged with civil disorder and mayhem. To thrust Judas through would have been easy. Instead Jesus kept His own council. Quietly He handed the traitor a piece of bread dipped in bitter herbs.

Judas slipped out into the bitter darkness to do his dastardly deed.

It was during this tension-charged night that our Lord initiated for all time the ceremony of Communion. This common sharing of bread and wine with His followers bore within it the very essence of the purpose for which He had entered human history.

It is best expressed in the words of Scripture:

> For then must he often have suffered since the foundation of the world: but now once in the end of the world hath he appeared to put away sin by the sacrifice of himself.
>
> Hebrews 9:26

The breaking of the bread and the drinking of the wine were for those men that night the anticipation of His agony to be endured: the bread broken speaking of His beautiful body to be mutilated and marred and abused by brutal men; the red wine quaffed depicting His divine blood, His gracious life to be poured out for the wretched sinning souls of all men.

That tiny band of followers could not comprehend the enormity of suffering He was yet to endure. Nor can we—who, subsequent to the events of Calvary, commemorate His death by breaking bread and drinking wine—enter fully into the awesome agony of those hours.

There is a point beyond which mortals may not pass in understanding the titanic transactions that took place at that terrible time. In simple obedience to the Master's desire His men broke bread and sipped wine with Him. And His followers ever since, likewise in compliance with His wishes, have respectfully commemorated the occasion.

In love and gratitude we gaze upon God's Lamb giving Himself in our stead. We see Him absorbing in His person the penalty for our sins, thus satisfying God's justice. We look and see displayed by His generous giving of Himself the mercy of our God, that everlasting love, that draws us to Him.

And so the long hours of that cataclysmic night moved on inexorably toward a colossal climax. It was like a time bomb, ticking off the minutes until the instant of explosion.

The young men were tense, edgy, and terribly confused. All their dreams and hopes and aspirations of participating eventually in a grand and glorious earthly empire ended in that upper room. Secretly some of them probably wondered if it had really been worth following the Master.

Where did they go from here? If He were to leave them, then what? Was there any future at all for His followers?

Jesus knew these thoughts were racing in tumbled chaos through their minds. He knew they were being tossed and tortured by the ebb and flow of fearsome emotions. He knew their wills and stern resolve to be His loyal fellows were undergoing enormous pressures and temptations.

Of the whole group, He alone remained calm, collected, in quiet control of Himself.

"Let not your hearts be troubled." His voice was gentle, low and reassuring. "You believe in God, believe also in Me." He looked around the room with loving concern. "In this world you will have trouble—but be of good cheer; I have overcome the world." The words were comforting even though the circumstances were most disquieting. "My Peace I give unto you, not as the world gives. Abide in Me and I in you. In this way you will produce much fruit."

In the dim candlelight a sense of His strength, His stability, His serenity swept into their troubled spirits. "Father," He prayed quietly, "I ask that they be one as We are one!" He went on softly: "I do not ask that You take them out of the world but that You keep them from the evil!"

Together—in unison—with beautiful harmony, they sang the great Psalm 136, the Hallel: *"For the mercy of the Lord endureth forever."* Warmed and comforted by its refrain, they got up and walked out into the night toward the Mount of Olives.

CHAPTER THIRTY-FOUR

Agony in a Garden

The hour was late. A hushed stillness had settled over the great sleeping city weary with the long day's excitement. Furtively and with whispers the small knot of twelve men made their way down the shadowed streets. Perhaps they were being trailed. They repeatedly cast nervous glances back over their shoulders.

Only when the limestone ridge of the Mount of Olives was reached did the disciples breathe more easily. Here the open terrain and long views reminded them a bit of their beloved Galilee. Often they had bedded down here beneath the gray green boughs of the gnarled old trees whose roots were knotted around the rocky outcrops. At one end of the ridge was a small secluded gardenlike spot called Gethsemane. It had long been the Master's favorite retreat. They headed for it.

Jesus made a remark that startled His men. "All of you will be offended because of Me tonight." In other words, Tonight every one of you will lose confidence in Me.

They were sure up to this point that He was in truth their Lord, their Master, their Messiah, their Anointed King, who would perform some mighty miracle to prove Himself.

But, in order that He might do what He had come to do, this would not happen. Instead, as the ancient prophets had predicted, the Shepherd would be smitten and His small band of sheep would be scattered.

Though this was inevitable and bound to happen, Jesus did not leave them in despair. Our Lord just never does that. He is the God of good cheer. He is ever the God of hope. So in quiet confidence He reassured their racing, trembling hearts: "But after I am risen again I will go ahead of you for a grand reunion in dear old Galilee." It was a word of comfort and consolation that came as a ray of light in this dark hour.

But Peter protested violently. "Offended in You, Master? Never! Others might lose faith in You, but never I. No, no!" He felt the smooth leather scabbard of the sword against his big strong thigh. If necessary he would whip the shining blade of steel from its sheath. He would attack any antagonist who dared to touch the Master.

Jesus knew this. With deep affection He looked at the big burly fisherman fingering the lethal weapon beneath the folds of his cloak. "Peter, I'm sorry to say it, but before the rooster salutes the dawn, you will have denied Me three times."

Anger welled up in Peter. His eyes blazed. His beard twitched. "Even though I should have to die with You, I will never deny You." The words came out hot and vehemently. The phrases were caught up by his companions and all eleven young men declared their total allegiance.

It was left at that. There was no further exchange, for now they had come to the Garden.

Each of the men, now bone weary from the long eighteen-hour day and the ominous news shared with them, began to look for a likely spot to lie down.

The Master looked on them with intense empathy. They had been so willing to follow Him. They had been so devoted to Him. They had been so loyal up to this very last night. They had been so charged with hope. But now the hour of trial was here. This was to be their ultimate test.

Softly He spoke in tones which were hardly audible to their tired hearing: "Satan, that ancient archenemy, has requested the right to subject you men to intolerable temptation tonight. You will be sifted like wheat tossed in the wind of tempestuous events." The Master's eyes filled with great tears. His strong face muscles writhed with strong emotion.

"But I have already prayed that your faith fail not!" Oh, what generosity! What graciousness! What concern and compassion comes to His people from our Lord!

Men's best protestations of fidelity are fickle. Our most earnest commitments are fragile, easily broken. The finest of our intentions fragment under pressure. Men are fallible. The fabric of our love and loyalty is torn in temptation. Our faith so often fails. Our God knows our frames, He remembers that we are but dust. And He prays for His people.

His commitments to us are infinitely more important than ours to Him. His concern and compassion far surpass our finite comprehension. Amid the ebb and flow of life's stresses and strains it is His strength that sustains us. And in this dark night of His own tremendous temptation the Master had not forgotten the titanic struggles of His men.

"Your flesh is very weak, but your spirits are so willing! You are My followers, My disciples, My loyal lads who love Me intensely, but that is not enough to sustain you against the onslaught of the Enemy." He looked at them tenderly. They were so very tired.

He urged all but three of them to settle themselves comfortably beneath the trees. Then taking His favorite three companions, Peter, James, and John, He withdrew from the others about a stone's throw.

A tremendous wave of anguish began to engulf Him. It was a sorrow such as no man had ever known before. This was an agony of the spirit, not of the emotions. It was a temptation of such titanic proportions that no mortal could ever comprehend it.

It is touching that He begged His dearest intimates to watch and pray with Him. He was engaged in the most appalling test of His character. His soul was in a struggle of eternal dimensions. On the outcome of this ordeal hung the destiny of all men.

He was not loath to let His friends see Him suffer. He had nothing to hide. The contest between self and selflessness was locked in deadly combat. It was the eternal contest between God and sin.

One would almost prefer to draw down reverently a screen of silence and secrecy over the agony of this hour. If it had been a mere man who there wrestled with his own will, we might do so. But it was God, very God, in that grim garden who was breaking through the enemy ranks of evil, Satan, self-will, and hell itself that encircled Him.

He was the gladiator in the arena of human history, fighting, single-handed, the fury of the foe determined to destroy Him. Only three sleepy, weary watchers were His visible audience from the world of men. But in the unseen world, massed millions of angels and countless members of evil spirits looked on askance as the Lord of Glory fell prostrate to the ground in agony of turmoil.

"O Father," He groaned, writhing upon the ground, "if it be possible, let this awful cup of judgment and utter condemnation pass from Me." His strong powerful frame shook and trembled; He was convulsed with the calumny of the hour. "Nevertheless, not My will, but Yours!"

What was the terrible turmoil He faced? Why was He so torn by this torment? What made Him recoil as He did from the ordeal?

It was that He, who had known no sin, was literally to be made sin. What for? That we might be made righteous with His righteousness. It was an excruciating exchange!

He who had been utterly honest, absolutely pure, completely just, He who knew no hate, no bitterness, no selfishness, no jealousy—who would be submerged, saturated, and stained with such sins—was horrified by the prospect. Just the thought of it was so abhorrent to His impeccable nature that in anguish He literally fell flat upon His face in agony.

Three times He staggered back up to His feet and went to His three friends. Three times He found them dozing. Three times they had already betrayed His trust.

Again He withdrew alone to wrestle mightily with His own will. "O Father, if drinking this cup of sin is to do Your will, then let it be done! If My taking men's sins will set them free from condemnation, let Me be bound and condemned in their stead."

The issues were clear. The contest was closed. He would conquer. But the battle was brutal: more brutal than any purely physical abuse He might later endure. This was a struggle of the soul. His will was the issue. Would He have His own way and save Himself? Or would He be utterly selfless and sacrifice Himself for sinful men?

Wave after wave of anguish engulfed Him. He fell to the rocky soil of the limestone ridge. His tunic was stained and His cloak reddened with great drops of blood-red fluids that oozed from His pores. Dreadful groans were wrenched from between His clenched teeth.

Once more He got to His feet and stumbled over to His three friends. Already He had begged them to watch and pray with Him. But they simply could not. Slumber had now completely overcome them. They slept soundly under the olive trees.

The third time He retired alone. He was at the point of triumph now. "O Father—I shall drink the cup. There is no alternative. Your will be done. Your will is always right and appropriate. Your will must prevail! I sacrifice Myself!"

In that total self-giving there was total victory. The issue had been settled. The conquest was complete. He had vanquished self. He had triumphed over the forces of the Enemy. God's will was done!

It is ever thus. God's will is irrevocable. Anyone identified with that will endures eternally. It cannot be otherwise. In that garden He guaranteed His own Resurrection.

Had our Lord had His own way that night, had He decided to indulge His own desire and set Himself free from doing God's will, had He preferred to protest and preserve Himself from the penalty of sin—then all of us earthmen would have remained prisoners to sin and perished therein. It was really that straightforward and that simple.

Yet it was not simple nor easy. It was the most fearsome contest ever witnessed in the universe. And when it was over, angels from the unseen realm came to minister to the conqueror. It was as if they, and they alone, were worthy to place garlands of glory and honor upon the brow of the victor. Because no men would ever do this. No men ever understood fully the enormity of the struggle in the dark of that night. In bitter contrast evil men would in a few hours pierce that same noble brow with cruel thorns in cruel jest. They would treat Him as a brigand, a criminal, and a man without a city.

The ultimate triumph that was to take place at Calvary was actually accomplished first beneath the gnarled old olive trees in Gethsemane. The final burst of victory that broke from His lips when He shouted from the cross, "It is finished!" was possible only because He first was victor in the sorrowful and lonely solitude of the garden. At Calvary scores of eyes were fastened on the Son of God suspended midway between heaven and earth. In the garden not a single human witnessed the Son of man's struggle and triumph at last over Himself.

When Jesus returned finally to His three friends He was calm and quiet. "Sleep on now, and take your rest!" He whispered to them softly.

As they did, He felt Himself totally restored in spirit, soul, and body. A great surge of revitalizing life and strength swept through Him. He was serene and strong and sure.

In unruffled tones He awakened His friends: "Let us be going. Here comes my betrayer, Judas, whom I have loved!"

CHAPTER THIRTY-FIVE

The Lynching

It was somewhere around two o'clock in the night—the darkest hour, when man's makeup is at its lowest ebb. In the distance, flickering flares of light moved eerily beneath the twisted, tortured trunks of the old olives. There were the low, hushed whispers of men's voices. A mob of ruffians armed with swords, clubs, ropes, and staves began to encircle Jesus and His sleeping men.

The Master knew they were coming long before they arrived. He could have made good His own escape with very little trouble, leaving His weary comrades to fall into the enemy hands. But He chose not to run. He elected not to save Himself. Instead, He stood calmly to meet the assassins.

The gang of ruffians gathered up that night by the Jewish leaders were the scum and offscourings of the city streets. They were not Roman soldiers. Rome had nothing to do with our Lord's arrest. The Roman authorities never laid a hand on the "Man from Galilee" until He had been delivered to Pilate, the governor, by the Hebrew hierarchy. The rough crowd were tough criminal types hired to do the dirty work for those who did not wish to stain their own hands. It was a horrible underhanded deal akin to what the Mafia might perpetrate.

Incredible as it may seem, here was a person with an impeccable character and flawless conduct about to be lynched by a mob of gangsters under the guise of religious propriety. It was part and parcel of the eternal hypocrisy of formal, cold, dead religiosity. Some of the world's most appalling atrocities have been perpetrated in the name of God. And this night in this grim garden, God very God, in Christ, in all His grandeur, was under assault by a lynch gang in the very name of deity.

Out of the grim-faced, hawk-eyed mob stepped Judas. In a treacherous, crafty show of false affection he called out, "Hail, Master!" It is a marvel he did not choke on the words. Christ was no longer his Master. His master was his own sin; he had sold himself a wretched slave to his own dread desires. Satan had sucked him in with subtle strategy. He was but a stooge to his own self and sin and Satan. These were his despotic owners that in a few hours would lead him to hang himself with a rope.

With a false flourish Judas flung his arms around the Master and kissed Him on the cheek. It was a prearranged sign. How strange that a symbol of affection and endearment common the world over should be used to betray Him who is love! The capacity of an evil heart to pervert that which is beautiful defies description. Here was degenerate human nature at its worst.

Our Lord's response to this dirty trick takes our breath away.

He did not back away from Judas. He did not recoil from his embrace. He did not react in anger to the hot, flushed kiss.

His reaction was the reaction that only God could make.

"*Friend*—My friend—My fellow companion for three long years . . . . Friend—why have you come here?"

Judas may not have realized it, perhaps in the frenzy and excitement of the moment he could not sense it, but he was being given a last chance to repent. It was an opportunity once more to reidentify himself with the Master. But he did not grasp it. It was soon gone, never to be offered again.

"He that is not with Me is against Me." These words of the Master would ring in his ears until he hanged as a corpse beneath some lonely tree.

Momentarily there was a strange hush after Judas kissed Jesus. It was as if the ragtag mob did not know quite what to do.

Jesus looked at them evenly. It was a look of terrifying intensity. It was a look of enormous dignity and strength.

"Whom are you looking for?" He asked calmly, the flickering

light of the torches lighting up His handsome face with its strong, rugged features.

"We are looking for Jesus of Nazareth," they chorused, brandishing their flares and swords. They jostled each other, then circled round Him menacingly, like a pack of pariah dogs.

"*I am He,*" was the Master's quiet reply. I am, that I AM. God very God. It was the simple yet profound manner whereby God had always identified Himself.

At the words His assailants fell back. The presence and power and person of the Omnipotent flattened them to the ground. Like Moses of old, and Elijah the prophet, they could not endure the glory of God immanent in this One.

At this point Peter whipped out his sword. He never was a coward. The big strong-muscled fisherman was quick to take advantage of the situation. The sharp steel flashed in the flickering light of the flares. There was an anguished scream. Malchus, a servant of the high priest, held his hand to his head. Hot blood gushed from the severed stump of his ear. An inch or two farther over and his skull would have been split in half by Peter's angry stroke.

Jesus was quick to take it all in.

"Put away your sword, Peter!" His command was short and sharp. "He who lives by violence dies by violence." This was not the place or time for a show of strength. Poor, poor Peter. He was always so eager to defend the Master. He was so fond of Him. It was so frustrating to be always fouled up. Almost in total despair and abject resignation he slipped the bloodied Damascus steel back into its scabbard. He hunched his shoulders in dismay and spat on the ground in disgust.

The Master, meanwhile, reached out quietly and touched Malchus. The wound was healed: the ear restored: the blood stanched.

It was the last miracle of healing Jesus was to perform. And He did it to the man who came out to help lynch Him in the dark. Oh, the amazing generosity and graciousness of Christ! It was a precise enactment of the very principles He had taught His men: "Love your enemies; bless them that curse you; do good to them that hate you, and pray for them which despitefully use you and persecute you."

Such action completely undid the crowd. The disorderly mob

staggered back to their feet. They milled about gesticulating wildly. An undercurrent of angry oaths and mumbling threats rumbled amongst them.

"Why didn't you arrest Me in the city in broad daylight? I sat in the temple teaching day after day." It was almost as if Jesus were taunting them to touch Him. "I never took anything from anyone—except abuse." His eyes flashed fiercely and His voice flowed low and strong and calm. "Yet here you come out with swords and staves to take Me as if I were a criminal."

Little did that motley mob realize that He had them at His mercy. Had He wished, the whole gang could have been wiped out in a moment. It would have taken but a word of His command to unseen angelic forces. In an hour, every man, woman, and child in Palestine that night could have been annihilated by armies of heaven.

"Don't you realize that I could simply ask for more than twelve legions of angels [72,000] and they would be granted Me by My Father?" His simple statement terrified His would-be attackers. "But that is not the way it is to be. Otherwise the ancient prophecies would not come to pass."

Whether the rough assassins realized it or not, Judas did—that now was the instant for counterattack. The Master would never go against the ancient Scriptures. He always submitted to the purposes of God prophesied of old. He would be duty-bound to allow Himself to be taken and bound by this cruel crowd.

"Take Him!" Judas yelled excitedly. "Take Him, and hold Him securely!"—and this he screamed to the surging mass of men closing in around his best friend.

The armed attackers surged forward and laid hands on Jesus roughly. They manhandled Him angrily. He was like a quarry who had held the bloodhounds at bay with regal disdain. Now they suddenly rushed in, impatient for the kill. They pounced on Him, grabbing His arms and throwing strong ropes around His wrists. They pulled His hands behind His back and lashed them together.

Others turned on the frightened, frustrated band of eleven young followers who hovered in the shadows of the trees. When they saw their Master overwhelmed they began to run. Like a covey of quail in fright they fled off in every direction, running and stumbling through the dark. With them was young John Mark. He was running stark naked. One of the mob had tried to grab him. But he slipped out of his garments and was gone like a young gazelle pursued by dogs. He had come to warn Jesus of the impending arrest and got caught up in the turmoil of the night's excitement.

It is an incredible scene of horror and outrage.

Villains cursing and swearing with obscene oaths against One who had done no crime, committed no offense.

Ruffians abusing with their rough cruel hands One whose hands had brought only blessing.

Chafing, cutting cords and clanging chains now manacled One who had come to set men free.

Abuse, belligerence, and vicious vengeance were heaped on One who had brought healing, help, and hope to others in despair.

So often it is thus. God ever reaches out His hands to touch, restore, comfort, and cheer. He gives and gives and gives. While men's hands are extended in greed to grasp and get all they can in selfish cruelty.

Yet, amid this mayhem, the Master went quietly, calmly, and without further ado to His mock trial. Now He was all alone. The last of His friends had forsaken Him. The terrible trail He trod from the garden to the grave He would tramp alone. But, though He trod it in torment, He also trod it in triumph.

He had not been taken as a martyr. He had chosen of His own free will to be brought to trial. It was not He who in very truth would be tried that awful day. It was mankind who stood on trial before the King of Kings. He was not at the mercy of men, except as He permitted Himself to be. They were at His mercy, partaking of it in a peculiar way they could not understand.

All through the subsequent hours of that dreadful day it was a strong, calm, self-controlled Christ who stood fully in charge of every crisis. To Him these events were not crises. They had each been fully anticipated. They did not, could not take Him by surprise. Rather it was He who quietly decided by His demeanor exactly what would transpire. Men do not take God by surprise. They do not decide their own destiny, except it be for their own certain destruction; these are other decisions long before determined of deity.

So as the Master marched, bound, back towards Jerusalem, He knew it was to His death, *but to set men free*. The streets were black. The pavements and narrow walled passageways echoed to the tramping feet and coarse language of the milling mob. Those hard rock walls had heard the innocent cries and sad sounds of other prophets who had lamented and perished in this wicked place.

But when evil reigns and men's hearts are full of hate, black is white, white is black; evil is good, and good is evil; falsehood is truth, and truth is falsehood.

In the midst of such madness the innocent Son of God would that day die as a criminal on a rough Roman gibbet.

Yet out of such bestiality God would bring life and light and love.

CHAPTER THIRTY-SIX

Before the High Priests

The mob sent by the religious leaders to lynch our Lord was accompanied by officers and a captain from the Sanhedrin. These were not Roman military men. They were really Jewish police used by the ecclesiastical hierarchy to impose their will upon the people. They closely resembled modern-day private detectives or plain-clothes operators.

They first led Jesus to the residence of Annas, the venerable old high priest who had held this august office long before Christ appeared on the public scene. Annas had five sons. Eventually each of these was to become a high priest in his own right. Annas was also the father-in-law of Caiaphas, who at this critical hour happened to be the chief high priest in Jerusalem.

Annas and Caiaphas each had his living quarters in the palatial high priest's house. This was a handsome and spacious building with sufficient room that both Annas and Caiaphas maintained their chief residence there. The two sets of living quarters were separated by a beautiful open courtyard.

It was through the gates to this so-called palace that the motley crowd pushed and jostled Jesus. Even though by now it was around 3:00 A.M., wily old Annas was up and wide awake, waiting for his victim to arrive. Undoubtedly it was he more than anyone else who had engineered the events of the night. He was by far the wealthiest man in Jerusalem. He had much more to lose than anyone else in the event of a popular uprising. Fear and terror had gripped his old heart since the first day three years before when the Master blazed into Jerusalem to cleanse the temple and overturn its treacherous trade.

Yes, it had seemed a long, long time to wait until this threatening prophet from Galilee could be brought to bay. But at long last He had been captured. He was caught in a net of vile intrigue. And Annas would be the first to try to pin some accusation on Him deserving of death.

It had not been easy to capture the Christ. Twice He had simply strode in mighty strength through maddened mobs bent on His destruction. The first time had been in His own hometown of Nazareth. There an infuriated mob wanted to fling Him over a cliff, but He simply walked through them unscathed. The second occasion was right in the temple courtyard in this cruel city. And again He strode through the screaming mob bent on His blood, incited to fury by the angry priests. No, He had not been easy to take. But this was the third try and it had succeeded.

Annas rubbed his hands with satisfaction, in typical Eastern fashion, as he heard the mob of men clamoring in the great courtyard outside his doors. Now was his chance to even the score and castigate this impostor. The great doors swung open. Jesus, already bloodstained, sweating, and disheveled was thrust roughly into the august presence of the veteran priest. In contrast, the latter stood immaculately attired in his ornate priestly garments.

Immediately he began to question Jesus carefully.

Meanwhile, outside, the band of rough men began to banter with each other. They slapped one another on the shoulders, laughed, joked, and congratulated themselves on their heroic achievements of the night.

The air was chilly. An armful of thorn brush was brought in by one of the servants, and soon a fire made from a handful of coals began to crackle in the courtyard. There were people milling about, some yawning sleepily, others holding out their hands to the warming blaze, a few squatting down in a circle close to the welcome glow. One of these, strangely enough, was John—Jesus' most intimate friend.

John, determined to see what would happen to his Master, had followed the gang into the city. Being quite well acquainted with the high priest's household, he had slipped easily past the servant girl who kept the door.

Peter, too, was as keen as John to be in on the action. But he was stopped at the door, unknown to the doorkeeper. And it was only when John came and spoke to the maid on his behalf that he was allowed entry. The sharp-eyed maid questioned Peter carefully: "Aren't you also, like John, one of this man's disciples?" Flatly the big fisherman denied it: "I am not."

Without hesitation Peter shouldered his way through the noisy crowd. He, too, was cold, and it would be good to get near that welcome fire and warm himself.

Inside the high priest's residence, Jesus faced Annas and his officers alone.

The grilling got under way.

He was asked about His disciples. The crafty old character thought that perhaps under pressure the Master might betray His men. But He did not. He never betrayed His friends.

He questioned Jesus carefully about His teaching and doctrine. Perhaps he could trip Him up on some petty point of the law. Little did he grasp that here before him stood the Son of God, who alone had fulfilled or could fulfill all the law of God.

Actually the latter investigation was utter hypocrisy. Being a Sadducee, Annas had little respect for the law, much less any interest in Christ's spiritual teaching for the future. Jesus knew this. He could see clearly through the old man's phony pretense.

Boldly He replied; "I always spoke and taught openly in the synagogues and temple. I kept nothing secret. I did nothing subversive. Ask those who heard Me. They know what I said. You don't have to interrogate Me. It is all common knowledge."

This unflinching, forthright response infuriated the bystanders. It was the truth, and the truth cut to the quick. One of the officers lashed out in anger. With stinging blows he slapped and smashed Jesus across the face in rapid succession. "How dare You address the high priest that way!"

It was the typical tough tactics used by the temple police to intimidate people. But Jesus was not about to be cowed.

Looking His accuser straight in the face, He shot back: "If I have spoken a lie, then prove it!" His voice was strong and sharp and stern: "If I have spoken truth, then you have no right to abuse Me. You will have to produce witnesses to prove your accusations."

The tables were turned.

It was no longer Annas who was trying Him.

It was He who had brought Annas to the bar of justice.

Witnesses. Where could they find witnesses to prove His crimes? And if in fact He had committed crimes, what were they? How could this One who was utter truth and absolute integrity ever be charged with a criminal offense? He could not. It would take some fancy footwork to fasten any allegation on Him that would stand up in a Roman court.

Annas was too old, too experienced, too crafty, too cunning to be caught out by Christ. He was wise enough and astute enough to know that he had more than met his match. This One was too hot for his sweaty old hands to handle. He would pass Him on to the Sanhedrin. Maybe Caiaphas, the active high priest, could catch Him off base.

Meanwhile, outside in the courtyard, the lynch gang, seeing Peter standing in the flickering circle of firelight, asked him if he was one of the Master's men. He shook his head. After all the warmth of the fire was too comfortable. He didn't want to leave. "But you are one of His followers," one of them insisted. Peter protested positively: "Man, I am not."

The morning hours had gone by in agonizing slowness. In the east a faint, faint glow of light began to lighten on the horizon. Peter wondered to himself what was going on in Annas' quarters. How inaction irked him!

Just then a kinsman of Malchus, whose ear Peter had slashed off with his sword, saw the huge-framed fisherman crouched before the fire. "Didn't I see you in the Garden of Gethsemane?" he growled angrily. His eyes were like needle points, penetrating Peter's false front. "You are mistaken," Peter protested angrily. "Man, I tell you I never knew Him." Oaths and curses followed.

"Well, your Galilean accent gives you away!" the accuser pressed Peter. Again vehement cursing and denial. Just then there was the raucous crow of a rooster hailing the break of day over the Mount of Olives in the east.

Precisely at this point the great doors to the high priest's residence swung open. Jesus, still bound with ropes and chains, was led across the courtyard. His handsome face was crimson, flushed from the captain's cruel blows. But His eyes were bright and clear. Crossing the open patio He turned and looked squarely at Simon Peter. There was love and longing and deep understanding in that glance. Then He was gone, led away into the great hall of Caiaphas, where the Sanhedrin was assembled.

It was a passing, fleeting incident but it pulverized Peter's pride. The big powerful man got up and strode away into the dim gray light of dawn. Outside and away from prying eyes a torrent of tears tumbled from his eyes. He was a man broken in spirit, contrite in heart. He had three times betrayed his Master, twice over that night. It was the low point of his life. He could sink no further in utter despair. His conduct was an absolute disaster.

Jesus now stood arraigned before the full Sanhedrin. They had been hastily assembled in the early morning hours. All but two of the ecclesiastical hierarchy were seated sedately in the great hall of the high priest's palace. They were arranged in a giant semicircle facing each other. And the accused stood in the center. Caiaphas presided over the proceedings.

It is noteworthy that even at this stage Jesus never asked for the services of a solicitor to plead His case. He never requested the privilege of bringing in witnesses to sustain His claims. He never once endeavored to clear Himself by conventional means. He realized that in essence He was undergoing a mock trial in a kangaroo court. He knew that He was the victim of iniquitous injustice. He never flinched in the face of bestial brutality.

In ancient times when Israel was a ruling nation, the Sanhedrin had the final power of life and death over its people. Ostensibly the Sanhedrin had been established to protect the people and to provide them with a degree of justice. If death was declared it could be by stoning, burning, or beheading. But after the advent of Rome's military might and jurisdictional rule, the Sanhedrin could only submit its offenders to the Roman governor for judgment and a final verdict. Nor would the Romans ever allow a local court of any kind to condemn a man to death. This was a prerogative permitted only to their own court of law.

So it was that in the dismal gray dawn of this dreadful day, this diabolical group of religious leaders was determined to destroy Jesus, no matter how devious its tactics.

He actually stood condemned even before a trial.

He was a man convicted before ever His case had been heard.

He was considered a criminal though no charges were laid.

He was seen as an instigator of subversion, yet without a single witness whose testimony could stand as truth before a court.

Such a scene was and ever will remain the greatest travesty of justice the world has witnessed. It was a spectacle of subterfuge and subversion at its worst. It was not the Sanhedrin who tried the Christ that dawn. It was He who calmly and in quiet control of the events, put them on trial for all time. Their actions have come down through two thousand years of history as some of the most base and dastardly ever perpetrated by mankind.

In their craven fear they fetched in ruffians off the streets of their sordid city to provide false evidence against this magnificent "man." The lies and distortions of truth spouted from these spurious perverts only added to their mounting frustrations. All of them, priests and scribes and elders along with the riffraff of Jerusalem, were thieves together. They were robbers trying to rob an impeccable character of an impeccable reputation. He had done no evil. He had committed no crime. He had said nothing subversive.

Some of them in their stupidity and spiritual blindness asserted that He had claimed He would destroy their precious temple then rebuild it in three days. Little did they know the temple to which He referred was not one of stone and timber, gold and cloth. Rather He referred to His own beautiful body, already beleaguered by cruel hands, abused by rough bestial men, soon to be crucified by their own decision. It was *this* temple, this residence of God's own Spirit, that in three days would be resurrected and restored.

But they were like beasts bent on blood. They were bloodhounds hot in their pursuit of hapless prey. No matter what, they would tear His life from Him today.

Amid all the confusion, amid all the false charges and counter-charges, amid all the cross fire of crafty accusations, Jesus stood silent. He was impassive. He stood erect, strong and serene. He alone was calm and self-controlled in the midst of all the agitation.

The members of the Sanhedrin were beside themselves with apprehension and excitement. It seemed nothing they said would stick. Was He going to outdo them after all? Would He slip from between their clawlike fingers? Could they not outmaneuver Him somehow in some sly way?

Caiaphas stroked his gray beard nervously. He cast his beady eyes about the great hall. There was one card left to play. It was his trump card. He would try it.

In sonorous, solemn tones he addressed Jesus: "I adjure You by the living God, to declare whether or not You are the Christ, the Messiah, God's Anointed."

A heavy hush hung over the hall.

The whole assembly was aghast—awestruck.

Jesus, being a Son of the Law, the Son of God, who had faithfully fulfilled all the law of God, had no option but to answer.

"If I tell you, you will not believe," He replied in a clear, unruffled voice. "And even if I ask you, you would not answer or ever let me go!" He looked at them with eyes that penetrated through all their pretense. "After this ordeal I shall be ensconced in power at God's right hand."

A look of horror mesmerized the assembly.

"Are You in fact claiming to be the Son of God—God very God?" they shouted in unison.

"You said it," was His quiet rejoinder—*"I AM."*

Those words electrified everyone. This was utter blasphemy! This was all they needed to nail Him to a cross.

In fake anguish Caiaphas grabbed his own ornate garment and tore it apart. It was a more symbolical gesture than he realized. He was to be the last of the old human high priests. This One who stood before him, bound, was to be the great new High Priest of God for all men of all time.

And before the day was out that other ornate cloth, the veil of the temple, would be torn from top to bottom, allowing all men to enter freely into God's Holy Presence without the help of crooks like himself.

So on the basis of absolute truth, declared without apology by Christ Himself, He stood condemned before this august assembly. It is a bit beyond us to grasp how God, very God, on the basis of

His own admission and forthright declaration should stand incriminated by coarse, crass men. On this horrendous day the earth was to grow dark and the heavens withhold their light from men who were absolute murderers.

The verdict of the Sanhedrin was unanimous.

He was guilty of death.

He was condemned to die.

They had won the day.

The case was closed.

To celebrate they decided to indulge in a ghastly game of terrible torture. Here were men who were supposed to protect the interests of their people subjecting an innocent person to appalling abuse.

They turned Jesus over to the street ruffians, their own private police and the other gang members who had lynched Him, for some horrible amusement. It was one way of repaying them for their grim part in His capture.

There is nothing so cruel as the bestial behavior of unregenerate men who play with hapless victims in their clutch. It is a common practice with prisoners. And we scarcely dare to look on.

The roughnecks blindfolded the Master. Mainly this was because they could not bear to look into those calm, quiet, knowing, searching eyes. They pummeled His weary body. They spat in His face until their foul-smelling saliva ran down over His flushed cheeks. They jeered at Him, challenging Him to prophesy who had last struck Him a stinging blow. They slashed and smashed His face until it was purple and swollen with great welts.

He, the Christ, was in a bear garden with beasts.

Judas had looked on, watching the revolting abuse heaped on the Master. He saw his friend tortured and taunted. He listened to the dreadful final condemnation passed upon the Prince of Peace.

Somehow his darkened soul and shriveled spirit had never imagined things would turn out this way. Perhaps he had even half expected Jesus to perform some mighty miracle at the last moment that would deliver Him from the jaws of His enemies. But He did not. Instead, He chose to die.

Shot through with remorse, Judas rushed up to the gloating priests. He flung the thirty pieces of silver at their feet. He was pierced through with a thousand painful pangs of a smitten conscience: "*I have betrayed innocent blood!*"

The crass leaders laughed in his face. He was but a lout. They had used him to achieve their own wicked ends. They could not care less what happened to him now: "That's nothing to us."

For Judas the hour of horror and darkness had come. In abject terror, grief, and remorse he went out and hanged himself from a scrawny tree.

The superpious priests decided the blood money should not contaminate their sacred temple coffers. What an absurdity! So they used it to purchase the potter's field. This was the dumping ground for broken pots, marred vessels, and shards of fractured clay discarded by the city potters. It was the scrap heap for pottery that might have served noble, useful purposes.

Appropriately, in keeping with the great prophecy of Jeremiah, it became the burial ground for strangers and the castoffs of society. Of these, Judas himself was the first. He had become a fractured, broken, shattered vessel, once of service to the Master . . . now discarded.

CHAPTER THIRTY-SEVEN

Before a Roman Governor

From the Sanhedrin, Jesus was hustled off to Pilate, the Roman governor.

It is imperative to know a little about the history of Pilate, the Roman administrator presiding in Jerusalem at this time, if we are to understand what took place in the praetorium. The events leading up to this trial of our Lord were rather complex, coloring Pilate's conduct in the face of the Jewish population.

Pilate had been sent by Caesar from Rome several years before, in A.D. 26. The two were great friends. Pilate quite literally worshiped and idolized Caesar. He was well-nigh his god, even though a very austere and tyrannical god. Caesar in turn held a peculiar affection for Pilate. Not only did he entrust him with the government of Judea, one of Rome's most difficult provinces, but he allowed Pilate the great privilege of taking his wife with him to Jerusalem. This was a special favor few Roman governors ever enjoyed.

Out of admiration for Caesar, Pilate had some of his armed forces outfitted with standards bearing the silver insignia of the emperor. Immediately this produced a tremendous outcry from the Jewish religious leaders. They protested that in Israel it had been decreed by Jehovah that there should be no other gods. Pilate was perpetrating a great evil in having these silver images in their midst, so under enormous outcries and protests from the priests he finally relented and had them removed.

Pilate's second mistake was to bring into his own residence some private tablets which served as votives to his god. Again the Jews found out. They were furious and sent angry representations to Rome. It was embarrassing for the governor. And the continued unrest put him in a bad light with Caesar.

In fact Pilate, who was a highly educated, exceedingly sophisticated Roman, despised the narrow-minded, bigoted Jews. He regarded them with great contempt. The rigid legality and austere life of Judea was abhorrent to a man who loved luxury, ease, and pleasure.

To indulge himself to a degree, he decided to divert one of the aqueducts leading into Jerusalem. There he built a beautiful set of Roman baths where he and his friends could disport themselves in typical Roman luxury. To the people of Judea this was again a pagan extravagance and rite, to which they objected angrily.

This time, however, Pilate had had enough of their protests and interference. He sent his armed men in mufti amongst the angry crowds. Whenever they found anyone raising his voice in hostility the offender was ruthlessly massacred and cut to the ground. The tough tactics took the fire from the people of Judea. But they also left behind a deep deposit of angry animosity and bitter hostility between the Jews and Pilate. The priesthood especially loathed Pilate intensely. So at this stage there was dreadful distrust and a vengeful vendetta between the governor and the governed.

In the warm bright light of early day, Jesus, shackled with chains, was led bound to Pilate, who sat in the praetorium. He, the Son of man, Son of God, knew full well that He was like a grain of wheat soon to be ground and broken between the upper millstone of Rome's power and the nether millstone of Jewish intransigence. It was part of the awful grinding, milling process whereby He would be crushed and made into the very bread from heaven.

"What charge do you bring against this man?" the governor thundered at the mob milling around Jesus.

Promptly they replied that He was guilty of several offenses. He was perverting the nation. He forbade the payment of taxes to Caesar. He claimed to be a monarch, a king.

Momentarily, Pilate was slightly amused. He had all sorts of informers moving amongst the Jewish populace. And if a single one of these charges had been true he would have known about it long before and taken appropriate steps to apprehend the offender. He was not dull or slow. He realized this was just a ruse.

So he indulged himself just a little and replied cynically, "You go ahead and judge Him by your laws!" It was really a jest which infuriated the priests. They knew they could not carry out their verdict. They saw themselves helpless to execute this One who threatened their position. And their frustration was doubly bitter because Pilate was playing games with them.

In anger and vehemence they screamed and ranted at him. It made him weary and fed up. These Jews were such a painful people, always arguing, quarreling, shouting, and protesting violently.

But Jesus was different. He stood before the governor calm and quiet. He did not utter a word. He did not scream or wave His hands. He did not shout out loud demanding His rights. It amazed Pilate.

He took the prisoner aside where he could question Him quietly. "Are you really King of the Jews?" It was the only charge that even interested the Roman. Jesus looked at him evenly. "Who told you this?" The words were without bitterness. "*I am a King*. But My kingdom is not of this world. I am here to bear witness to that truth."

Pilate, a student of philosophy, was arrested by this last statement. "What is truth?" Little did he realize that utter truth, absolute veracity, total integrity personified, stood before him shackled. He, the Christ, though bound by men, could set free the spirits and souls of ten thousand times ten thousand of those who came to trust Him as *the Truth*.

Taking Jesus out before the murmuring crowd, Pilate declared flatly, "I find no fault in this man!" How could he? But the mob was not to be put off this easily.

Twice now Pilate had played around with them. And they were livid with rage. In typical Jewish fashion they gesticulated wildly, shouted angrily, twisted their beards, and spat on the ground.

"He incites this whole nation!" they roared. "From Galilee to Jerusalem He has propagated His views." At the mention of the name *Galilee* a fresh thought flashed through Pilate's sharp mind.

Herod was visiting in Jerusalem. He had formal jurisdiction over Galilee. If indeed this prisoner was from that province, then He could easily be passed off onto that foxy fellow, who had disposed of John the Baptist so easily. After all, Pilate had enough on his plate just governing Judea. Why should he be bothered with petty problems from Galilee? And anyway, it would flatter Herod's proud ego to have Pilate show him this deference.

Jesus was handed back to the angry mob. They pushed and shoved Him down the streets to Herod's headquarters. When the crafty impostor was informed that Jesus was to be presented to him, he was excited. Ever since he had beheaded John in the dungeon of black Machaerus, he had wanted to meet Jesus. Some claimed that this prophet from Galilee was none other than John the Baptist risen from the dead.

With gloating eyes and racing heart Herod gazed upon the bruised face and bloodstained clothes of the Galilean. He did not know it, but there before him stood the King of Kings whose life his jealous father had tried to snuff out as a babe in Bethlehem.

Though the evil monarch quizzed Jesus carefully, the latter refused to reply. Jesus had answered Annas; He had answered Caiaphas; He had answered the Sanhedrin; He had answered the Roman governor. But to Herod He would not speak.

Herod was a cruel, cunning, perfidious impostor from the deserts of Arabia. He was no rightful ruler. He was less than scum from the dregs of a dreadful desert family. And to him Jesus would not deign to speak a single syllable.

The amazing thing—the incredible thing—is that Herod, deep down in his black, dark heart, knew Jesus was innocent. More than this, he knew this One from Galilee was a great, good man. Just as he had known that John the Baptist was a good man.

He commanded his soldiers to robe Jesus in a glistening white garment. It was a gesture that spoke more loudly than any royal proclamation he may have made. As He stood there adorned in the cloak of Jewish royalty—for Jewish kings were always uniquely garbed in shining white—Herod declared: "This is a king of the Jews!"

Of course it was an act perpetrated in jest. It was done in mocking. There was nothing like games of torture to pass the tedious hours away. And Herod's men of war found it very funny to belittle the prophet of Galilee garbed like a king, with swollen face and blackened eyes. They taunted and tormented Him unmercifully. After all, if He thought He was a king why not let Him play the part for an hour or two?

Then Herod shunted Jesus back to Pilate, with the verdict that the defendant was indeed an innocent person. This identical endorsement of Pilate's position provided common ground between the two rulers. And that day a bond of friendship was forged between them. A white robe on an innocent man brought two crafty, cruel governors together in mutual agreement and peace.

But this did not placate the priests. Incensed and enraged beyond measure by the endless delay in bringing Jesus to death, they ranted and raved for His blood. Their screaming and shouting roused the rabble crowds gathering from the streets. The morning was wearing on. And they wanted Christ crucified before the whole city was inflamed.

A fourth time Pilate tried a political ploy to rescue Jesus. It was customary on great occasions of this kind to release a political prisoner to the people. This is an ancient ruse still used to this day to assuage an angry populace. Pilate released a prisoner from time to time as a sop to the people.

There was being held in custody at this very hour a violent revolutionary named Barabbas. He was a robber brigand but a popular hero because of his audacity in defying the Roman authorities. Pilate had considered freeing him. Now he had a new idea.

He went before the wild and belligerent mob. Holding up his hand for silence he shouted, "Whom would you rather have released to you—Jesus or Barabbas?" It was a cunning move. He was more than half convinced the crowd would opt in favor of the good man from Galilee. But he was wrong. He had misjudged the mood of the mob that morning. They were bloodhounds baying for the blood of an innocent victim.

"Barabbas!" They screamed in unison, waving their arms. "Give us Barabbas!"

Pilate's political ploy had boomeranged. He was being crowded into a corner by the rising roar of the masses. What could he do now? He was getting desperate. Not only did he want to save Jesus for His own sake, but he wanted to save Him to settle the old score of hatred he held for the Jewish priesthood. If only he could prove them wrong. Then the old vendetta would be evened.

Pilate tried a fifth trick. It was a low-down trick. It was the sort of thing exported from the grisly arena of Rome's ghastly coliseum. He would make a public spectacle of Jesus. If he shed enough of His blood and flagellated enough of His beautiful body in an orgy of agony, the people's lust for bloodshed and carnage might be satiated. Sometimes a point can be reached where human beings, even the most brutal, will revolt and vomit up the violence on which they gorge themselves.

In a gesture of false grandeur the governor queried the quarrelsome crowd: "What shall I do with Jesus, who is called Christ?" As if to answer his own question he ordered the tough Roman legionnaires to bind and flog the defenseless man.

It was an appalling performance. Jesus was lashed with ropes to a pillar so that His body could not bend beneath the blows.

The glistening white robe was removed roughly. His naked, mutilated back was laid bare to the grimacing onlookers. The soldiers picked up the cruel oxhide whips that carried fragments of bone. These would plow blood-red furrows in His back, just as predicted by the psalmist of old: "The plowers plowed upon my back . . . ." (Psalms 129:3).

A Roman flogging, next to a Roman crucifixion, was amongst the most inhuman of tortures ever devised by bloodthirsty beasts. The cruel thongs cracked and whined as they wrapped around Jesus' back and buttocks and legs. With each lash the flesh was laid open as though gashed with a gangplow. Blood gushed from the gaping wounds. It ran down His strong thighs. It trickled around His ankles and gathered in dark, black pools on the stone pavement.

The sound of the lashes could scarcely be heard above the lusty cries for blood from the maddened crowd.

Instead of relenting they roared for more. Pilate was dumbfounded. "Crucify Him! Crucify Him!" they began to roar. "Away with Him!"

In an abject gesture of craven fear, cowardice, and disbelief, Pilate called for Jesus to be unbound from the pillar. He was an appalling sight. Surely someone, somewhere, somehow would be moved to pity. But there was none!

> . . . he was wounded for our transgressions, he was bruised for our iniquities: the chastisement of our peace was upon him; and with his stripes we are healed.
>
> Isaiah 53:5

In the indecision of this hour a messenger brought word from Pilate's wife. She had experienced a most-disturbing dream. This man on trial before her husband was an innocent person. He should not be responsible for the death of such a victim.

Pilate was on the horns of a dilemma. It was still within his power to release Jesus. He could still rescue Him. He could declare Him innocent and under the protective custody of Rome's might. He, the Christ, might have been allowed to walk away a maimed, mutilated, but untouchable man.

But to do this was to jeopardize Pilate's own future. If the Jews sent still another public protest back to Caesar, Pilate's political career could be crippled. Caesar might question his capacity to govern.

In fact the very shouts reaching his ears now bore that out. "If you let this man go," the Jews yelled, "then you are not Caesar's friend." The accusation made Pilate frantic with fear. *"We have no king but Caesar!"*

He called for a basin of water. Using an ancient gesture of absolution, he dipped his hands in the clear liquid.

"I am innocent of this man's blood!" he growled angrily. *His blood be upon you*, he thought to himself. He had done everything he could by way of compromise to rescue Jesus. But he had not done everything he could as a man. He could have sacrificed his own career, his own reputation, his own future for the Christ.

"He that saveth his soul will lose it. And he that loseth his life for My sake will find it." These were the words of the Master, who now stood before him in silence, in strength, and in supreme dignity.

The commingled voices of the brutal crowd now reached an absolute crescendo: "His blood be upon us and our children!"

They roared, yelled, screamed and gesticulated wildly. "Crucify Him! Crucify Him! Away with Him!"

Pilate relented. Turning to his mercenaries, he gave Jesus into their hands to be crucified. Roughly they tossed a purple robe around His bloody back. Its coarse cloth turned crimson with blood. They quickly made up a crude crown of Christ's-thorn and jammed it down over His noble head. Blood spurted from the sharp spear points and ran down into His gentle eyes. They beat Him with a rod to further deform His swollen face and feet and hands— the face and feet and hands that had brought so much love and mercy and hope to others. They covered Him with foul language, oaths, obscene taunts, and spittle from their own vile mouths.

Pilate a few years later was recalled to Rome, then exiled in disgrace to Gaul. There he, too, like Judas, hanged himself in despair, a man responsible in part for the death of the innocent Christ.

"There is a way which seemeth right unto a man, but the end thereof are the ways of death" (Proverbs 14:12)!

CHAPTER THIRTY-EIGHT

God on a Cross

The hour of black ignominy had come. God in Christ was at the mercy of the mob. He had no further protection from Pilate. He was to be tortured to death. The ghastly and revolting instrument of that dreadful, slow, excruciating death was the notorious Roman gibbet.

The Romans, ruthless, violent, crass slayers of men and women, were famous for their crosses. They had devised crosses of all kinds. And with barbaric bestiality they had invented various methods of crucifixion that prolonged the victim's appalling pain while pinned to the tree.

On this dreadful day they found three crosses.

One was for the Christ of God: the King of the Jews.

The other two were for crude criminals.

Three victims dying at once would be quite a spectacle for the Passover crowds. They would get more excitement and cruel fun from this cruel city of their fathers than they had ever imagined.

It would be quite a sight to see three forlorn figures, like grotesque scarecrows, suspended halfway between heaven and earth. The gruesome and grim picture of three trees blackened with human blood standing stark against the eastern sky would engrave an indelible imprint on ten thousand memories. On the bare outcrop of rock called the Place of the Skull—shaped roughly like a dead man's skull and named Calvary or Golgotha—there would fall, drop by drop, the blood of three men. One was the Son of God.

Dragged and pushed out of the praetorium—away from Pilate's protection—Jesus half stumbled down the marble steps out into the dusty, dirty streets. Drops of blood from His torn back marked every step. With each move He made, the ugly lacerations opened up and oozed blood mingled with lymph.

There were angry shouts from the Roman guard. The mob had to make way. A rough-hewn pole with a crude crossarm was carried through the crowd. Brutally it was shoved over the Master's great strong shoulder. Part of the torture was that each prisoner struggled painfully beneath the deadweight of his own instrument of agony and death.

The heavy tree bowed His strong back. Its weight cut into His mutilated flesh. The splinters were sharp knives shredding His shoulders. Valiantly He strained to drag the dreadful burden bumping on the pavement. A lesser man would have surrendered sooner. He struggled on. But loss of blood, and physical exhaustion from long hours of abuse, left Him weakened. Finally He collapsed. The cross crashed down on the ground. Shouts of commingled jeers and taunts rose up from the mob around Him.

There was the God of Glory, lying slumped in the dust of Jerusalem's filthy streets.

What had brought Him to this state of degradation? What had so humiliated this King of heaven? What had so crushed the broken body of this brave One?

It was the selfishness of the race He had come to save.

It was the selfishness of His people, Israel.

It was the selfishness of Judas, who betrayed Him.

It was the selfishness of the high priests, scribes, Pharisees, and Sanhedrin, who falsely accused and condemned Him to die.

It was the selfishness of Herod, who interrogated Him.

It was the selfishness of Pilate, who tried to save his own skin.

It was the selfishness of uncounted millions who would not choose to turn to God in response to His great compassion.

But more imperative, more compelling than any of these, it was He Himself who chose to come to Calvary. It was He who chose to endure such abuse at the hands of cruel sinners. Why?

Because His very character was utter selflessness. He was caring Love. He could not do otherwise. He had to be true to Himself.

Crumpled up under the cross, Jesus appeared a revolting spectacle. Some of the masses milling around Him spat on Him in derision. They taunted Him with insults. The other two criminals could carry their crosses; why couldn't He? Little did they know this One bore not only heavy wooden beams but the even more intolerable weight of all the world's wickedness. Those broad, bleeding shoulders and that flagellated back were bent not just by a wooden cross but by the more colossal cross of men's sins.

Yet He never whimpered. He never begged for mercy. He never pled for release. The maddened mob might crush His body, but they could never break His Spirit. "In this world you will have tribulation. But be of good cheer. I have overcome the world."

Women and men and youngsters whose lives He had touched and transformed followed at a distance. They seemed powerless to help. Deeply moved at His plight, some of them burst into tears. Unable to control their emotions, they broke into anguished groans and heart-tearing wails.

It must have touched one tough Roman's sotted soul. A brusque command roared out from the centurion's throat. His soldiers seized a great burly black man standing in the crowd. He was a Cyrenian, a country man accustomed to hard work and large loads. This huge Simon was pressed into carrying the cross. Eyes filled with compassion for Christ, he was glad to do it.

Staggering to His feet, Jesus turned to those around Him who were wailing and lamenting. His look was tender. "Don't weep for Me," He spoke serenely and sincerely, "weep for yourselves. Events even more awful than you see today will overtake this terrible city."

One day, not very far distant, there would stand starkly outside this grim metropolis not just three crosses but thousands of crosses. Fastened to those crosses would be not the beautiful body of God's Son but the famished bony carcasses of the cruel people of this murderous city.

At long last the three victims staggered slowly up the rough side of Golgotha. The three crude crosses were dumped on the ground. Their timbers rattled on the stones as though sounding a dreaded death rattle.

Military mercenaries with grim faces and hard looks held the three men. Others pulled heavy hammers and giant iron spikes from a soiled bag. The butchery was about to begin.

As a final gesture of commingled mercy and malignancy they also drew a bottle of mixed vinegar and gall from the filthy bag. The vinegar was intended as somewhat of a sedative. The gall, bitterness of bitterness, added to the anguish. It was proffered to Jesus. But He turned from it with distaste, after it touched His lips, swollen and bruised and bleeding.

For the first time since the early hours of that momentous morning a hush fell over the militant mob. The Roman centurion had ordered them to stand back away from the ghastly rock. The actual act of crucifying a man was so terrible the sufferer was entitled to endure the agony in some solitude. It was the verdict of Rome that He die this way. It was the power of Rome that prevented the pariahs from pouncing on His person.

Jesus was stretched out prostrate on the cross beams. Of His own accord He extended His hands to take the spikes. With the ominous sound of iron on iron, the nails pierced His sinews and flesh. Blood spurted from the wounds as the spikes sank into the tough wood. He writhed in pain. Then His feet were laid flat on the wood with His legs drawn up. Two more terrible spikes did their dreadful work.

Like the thousands of other lambskins stretched in the midmorning sun that day, so the Son of God lay stretched beneath the burning skies of Judea. God's Passover Lamb was there for all to see.

With a sickening shudder the soldiers raised the cross upright. With a revolting jolt its base was dropped in a hole. The deed was done.

"Father, forgive them, for they know not what they do!" A more incredible cry has never come from any lips! Instead of vituperation or vehemence, here was God revealed. Here was the character of Christ in colors so vivid no man could ever mistake them. Such forgiveness! Such generosity! Such greatness! Such magnificence! This was no mere man on the cross. This was God in all His grandeur!

Even the Roman centurion, looking up aghast at such a person, his own proud spirit humbled, mused to himself: "Surely this man is the Son of God!'' If Jesus' own compatriots did not appreciate who He was, a pagan did.

The forgiveness of our God, extended to sinning, stumbling, selfish men, entailed a fantastic cost. That cost was the blood, the sweat, the suffering, the excruciating agony of the perfect One, paid in the place of the imperfect. How few there are of us who ever understand the pain we impose upon Him who loves us and gave Himself a ransom to redeem us from our sins.

In blindness, ignorance, and spiritual confusion, we crucify to ourselves the Christ of God just as surely as did the soldiers with their hammers and nails.

Throwing a few broken stones in the hole at the foot of the cross, they stabilized the upright pole standing stark against the burning sky. It was the most ghastly altar upon which any human sacrifice had ever been offered. God very God hanged there suspended between heaven and earth as the supreme substitute. He Himself was atoning for the awesome sins of all mankind, making reconciliation between God and men.

The soldiers casually dusted off their hands. The whole business was a messy one. But they were hardened to it. The groans coming from the three crucified victims never even stirred their sensual souls. Like jackals at a kill, they prowled around looking for some last scrap to pounce upon. They found it. It was the Master's clothing. Even though it was blackened with blood stains and besmirched with dust from the city streets, they grabbed it up in glee. It was loot!

With swift, sharp strokes they severed the long white mantle into four parts. The tunic was too well made to tear up. Drawing dice from their pockets they laughingly flung them on the outcropping rock of Calvary to decide who should take the booty—bloody though it was.

What they had done precisely accomplished the prophecy made by David nearly eleven hundred years previously: "They part my garments among them, and cast lots upon my vesture" (Psalms 22:18). He, the Christ, had come into the world, born into utter poverty, with nothing. He was to leave its unfriendly environment in exactly the same way, utterly destitute. He was the poorest of the poor, not possessing even a change of clothes.

The soldiers jeered and made light of the rags in their hands. They were torn, stained, and valueless. But at least their dogs at home would try to lick the blood from the cloth before lying down on them to cushion their scrawny frames from the hard ground. Even brute beasts would benefit from this dreadful day.

In man's eyes all this seemed so repulsive. In God's estimation it represented the final and total redemption not only of men but of all of the universe. By His own demise there was guaranteed not only a new race of men, re-created in Christ Jesus with new hearts and minds and emotions but also a new heaven and earth in which dwelleth righteousness.

The crucifixion was accomplished by 9:00 A.M. The high priest's hopes of getting the grisly affair over with before the city was astir had been pretty well realized.

The soldiers sat bored, making coarse jests, waiting for the victims to die. They found it very funny that Pilate should have insisted that a plaque proclaiming THIS IS JESUS, THE KING OF THE JEWS be tacked to the tree above the Galilean's head. It was a crude joke, the kind of cynical gesture Romans reveled in, to insult their subject people.

The words were inscribed in Latin for the soldiery to read; in Greek, the lingua franca of the whole civilized world, that any passerby might understand; in Hebrew, as a grim reminder to the people of Israel that heaven's royalty had come amongst them but had been rejected.

This made the high priests furious. They looked on from afar, somewhat satisfied at last that they had forever stilled this troublesome troublemaker—or so they thought. They stroked their beards in soft self-assurance. Yet they were never satisfied. Again they sent a delegation protesting to Pilate. If he insisted on an insignia, it should read HE SAID HE WAS THE KING OF THE JEWS. Pilate's curt retort was: "I have written what I have written." And it was better than he knew.

As the morning wore on, so did the suffering intensify. The burning thirst: the torn muscles: the screaming sinews: the wildly pumping heart: the heaving lungs—all struggling to sustain life while the very lifeblood drained slowly away. It was an inferno of agonizing abuse. The Master writhed on the cross, His great frame heaving with the strain.

Yet He was not concerned just with Himself. Infinite love, tender compassion, flowed from Him even in this torment. Looking down, He gently entrusted His mother, Mary, to John, His favorite disciple. Helpless to help their beloved, the grief-ridden women and devoted disciples who dared to approach near Golgotha sobbed openly. What if the soldiers did stare at them? What if the priests and scribes did scoff at them? They would be loyal to the last.

Just as in His life, so in His death, Christ polarized people. For others passed by, going to and from the city, mocking and jeering the prophet on the pole. They wagged their heads, grinned, and flung taunts in His teeth: "If You are the Son of God who can demolish and rebuild our temple in three days, free Yourself from those iron spikes!" They laughed with disdain. "Come down from the cross!" they scoffed.

The onlooking priests, scribes and elders were equally scornful. Rubbing their hands with gloating, they chided, "He saved others; Himself He cannot save. If He is God's Son, then why doesn't God rescue Him?" They prodded each other with proud looks of accomplishment. "If He would just come down off the cross, we might just believe on Him." It was a diabolical diatribe. Little did they know that millions upon millions of lost men and women would look to this One and be saved. How little did they realize that multitudes without number would believe on this One and find a new life of eternal dimensions. For their sakes, He would not, could not, save Himself.

At first both of the criminals crucified alongside Him reviled Him. But as one observed the enormous strength, serenity, and generosity of Jesus, he repented. This was no ordinary man dying alongside Him. It was God! No fierce tirade came from Him, no oaths or curses against His persecutors, no vilification or vengeance.

The dying thief begged for pardon. He received full forgiveness. He saw a Saviour. He found an open entrance into a new life. "This day you will be with Me in paradise." Those were the most refreshing words. They did him greater good than any earthly consolation. Even in death, new life was transmitted from the Master to a mortal man.

About noon, when the whole world should have stood stark in the blazing light of the midday sun, a strange darkness began to envelop the earth. It was not a sirocco wind blowing in with clouds of dust that obscured the sun. It was a darkness that could be felt and feared. It was a darkness palpable to human senses and human spirits. It gripped the populace with a peculiar foreboding. Titanic transactions far surpassing anything mortal men could comprehend were taking place in the unseen world. God was dying for men. And men could not see or understand.

CHAPTER THIRTY-NINE

Darkness and Death

Sometimes it would seem impertinent for us to discuss the life of our Lord during these three hours of darkness. One would almost prefer to draw an opaque veil of privacy over His anguish. Certainly no mortal can explain the eternal exchange of death for life and life for death made in the suffering of God. At best we approach the death of Christ with enormous reverence and awe. We admit freely that here we face a mystery of momentous magnitude.

If we could understand and explain it all, then it would be finite. It would be less than divine. But because it is beyond us fully to grasp, we bow before this monumental event in humility and gratitude. Humility because of the honor He bestows upon us in even letting us see a little of what took place. Gratitude because it was for our sakes He endured it.

As the darkness deepened over the whole earth so did the struggle in the unseen world of the Spirit.

The death He was dying there was not just a physical demise. In no way could ordinary physical death compensate or expiate for our misdeeds done in the soul or our wrongs committed in the spirit. The death referred to so often in Scripture as being the consequence of sin is not just the termination of physical life. There is also moral death, in which a man is dead—totally indifferent—to the quickening Spirit of God; and beyond that is spiritual death, which is eternal separation and alienation from God our Father.

Our Lord had to taste and drink of all three this dreadful day.

To have done less would have been to leave His work on our behalf incomplete.

It is a measure of His majesty and might that, repugnant as it was to Him, He did not flinch from drinking of all three deaths. In fact He drank them to the dregs. In keeping with His fierce determination so to do in the Garden of Gethsemane, He would go through with it, no matter how dark and desperate the ordeal.

Four times our Lord spoke from out of the deepening gloom. *"I thirst,"* He groaned, twisting with torturous fever. The bystanders put a sponge full of vinegar to His burning lips. But it was not just physical thirst He felt. It was a terrible thirst for righteousness. He who knew no sin was being made sin for us. Why? That we might be made righteous with His own poured-out righteousness. In this titanic transaction He was being drained of His own impeccably pure life. He was as water, the water of life, poured out on the earth to parched men who thirst for His life . . . His righteousness.

To undergo this was to endure a moral death of the worst sort. He suffered it for my sake. He had in truth become the fountain of life, giving righteousness to all who thirsted for it, while in turn being made the cesspool of all men's sin.

There was a long silence. Only low moans came to the ears of those who hovered fearfully in the foreboding darkness.

Then there burst from Him an anguished cry: *"My God, My God—why have You forsaken Me?"*

Some who heard it were startled. "He is calling for Elijah the prophet of old!" Again they raised a sponge of vinegar to His face on a slender reed. But He turned away from it. No human remedy was to be found for the anguish of His Spirit. How He recoiled from His own repulsiveness!

Like one separated from Himself, so He saw the sins of men laid upon Him now, dividing Him from His Father. It was an alienation unknown before. To taste this was to taste spiritual death for all men. To sense the forlorn and abhorrent aloneness of His Spirit was to enter a living hell. That hell was alienation from Himself, from God. Its anguish consumed Him.

The onlookers could not grasp how grim was this ordeal. Some even taunted Him: "Maybe Elijah will come and rescue You from Your torture—but it's not likely!"

What they did not know was that in drinking of this death, absorbing its penalty, He was demolishing the power of the Evil One who held men captive in fear of death. *He was drawing from death its dread.*

In His own Spirit He was exhausting, too, all the judgment of God against mortal sins of men.

"O death, where is your sting? O grave, where is your victory? . . . Thanks be to God who giveth us the victory through our Lord Jesus Christ!"

To those who stood close to the three crosses in the darkening hours, the events that followed one upon another appeared as a diabolical disaster. But in the realm of the eternal, great and mighty triumphs were taking place.

The Christ had not retreated from before the powers of death. He had experienced and entered fully into both moral and spiritual death of the first magnitude. He had done it deliberately and on the scale of the infinite. A way had been broken, shattered through all the ranks and ramparts of evil arrayed against Him.

With a shout of triumph He exclaimed, *"It is finished!"* The enormous transaction had taken place. All that He entered human history to achieve had been accomplished. Nothing more remained. By His perfect doing and perfect dying, full and wondrous redemption was available for all who would accept it. Not only redemption for the race of earthmen, but redemption for heaven and earth as well. God's rescue operation was complete.

Then in quiet repose, the anguish past, His noble head, though bruised and marred, was gently bowed. *"Father, into Your hands I commit My Spirit!"* It was the finale. Not the end of Christ. Not the end of God's Son. But the end of His role as God incarnate . . . the suffering servant . . . God in man . . . heaven's Sacrifice. With calm deliberation He dismissed His own Spirit from its earthly residence. The earthen temple was terminated. And now He tasted physical death.

There is a majestic mystery here. This death, too, could not hold Him. No more could it bind Him than could the forces of evil over which He triumphed in partaking of both moral and spiritual death. He was the victor. His body would not undergo decay. He stepped strongly through the doorway of death into a brand-new dimension of life. In so doing He opened a way for all of us who will receive Him!

CHAPTER FORTY

In the Shadow of the Cross

At the instant His Spirit was released, enormous repercussions reverberated through the earth. The forces both of men and nature were shaken. The Spirit of God, almighty in splendor, swept across the country with terrifying impact.

In Jerusalem, at the very heart and center of its religious life—in the holy of holies of the temple, in that innermost sanctuary where only the high priests dared to enter—there was a tremendous tearing, ripping sound. No such rending had ever shattered the silence of this inner sanctum before.

The great heavy temple veil was torn apart from top to bottom. Its dense, thick fabric woven of the finest, strongest linen was torn in half like tissue paper. There it hung open, revealing to all who cared to see, the sacred ark with its mercy seat.

This was a sight which up until this momentous hour had been reserved exclusively for the high priest, and then only once a year. He came then to enter the holy of holies on behalf of all the people. But God's greatest and final and last High Priest had once for all sacrificed Himself. And there was now no longer any need for an earthly priesthood of corruptible men. An incorruptible High Priest, our Living Lord, had entered once for all, forever, into the presence of God on our behalf.

It was a thrilling triumph!

Its meaning was not lost upon Annas, Caiaphas, or their associates. Their end had come. Naively, they had assumed earlier in the day that Christ's end had come. The opposite was true.

The Jewish priesthood from this time forward was merely an anachronism. It was a pathetic performance without content or meaning. No longer did anyone require their service to meet God at His mercy seat. Men now could come unashamedly, boldly into His presence through a new and ever-living intercessor—our Lord, the Christ.

What an emancipation! What a deliverance!

But not only was the society of men shaken at this cataclysmic hour. So was the very earth itself.

The hills of Judea and the sweeping valleys of Galilee, where the Master had tramped so many weary miles, shook and shuddered beneath the impact of a mighty quake. Perhaps it was a gigantic faulting of the ragged edges of the ancient Rift Valley. But in that frightening hour the fiercest of men were afraid. Great rock ridges were split apart. Deep dongas were opened up as the earth faulted and burst asunder. The houses of Jerusalem rocked under the earth tremor. Even the three crosses on Golgotha swayed eerily in the dim light.

The tough Roman centurion and his armed men were alarmed. They were men of might who knew power and respected force. Confronted with these cataclysmic events their pagan hearts panicked. "Truly, truly," they exclaimed, "this man was the Son of God!" They had crucified deity. It was a diatribe, a desecration, a dastardly offense they had committed.

The searching, seeking, questing heart of the Roman centurion was reassured that on the cross above Him was indeed *the Christ, the King of the Jews.* He had suspected this from the very beginning of Jesus' trial before Pilate. The beautiful behavior and brave conduct of Christ had made an enormous impact on his searching spirit. Never before had he seen a man die with such superb strength or serenity. Never had he witnessed an innocent man so wrongly accused or badly abused by his government and officers accept the penalty without recrimination. Only a God could conduct Himself with such enormous dignity!

As the centurion, cloaked in iron mail, looked up at Jesus, his hard heart was broken. Outside he was all metal. But within he was contrite in spirit, humbled in soul. He, a heathen officer, an emblem of a supposedly invincible empire, bowed his proud head in the darkness. He was the first gentile believer in the new Body of the Living Christ being formed on earth.

The earthquake shook open many mausoleums. Their walls were cracked, the barricaded doors were broken. The quickening Spirit of the Living Christ swept through them in energizing power. Corpses sprang to life. Saints long interred emerged from their deep sleep. It was a rerun of what happened to Lazarus, a preview of what the Master Himself was about to do in His own Resurrection. A new era of hope, life, and eager anticipation engulfed the entire unseen world. Christ was not dead. He was alive! Yet most of His closest intimates never knew it!

All that the tearstained women could see in the late afternoon light was a corpse upon a bloodstained cross. All that His despairing, discouraged disciples could understand at this pathetic point was total disaster and dismay. Their Master was dead. Their future was dark. Their dreams had crumbled to dust.

What now? Where would they go? What could they do?

Jesus had other friends and admirers in Jewry. But as so often happens in human affairs, they had not always acted in honor. There was Joseph of Arimathea, an immensely influential man in the Sanhedrin. For some unknown reason he had not been present at the dawn council that convened to condemn the "man from Galilee." If he had, no doubt he could have vetoed their dastardly decision. But he was simply not there to exert his influence. Why will never be known. Perhaps he feared a showdown. He feared for himself.

He was an ardent devotee of the Master. And as the long evening shadows began to cast themselves across the countryside he came privately to Pilate. He requested the privilege of taking his Master's body from the tree to embalm it with honor. Because of his great prestige in Jerusalem, Pilate could hardly deny him this request. Normally the Romans left the corpses of convicts on their crosses. Carrion eaters such as crows, vultures, jackals, hyenas, and scrounging dogs consumed the decomposing flesh of the victims.

If Jesus was indeed dead, then Pilate had no objection to His body's being given an honorable burial. After all, He was *the King of the Jews*—incognito.

He really would not run into opposition on this, even from those painful, pesky priests. For since it was the Passover Sabbath approaching, a very special day to them, they did not want it either polluted or contaminated by three corpses on crosses. Would he please, then, have them all removed? Everything, then, would seem to be just the same as ever, beautiful as though no bestiality had ever marred their cruel city or its environs. All of it was part and parcel of their perpetual, phony pretense.

So Pilate dispatched soldiers to carry out this assignment. In typical Roman cruelty they shattered the shin bones of the two criminals. Neither of them had yet fully expired. This final act of brutality was the shattering shock that generally brought sudden death.

But when they came to Jesus' body, they noticed life had left. It surprised them. How come He had died so quickly? They did not know, could not know, He had borne more than the agony of the cross. He carried with Him there, as well, the even more devastating cruelty of the sins of the world. His had been a double death. Yes, even more than that, a triple death of body, soul, and spirit.

In a ghoulish gesture of inhuman humiliation one of the soldiers plunged his Roman spear into the bleeding side of *the King of the Jews*. Commingled blood and body fluids spurted from around the sharp spearhead. It was the last act of violence to be perpetrated against a loving God.

In that act, prophecies more than a thousand years old were fulfilled in minute detail: "A bone of Him shall not be broken," and, "They looked on Him whom they pierced."

Satisfied that the requirements of Rome had been fulfilled, Pilate gave permission for Joseph of Arimathea to remove the remains from the cross.

Joseph was not the only "secret disciple" Jesus had. He was soon joined by Nicodemus, the one who at the start of his Master's public ministry, three years before, had come to interview Him secretly by night. He had been reluctant to declare his devotion to the Christ openly. His enormous wealth stood in the way. He was afraid to lose his money and possessions. He and Joseph were men of divided loyalties and divided affections. Both had betrayed the Master as much as any of His twelve young companions.

How much they could have helped His cause while He was alive! Now that it was too late, they had second thoughts. In their own stumbling, shaken, distraught way they tried hard to make amends for their gross omissions.

It was a touching scene. Two of Jerusalem's most distinguished leaders laboring in the darkening twilight to loosen the shattered remains of their Master from the horrible spikes. It was a revolting task. But it was carried out in tenderness. And, no doubt, the descending night hid copious tears falling from their tired old eyes.

Nicodemus brought a huge amount of embalming spices as well as long winding-sheets of pure white linen. Carefully, tenderly, they wrapped the body in layer upon layer of linen with lavish amounts of myrrh and aloes interspersed between. The noble head was bound round separately as though encased in a turban.

The corpse was carried away into a gorgeous, gleaming, brand-new mausoleum. It was situated in a pretty private garden. Such honors were reserved only for royalty. So, with great dignity, to the best of their ability, these were now bestowed on the Master.

The women from Galilee followed at a distance and marked the place where their beloved One had been interred.

So, too, had the priesthood. They were determined to prevent any chicanery: this deceiver's disciples would no longer be permitted to pervert the people. Receiving Pilate's consent they had the tomb sealed with his insignia. Then as a last precaution, a contingent of guards was set on watch.

For Jesus' friends and followers, that weekend marked the low-water mark of their lives. Never, never had their hopes and aspirations been at such a low ebb. Though the Master had always inspired them, always uplifted them, always given them enormous hope, always cheered and stimulated them with prospects of a new and wider dimension of life—nothing had come of it.

They seemed to be at a dead end.

Their legacy was despair.

Their future was dim.

They were gripped by fear.

They could see only defeat.

They felt only dismay.

As so often happens with us mortals, we tend to live only in the dimension and to the degree of our human feelings. We are governed and controlled by our physical senses and human emotions. Living by faith in the utter reliability of our Lord is a bit beyond us. We are victimized by our rationalization. We believe only what our senses tell us. Beyond this we dare not trust ourselves, much less trust God.

And so we do not see the great hand of God at work "behind the scenes," we cannot believe His mighty Spirit is active in energetic endeavors unknown to us. We are reluctant to concede that Christ can bring life out of death, light out of darkness, love—vibrant, dynamic love—out of despair.

And had anyone told these friends of Jesus what was actually happening in the unseen realms that weekend, they would not have believed.

Within sixty hours they would be shouting, *"He is alive! He is alive!"*

Within fifty days their little frightened band would be turning Jerusalem upside down like unleashed lions. In a single day three thousand new believers would be added to their numbers.

Within a few years all the known world would know of Jesus, the Christ. And within a century, pagan Rome would be a citadel of Christianity, bowing before Him . . . whom they had crucified!

CHAPTER FORTY-ONE

"He Is Risen!"

All during the Passover week despondency and darkness had thickened around the disciples. A steel ring of despair had closed in inexorably around the cross. It was as if all the forces of evil, the cohorts of hell, had been arrayed against them. They were a battered band who were sunk in sorrow and mourning for the Master. To them it seemed a dead end as they watched their Lord laid away in the garden grave.

Then came the first day of the new week.

What had transpired over the weekend they knew not.

God's great outstretched hand had been at work.

The forces of men and evil arrayed against Him had been thrown into total disarray.

A glorious conquest had been achieved by Christ. It was a victory that would revitalize His men, startle the world, and electrify all His followers in the centuries to come.

But during that dismal weekend Jesus' friends did not know this. They could not see the mighty hand of God at work behind the scenes of their despair. They did not detect the fact that this, their darkest hour, preceded the most majestic dawn of a new day in all their lives.

They were all devout Jews. The Sabbath had come. Being the Passover Sabbath it was especially sacred. True to tradition, they had remained quietly in their quarters. They were in small groups here and there, lodged in the city, waiting for the beginning of the new week to travel home. Many of the Master's friends had come down to Jerusalem all the way from Galilee for the great festival. This explains why people like Mary His mother, Mary Magdalene, and Mary the mother of James had been at the cross.

His frightened followers huddled in little knots in their rented rooms. Over and over they relived and recounted to each other the drastic events of the preceding week. Each had witnessed the final dreadful drama from a different perspective. So they sat, often in tears, deeply mourning, telling each other their tales of grief. Some of the weaker, emotional ones wrung their hands in despair. Others shook their heads, fighting back the burning tears that welled up in their eyes.

It seemed the religious leaders of Jerusalem and Judea had finally vanquished Christ and held the field.

The Master had met an ignominious end.

And for them there was no future.

It was back to the old life.

Back to boats for Peter and his pals.

A return to the regular, boring routine of home for the women.

What none of them knew was the titanic triumphs taking place out beyond the narrow horizons of their little selves. They could not see much beyond their tears and heartache. They were so preoccupied with their own personal problems and grief they could not grasp what was happening at the grave. They were sunk down in sadness. Outside, God was active in great glory.

The divine events of that weekend rival in majestic mystery those stupendous exchanges which took place at Calvary. They are beyond our human capacity to fully comprehend. It was God moving in enormous power, yet without public fanfare or display. It was God achieving His purpose, overwhelming every force set against Him, yet unwitnessed and unheralded except by angelic hosts.

Not for an instant should it be imagined that Christ lay inert in that tomb that weekend. Far from it! Death could not hold Him! The graveclothes with their myriad windings and heavy spices could not restrain Him! The great stone at the door could not stop Him! Decomposition and bodily decay could not taint or touch Him!

Quickened, enlivened, energized by God the Father, God the Spirit, and God the Son Himself, He simply cast off the constrictions surrounding Him. He was alive in a radiant new dimension of supernatural living, instantaneously.

No man's hands unwrapped those heavy spices around Him.
No man's hands unwound those windings that bound Him.
No man's hands removed the bindings about His face.
No man's hands loosed Him and let Him go.
No man's hands rolled the great rock door away.
No man's hands broke the seal set upon the tomb.
No man's hands struck the guards to the ground outside.
This was only and all the work of God!
It had gone on in the absence of human interference.

It was as though the divine chrysalis had quietly emerged from the confines of its cocoon, without splitting the case or disturbing the wrappings.

He simply was not there. He was risen.

He had enormous enterprises to engage His energies. He moved throughout the unseen spirit world ministering and manifesting Himself to those who had been imprisoned since the days of Noah.

And the only reason for opening the grave was not to release Him, but to reveal to His friends that *He is alive*.

There was a startling earthquake. It shook the tomb. It terrified the temple guards. The blinding presence of supernatural radiance from visiting angels overwhelmed the soldiers. They fell prostrate on the ground. Overcome with apprehension, they lay still, stunned with amazement, inert with fear.

It was a swift, resounding endorsement of all that had taken place at grim Golgotha. It was God's way of declaring Christ's work completed. It was the supernatural sign that He who died on the cruel cross was the Christ of God. It was confirmation to doubting men that God Himself had interposed His own life in their stead, dying that they might live.

Because of all this, the dramatic change that sweeps over the scene takes our breath away. Mourning turns to joy—inexpressible joy. Doubt and disbelief turn to wondrous assurance. Darkness turns to jubilant delight. *He is alive*.

Mary Magdalene and Mary the mother of James could scarcely sleep. Impatiently they tossed and turned on their lumpy pallets. At the sound of the first cockcrow, they got up. The dawn of the first day of the week was about to break. Quickly they gathered up the little bundles of spices they had prepared. Groping through the gloom, they stumbled along toward the mausoleum where they had watched Joseph and Nicodemus inter the Master.

Just remembering the scene brought tears. It was not easy to love anyone as much as they did, then lose Him. Especially in such a cruel, dreadful death.

Highly charged with emotion, blinded with grief, strung up with sorrow, it perhaps never occurred to them that they could not possibly roll the great stone door back from its opening. This was a task for big strong men.

But when they got to the grave the entrance was wide open. The sight startled them. They were afraid. A brilliant white presence spoke: "Fear not. You are looking for Jesus who was crucified. He is not here. He is risen!" It was impossible to believe. They threw their hands up to shield their eyes. The angel reassured them: "Come, see the place where the Lord lay. Remember? He said He would rise! Go quickly and tell His disciples."

The impact was one of commingled fear and joy.

Like a startled doe, Mary Magdalene raced away back to find Peter and John. Panting wildly, she blurted out to them, "They have taken away the Master. And we don't know where they have laid Him."

She couldn't grasp what had happened. She was so distraught with combined apprehension and hope that she was well-nigh incoherent. Not waiting for further details, Peter and John sped off.

Running hard, the two young men kept neck and neck most of the way. Their feet pounded hard in unison as they raced toward the tomb. Their breathing came in hot and heavy pants. Little by little, John, the younger of the two, pulled ahead of Peter.

A score of questions raced through their minds as they ran: Was Mary so overwrought with emotion that her mind had snapped? Could the high priests or elders have stolen the body so as to further mutilate the Master? Was it a last vile insult to add insult to injury? Where were the guards? If the Lord had indeed risen, where was He? Would they find Him? Could it really be He was alive?

Coming to the sepulcher first, John stooped quickly and glanced into the grave. Sure enough, Jesus was gone. Only the graveclothes remained. But the full impact of what he saw really did not register. He stood outside a bit dazed. He was Jesus' closest friend. This was tough to take.

Peter, big heavy Peter, came pounding into the garden. His great hairy chest was heaving. Sweat stood out on his brow. Hardly pausing, he pushed on past John at the door entering right into the tomb. He was determined to see all there was to see. What if it was the home of the dead.

Like John, his attention was arrested by the undisturbed graveclothes. They were lying there exactly as they had been wound around the Master's body. They were still enfolding the spices. They had simply collapsed slightly, like an empty cocoon. And separate from them, the head windings, like a collapsed turban rolled in a careful roll, lay exactly where the Master's head had rested.

John joined Peter inside. In amazement they both stood stunned by the sight. It was exactly as He had said. *He is risen.* He had simply moved out of the wrappings—out of the windings, out through the rock walls—in a transformed, spiritual body.

Then they believed!

It was enough. Now for the first time the ancient Scriptures were understood:

> Therefore my heart is glad, and my glory rejoiceth: my flesh
> also shall rest in hope. For thou wilt not leave my soul in hell;
> neither wilt thou suffer thine Holy One to see corruption.
>
> Psalms 16:9, 10

It all came home to them with great clarity. Now they knew. Now they were satisfied. Now they were overjoyed. *He is alive!* So they turned back and left the empty tomb.

Mary Magdalene, meanwhile, came back. She stood outside the

sepulcher sobbing softly. Somehow she was still terribly confused. Tormenting questions tumbled frantically through her fevered mind: He was gone, but where had He gone? Who had taken Him? Why did they do it? Where had they put Him? If He was alive, where could she find Him?

In blind hope she stooped down and stared into the tomb again. Two angels were there, one sitting where her Lord's head had rested, the other where His feet had been. When asked why she wept still, her reply was that her Master had been removed and she did not know where to find Him.

Gingerly, almost ashamedly, she withdrew from the mausoleum. Then turning around she saw someone whom she assumed was the gardener. Gently He asked, "Why are you weeping? Whom are you looking for?"

In her grief she did not recognize her Lord. "If it is you who have taken Him away," she pleaded softly, "tell me where, so I can take care of Him." She burst out sobbing.

Jesus then spoke her name: "Mary." It was the voice of old. The syllables were sweet, familiar, tender and reassuring. It was He!

"Rabboni!" she exclaimed, startled—*"My Lord! My Master!"* This was the loftiest adulation she could confer on Him.

In ecstasy she would have flung herself at His feet. In rapture of recognition she would have embraced Him, washing His feet with her tears, toweling them with her hair, just as she had done long ago in the house of Simon the Pharisee.

But He would not allow her to touch Him.

From this day on Mary would no longer live in her emotions. She would no longer be governed by her feelings. She would live by implicit, unfaltering faith in Him. He was totally trustworthy, absolutely reliable.

Jesus looked at her tenderly and with enormous empathy. "Go to My brothers—those fellows who though they tried so hard to follow Me to the end, failed so often; yes, My brothers—and tell them I ascend to My Father and your Father, and to My God and your God!"

Oh, what condescension! Oh, what graciousness! Oh, what incredible generosity!

Mary raced away to find the disciples. She had seen Jesus. She had spoken with the Master. He is alive. He is here. He has a wondrous bit of great good news for His forlorn friends.

She was the first missionary of the new era. And with winged feet she flew away to find her friends and share the good news that ". . . *He is alive!*"

But like all missionaries who have followed her during the ensuing twenty centuries, Mary found that she was not fully believed. Her glowing account of her encounter with the risen Christ seemed, to some, as idle tales. In fact they may have felt the poor woman's mind had been overtaxed by the recent tragedy.

It is the artlessness, the candor with which the events of that Resurrection day are reported that convince one of their validity. Distraught, grief-stricken men and women overcome with emotion are suddenly galvanized with gladness and joy. Their instantaneous transformation from victims of tragedy to participants in triumph are well-nigh unbelievable. Some of those who did not actually see the Master or go into the deserted tomb would have liked to believe but could not. As Thomas was to declare boldly later on, he needed absolute tangible, empirical evidence that the thrilling stories being circulated were true.

These followers of Jesus were an excited crowd. It was obvious that supernatural events of some sort had occurred. What was difficult for them to understand at this point was that their Lord had not come back to life in the same way that Jairus' daughter had, or the son of the widow of Nain, or even Lazarus. Each of these resurrections had simply restored the individual to his or her former earth life. They had been brought back into correspondence with their earth environment.

The Master's Resurrection was the first occurrence in human history of an individual's rising into a brand-new dimension of life not in any way dependent upon earth for survival or sustenance. The Lord's body was utterly unique, diametrically different from that ever present before amongst men. He was no longer restricted in any sense by the time/space concepts of earthmen. He could appear and disappear at will. He could pass unhindered through the rock walls of a tomb or through the stone walls of a house. He did not depend on earth's environment for nourishment or bodily sustenance. Yet He could eat and relish bread, honey, and fish. He could appear as an apparition, unknown and unrecognized by His former intimates. Or He could speak in His old familiar tones and present Himself as their dearly beloved friend, marked with all the scars of the cross. Distance was of no consequence. In an instant His spiritual body could be here then suddenly gone. Likewise, the reverse was true.

It is not the least surprising that such unusual behavior really baffled His followers at first. Never before had human beings ever seen or heard of such conduct. They were totally unprepared for it. It was impressive, somewhat disturbing, even frightening at times, and certainly almost unbelievable.

In His generous and gracious way the Master was to spend nearly six weeks appearing and reappearing to His friends. Sometimes it was in Judea, sometimes in Galilee. At times it was indoors, at other times outdoors in old well-loved settings. Eventually over five hundred of His associates had seen Him in person, heard Him speak, and thus became convinced of His presence amongst them . . . no longer as the Son of man in mortal guise, but as The Lord of Glory in spiritual attire.

But outside His immediate circle of acquaintances, ugly and underhanded tactics were used to discredit what had transpired. The struggle for truth still went on. The ranks of the religious leadership of the times were determined to destroy the evidence of His Resurrection.

The guard which had been commissioned to keep watch at His grave had been utterly overwhelmed by the earthquake and dazzling arrival of the angels. Frightened and mesmerized by the unexpected display of divine power, they fell prostrate outside the mausoleum. All their military might and power was helpless. They could do nothing to prevent what took place. Like little lead soldiers, they lay flat on their faces, inert, while the forces of the eternal God carried out His sovereign design.

Though the Master had declined to ask for angels to assist Him that awful night He was lynched by the mob, He did not mind at all their presence at His vacated tomb. They were incontestable evidence, both to the women who came and to the smitten soldiers, that God was in action here.

When later in the day the angels had withdrawn and these would-be tough mercenaries had picked themselves up from the ground, they realized they were in a dreadful dilemma. The empty tomb could cost them their heads. Men were not set on watch just for fun. They had been sent there to prevent the very thing that happened. It was a dereliction of duty. Death was the penalty.

Trembling, and now doubly afraid for their very lives, some of them marched back into Jerusalem to report the events to the chief priests. It was a ticklish situation. The consequences could be calamitous. Would they be believed?

Strange as it seems, they were. In the depths of their hard old hearts the high priests and elders must have suspected all along that they had indeed been dealing with divinity in their conflict with Christ. This makes their conduct even more despicable. And now when the guard reported that this One had indeed risen from the dead in a miraculous way, they were believed by the authorities.

To forestall this from becoming common knowledge the ecclesiastics decided on deception. Their record in dealing with Jesus was already so black, they really could not darken it much further. If they had the soldiers put to death it would be a public admission of divine intervention. The whole populace would be alerted to the fact that the prophet from Galilee was in truth God very God because of His supernatural Resurrection.

So they resorted to cunning subterfuge. They would bribe the guard to lie about what happened. Instead of telling the truth, they were hired to circulate the falsehood that they had slept on duty. And while they slept, the Master's men had slipped in to spirit His body away. The soldiers would be their scapegoats.

It was a pathetic ploy. The only thing that influenced the soldiers to so discredit themselves and tarnish their own reputations was the huge sum of money offered to buy them off. But even in this there lay an enormous risk. When word got back to Pilate that the seal of Rome had been broken without permission, their very lives would again be in jeopardy.

The crafty old priests felt sure even Pilate could be bought off. If he began to make noises and protest the performance, they would oil his palm with enormous sums from the temple treasury. Even a Roman governor was not above intrigue and bribery.

These malicious men had cunningly congratulated themselves on buying Christ's betrayal for a mere thirty pieces of silver from Judas. But it cost them uncounted thousands to try to conceal the fact of His Resurrection. And then they failed! Men eternally try to play their petty games with God and ever end up the losers.

Matthew, who had always had so much to do with money, later reported how this false tale was commonly current in the country. Yet despite their most despicable efforts, these priests and elders were to see their city electrified by the Resurrection on the day of Pentecost, only a few weeks later: electrified by the fearless preaching of Peter, who now had seen his Master risen—Peter, who had known complete restoration; Peter, who moved now in the power and energy of the resurrection life of His risen Lord.

CHAPTER FORTY-TWO

Jerusalem in Ferment

Before Jerusalem experienced the great visitation of God by His gracious Spirit at Pentecost it was like a hot pot of humanity seething with ferment. Counteracting crosscurrents of conflicting reports boiled beneath the surface of its sophistication. Enormous issues were at stake. And though the Christ had been crucified, somehow He simply had not been stilled. He was present in spiritual form amongst His followers. Far from being neutralized by the authorities, He remained as much at work as ever.

Evidence of this was brought back into the city that morning by a number of women who, along with Mary Magdalene, had been to the ornate mausoleum. They were returning to share the news of the Lord's Resurrection with His disciples when He accosted them along the way.

The encounter, so unexpected yet so familiar, with His old hearty greeting, "All hail!" overwhelmed their racing hearts and fluttering emotions. In adoration they fell at His feet on the dusty road, worshiping in awe and wonder. He is alive!

The Master's words, as always to His own, were warm, reassuring: "Be not afraid!" He smiled at them tenderly. He understood it was well-nigh impossible for them to believe it was really He. "Please go tell My brothers, My beloved Eleven, that I'll meet them back up in Galilee."

In commingled joy and disbelief that they had really seen Him, the women remained momentarily prostrate at His feet in worshipful submission. Here indeed they were in the presence of their living, eternal, indestructible deity. At His birth, shepherds and wise men had bowed before Him as a babe. Now at His rebirth, women who had become His intimates recognized His divinity and bowed before Him in worship.

Quickly they, too, like Mary Magdalene, scurried off to scatter the exciting good news to their friends and all of Jesus' followers. The word swept through the city, borne on the whispered lines of underground communication: "The Lord is risen! We have seen Him! He has spoken to us! We have touched Him! He is going to have a grand reunion in dear old Galilee."

It hardly seemed possible. It was hope and cheer. They needed that just now, because other black, ominous, threatening reports were also reaching their ears.

The religious authorities were in a rage. Their cruel, crafty designs in crucifying Jesus of Nazareth had boomeranged. Just three days before, the priests, elders, and Pharisees were dead sure they had silenced this "deceiver." They had Him on a cross. They had taunted Him there with cruel jests. But somehow they just had not had the last word.

First there came the unsettling report from their own mercenaries that He had escaped the tomb.

Then the disturbing news that angels and an earthquake had opened the mausoleum.

Perhaps for them the most frightening aspect was the forbidden breaking of the Roman seal. Pilate would be furious.

For this someone would have to die. No one flouted Rome's might without devastating consequences.

Of course they could placate Pilate with princely sums of bribing money. It would practically bankrupt them to do it.

The soldiers who sold their own reputations would circulate falsehoods. They would claim that this little frightened, furtive band of eleven lads had stolen the body. The absurdity of it didn't matter: To think that in spite of the dreadful consequences of breaking a Roman seal they would dare such a steal. Of course not!

But to make their story stick, the authorities now were bound to pursue and prosecute these innocent men. Since they broke the seal, it was they who would have to die. How terrible is the downward trail of deception.

And now to compound their dilemma even further, word filtered through to the ecclesiastics that in very truth He whom they had crucified was very much alive. The first of their members to hear of this would no doubt have been Joseph and Nicodemus, who had interred His body. In their half ignorance they had bestowed on the Master what they considered a dignified burial. But one doesn't just bury God! Simply stating that He is dead does not make Him so! Men in their pathetic pride have tried that little game many times. Unfortunately for them, God just doesn't disappear that easily. He doesn't just go away.

So the Sanhedrin was in an awful stir. He is alive! And for the Sadducees, this was a mortal blow. They had always scorned resurrection. It just could not be. Yet here Christ, the Crucified One, was risen. All their finest and most intricate objections had been confounded. And so confusion was heaped upon confusion.

Politically there were tremendous issues at stake. If Pilate was bribed and Caesar ever discovered it, either the governor or Jerusalem would have to go. Caesar would tolerate no such chicanery. Eventually both Pilate and this perverted city perished beneath his cruel hand.

Economically, the ecclesiastical hierarchy faced ruin. They had paid only a pittance, the price of a mere slave in the market, for the Saviour of mankind. But now they were shelling out enormous sums to silence their accomplices in crime. And for years to come it would cripple them financially. Their temple coffers and own private fortunes would be hard hit.

Socially and religiously, the ruling priesthood were to be utterly discredited. Too many undeniable reports kept coming in from irrefutable sources that Jesus had been seen. He had spoken to His followers. He shared meals with them. And because of all this the blood ran cold, and black fear gripped this grim city.

Because the Passover Sabbath was past, pilgrims began to leave for home. The streams of flowing humanity that had converged on the city the week before were now reversed. Hordes of visitors spilled out of the great gates. Columns of caravans, little knots of family groups, and occasional pairs of pilgrims started off down the hot roads that led to faraway places. In a matter of a few hours, that first day of the week, Jerusalem would be almost emptied of its excited, festive throngs.

For most of the pilgrims this had been the most unusual Passover. Even for the very aged who had come up to Jerusalem faithfully year after year there had never been a festival to quite match this one for color, excitement, hope, despair, and bewilderment.

The week before the milling masses were sure the Messiah had come. In jubilation they joined their voices in shouting, "Hosanna to God in the highest!" For a day or two it looked as though the King had come. How they thrilled to the towering figure of the flaming prophet from Galilee as He taught in the temple!

Then, somehow, in some strange way, the whole atmosphere had suddenly changed. This "deliverer" had been delivered by some scoundrel into the hands of the authorities. Between the priests and the hated Pilate, He had been brought to trial, charged with sedition, and suddenly crucified. In stark horror they saw three crosses outside the city walls, silhouetted against the eastern sky. Somehow it just didn't make sense. Must good always be offered as a sacrifice to evil? Must the poor ever perish?

And now suddenly this first day of the new week, rumors were flying fast and freely that this One, crucified, was alive. Some had been to the tomb and found it vacated. The graveclothes, undisturbed, were still there, but the body was gone. Angels, an earthquake, sightings of the Master, His intimate conversations with various women—all made people wonder. Nothing like this had ever been seen or heard of before in all of Israel's history. How much could a man believe?

Two men traveling down the rocky road to Emmaus, their heads bowed and close together, were discussing all of this. "And we thought implicitly, He was the Redeemer." They tugged at their beards and shrugged their shoulders in despairing wonder.

At this point they were joined by a third person who had overheard their conversation. He questioned them closely why they should be so disturbed. They seemed surprised at His apparent ignorance of the exciting events of the previous week. Perhaps He was a total stranger? Little did they realize their companion was the central figure in the great drama.

The Master, remaining incognito, allowed them to recount all that had transpired. "We had trusted that it was He who would redeem Israel." They shook their heads in dismay. "Some women who were at His grave at dawn claim that He is alive. Several disciples went to see—and sure enough the tomb was empty, but they didn't see Him."

The Master picked up the conversation. With tremendous force and vehemence He went back over the ancient record of God's dealing with Israel. He pointed out the prophecies relating to Himself. The Scriptures burned with the fire of truth. The men began to wonder at their own unbelief.

Reaching their humble home they invited their unknown companion to come in and share a simple meal with them. Taking a bit of bread in His hands He blessed it, broke it, and handed it to them. In an instant they saw and recognized their royal guest. He is here. He is alive. Then He is gone.

Without delay they set off to retrace the seven miles back to Jerusalem. They simply had to share the good news with their friends. Charged with excitement, they rushed into the home where Jesus' eleven men were still huddled together. "He is risen! He is risen!" they exclaimed. "We have walked with Him. We have talked with Him. *He is alive!*"

CHAPTER FORTY-THREE

The Master's Reunion With His Men

The Master's young men were torn with misgivings. Most of them had had enough of Jerusalem. It was such a cruel and forbidding city. They had come here again and again, always to encounter caustic confrontations. Always there had been conflict between their Lord and the religious leaders. And at last it looked as though they themselves had become the great losers.

They had lost their careers for the Christ.

They had lost their comfortable old lives.

They had lost their leader.

They had lost credibility . . . or had they?

Most of them were eager to join the throngs leaving the city. They were keen to get back to their familiar old haunts in Galilee. The rolling hills, the open plains, and the sweet sight of the lake lying blue beneath the northern skies would be a balm to their bruised and battered spirits.

On the other hand there were all these various reports that came drifting back to them about the Master. Obviously He was no longer a corpse in the tomb. Peter and John had seen the empty graveclothes and believed He had risen. Mary Magdalene and the other women had actually seen and talked to Him, or at least claimed this. Highly charged, emotional women cannot always be believed. It might be pure fantasy or wishful thinking. Then came Cleopas and his friend to report that they had actually walked, talked, and dined with Him.

Because of this the men felt unsure, wondering if perhaps they shouldn't stay around Jerusalem just a little longer in case He did want to make Himself known to them.

It was dangerous! They were marked men. Because of the false report that they had dared to smash the seal of Rome on the tomb, their lives were in jeopardy. Fearfully they huddled in their quarters.

Then suddenly He stood amongst them. In His quiet, strong, low, level tones He greeted them: "Peace be unto you!"

They were terrified. His unexpected appearance made them jumpy. Their hearts pumped hard. Their pulses raced. Their eyes dilated with apprehension. Some of them threw up their arms to shield their faces. Others drew back from Him in alarm.

This was surely an apparition . . . a spirit being!

Not since the night of the great storm on the lake, when Jesus had come to them walking across the wind-whipped waves, had they been so distraught. *Is this really the Master?* was the question that raced through all their minds.

They simply were not sure.

Then He spoke again: "Why are you so troubled?" He looked at them with affection. "Why do questions arise in your minds?" He stretched His hands toward them in a gesture of goodwill and reassurance. "See, My wounded hands and feet. It is I Myself." He smiled warmly and invited them to touch Him. "Handle Me; see I am not just a spirit being. I have a body of flesh and bones!"

The Master's gracious gesture overwhelmed them with commingled gladness and misgiving. Gently they ran their hands over His hands, their fingers over His feet. Sure enough, it was their friend! The same old strong muscles and stout sinews were there.

It was true, yet it was not true. He is here. Yet it seemed too good to be true. Broad smiles wreathed their worried faces. They grinned with glee, gazing into His great eyes with sheer joy. They slapped one another on the back and shook their heads in wonderment. *"He is alive!"* They kept repeating the phrase to each other in excited syllables: *"He is alive!"*

To further confirm the tangibility of His person, Jesus asked for something to eat. Quickly they placed before Him some broiled fish along with a sweet piece of wild honeycomb. It was their favorite fare. And He too relished the simple meal.

It was too bad only ten of His eleven men were there for this festive reunion. Thomas was out. So he missed the chance to touch the Master and watch Him eat. But, no matter. In due course, he too would have his turn. For really, he was no more of a doubter or skeptic than any of these ten who had been so taken aback.

Jesus enjoyed His meal. He separated the sweet tilapia flesh from the bones. He munched happily on the waxy honeycomb. It was a delicious combination. Then He began to discuss one or two spiritual issues with His fellows.

As of old, He carefully reiterated the validity and authenticity of the Old Testament writers: Moses in the Pentateuch, David and the other poets in the Psalms, the great prophets in their predictions— all had foretold accurately the events of His birth, childhood, life, ministry, death, and Resurrection.

What He was trying to have them see was that in very truth He Himself was the fulfillment of all the ancient prophecies of their people. Not only had He accomplished and carried out in precise detail all those predictions, but also—even more—He was the actual embodiment of the *Word* spoken. He was *the Word made flesh!*

When this realization dawned upon their dull hearts and awakened their slumbering spirits it was a tremendous stimulation to them. He, their Master, their Lord, their God, was the enfleshment of *the Word*. That Word had been from the beginning with God. That Word was God. That Word was the very articulation of the express person of God, first in human language, now in human form. That Word was now completed. It was fulfilled. They had seen it lived out in its entirety in a human body. It was the visible expression of the invisible God.

This was He who had dwelt amongst them, who at this very hour sat with them, talked with them, ate with them, shared a meal with them. And they saw His character, His conduct, His Glory, as that of God the Father, full of grace and truth, the express image of God's person!

This was God, very God, who gave His life that men might live.

This One they had seen, heard, and handled. This One they would bear witness to with unabashed bravery the rest of their days. *He is alive!*

It was eight days, eight long days of waiting and wondering intermingled with joy and gladness, before Jesus again appeared amongst His men. This time all eleven were assembled together behind locked doors. Thomas was amongst them.

It had been a trying week for Thomas. He had felt very much out of things. His ten young companions were all excited about having seen the Master alive. It was all they could talk about, it seemed. Whereas for him, the last memory he had of the Lord was when he saw Him hanging on the cross, a corpse, later to be taken down and laid away in a grave.

Thomas had always been a bit of a pessimist. He was inclined to see the dark side of things. He was sure when Jesus announced the last time that He would return to Jerusalem after Lazarus died that all of them would be killed there. And certainly they came close to it the night the Master was lynched by the mob. It was only by a hairbreadth that any of them escaped. And even now they were under surveillance.

During Jesus' last discourse with them that fatal night He had said He was going to prepare a place for them all. "Don't let your hearts be troubled; you believe in God, believe also in Me." Words that should have reassured Thomas only served to deepen his despair.

Thomas had expressed deep skepticism: "Lord, we don't know where You are going; and how can we possibly know the way?"

In reply the Master reiterated truths which somehow still escaped this young cynic—truths which since then have polarized uncounted millions of men and women: "I am the way, the truth, and the life; no man cometh unto the Father, but by Me." At this point in his life Thomas was still not at all sure such a way existed.

Over and over he had protested to his pals: "Unless I shall actually see in His hands the imprints of the spikes, and put my finger into them, and thrust my whole hand into the gaping spear wound in His torso, *I will not believe!*"

He always said this with a certain self-assured vehemence. He was almost cocky about it. He was from Missouri; he simply had to be shown. If the Master was indeed alive, empirical evidence would have to be supplied before he would believe.

As in Christ's life, as in His death, so also in His Resurrection, men demand positive proof of His deity. They insist that somehow they be convinced of His reality. In ignorance and pride they still expect God to be subjected to the test of their finite senses. It is of course a colossal conceit and an outrageous absurdity, but always men do it.

Even in this so-called enlightened twentieth century, skeptics and cynics call blatantly for God to undergo the so-called scientific method of ascertaining His reality. In blindness they bray that only if He can be measured by our fallible five senses can He be known. How then shall hope, love, cheer, goodwill, beauty, faith, loyalty, justice, integrity, peace, or courage be placed in a laboratory retort or under a microscope for human analysis? How can they be measured, weighed, or defined? Yet these are the greatest realities in the universe. They are the very essence of the character of Christ. In short, they are God.

The modern skeptic in his scientific arrogance who boldly insists "Show me God!" who taunts and jeers his fellows with "Prove God to me!" is but the counterpart of Thomas, who protested again and again, "Unless I touch Him with my hands, I shall never trust."

To so speak is a monumental affront to God. He is fully aware of men's skepticism. He hears the puny challenges flung at Him. And the Master had known every protest poor young Thomas had ever made. Yet, in spite of it all, He came to him in peace and goodwill again. This is always His way!

Suddenly this evening the Master was standing there once again amongst His men. He had come unannounced through closed doors. "Peace be unto you!" What a comforting greeting! It set everyone at ease.

This time the young fellows were not afraid. Their best friend was back. It was so good to sense His presence, to hear His hearty voice, to know He was there.

Only Thomas was a bit taken aback. It was a bit embarrassing to be the only one there who felt a little ill at ease.

Jesus looked straight at him. "Thomas . . . ." His name alone when spoken with such affection was enough to melt the young fellow. "Thomas, stretch out your hand. Touch the nail prints in My hands with your forefinger. Place the palm of your hand in the opening in My wounded side.'' As He spoke He beckoned to the blushing young man. "Don't be without simple faith in Me, my boy. Just believe!''

It was too much for Thomas.

He didn't need to touch the nail prints.

He didn't have to feel the flesh wounds.

It was enough. The Master is here. *He is alive!*

There burst from Thomas an ecstatic exclamation of unabashed belief: *"My Lord! My God!"* Without a shred of embarrassment he knew that he stood in the presence of deity. This is God: He has come: *Rabboni!*

Quietly, without reproach or recrimination, Jesus remarked, "Thomas, you have believed because you have seen Me. Millions upon millions who never set mortal eyes on Me will still believe. They are fortunate!''

In that room that night Thomas was transformed: from a skeptic to an unshakable believer. With the assurance "He is alive," he was to take the great news of the risen Lord as far as India. He was no longer the weak-kneed cynic. A fearless saint, his life for God was to minister to millions in the great subcontinent of Asia.

CHAPTER FORTY-FOUR

Breakfast by the Lake

In accordance with the Master's wishes, His men had returned to Galilee. He had told Mary Magdalene and the other women who came to the tomb that He was looking forward to happy reunions with His friends in their old familiar haunts in the north. Only one detailed account, out of the many happy occasions on which they met during those final forty days, has been left to us.

John, the aged apostle, now a beloved and venerated leader, in concluding his story of Jesus makes this so clear. He reiterates twice over that the Lord performed many signs and miracles in the presence of His followers during this brief interval between His Resurrection and Ascension. He insists that they were so numerous it would be well-nigh impossible to record them all. But those reported were recorded in detail, that anyone reading them might believe in the reality of the Living Lord who moved amongst His people so freely.

For the disciples it was a delight to be back home again. The dark events of the Passover week in Jerusalem were like a dreadful dream. It was a positive relief to be away from the fierce hostility of Jerusalem. Once more they could hold their heads high with assurance and breathe more easily in the relaxed surroundings of their home villages.

Galilee was home to these men. It was the region of their births and carefree boyhood days. They loved the gaiety and good cheer of the north country. Their humble little whitewashed houses clustered around the Lake of Galilee were full of joy. The lap of the water on the beach and the rustle of the wind in the reeds were soporific sounds that soothed their souls. The flaming sunsets and sunrises, the sight of sails catching the breeze were balm to their spirits. The gentle rocking of the boats and the aroma of the fishnets drying in the sun set them at ease. It was good to be back!

Amid all these old familiar sights and sounds it seemed that somehow they could just go back to their same old life again. It would appear to be the natural, normal thing to do. But it simply was not so. After a personal and profound encounter with the Christ, men and women are never the same again. Something very deep within the spirit has been touched and transformed. So once the hand is set to the plow, and the feet have walked in the opening furrow of a new life of following the Master, one does not turn back.

No, it just is not that easy.

But the disciples thought it was. They thought they could.

One morning, Peter in bluff and blunt language boldly asserted again: "I'm going fishing!" Because of his charisma and innate leadership, whatever he suggested the others quickly followed. "We'll go with you!" half a dozen of them chorused.

So back to the lake. Back to the nets. Back to the boat. Back to the old skills and tricks of taking tilapia from the dark waters.

It was hot and heavy work. The night was still. Warm desert air hung on the lake. Stripped naked, the seven men strained and sweated at the oars all night. Raising and lowering the great heavy nets was hard toil, made doubly hard when every time they hauled in, not a single thrashing fish was caught in the mesh. The fellows cursed their poor luck. They were fed up with frustration.

Persistently they tried all their old fishing tricks. They moved out into deep water. They shot the net near the shore. They lowered it both port and starboard. But all to no avail. They were skunked. Nothing worked. And the longer they toiled, the more tired they became.

A faint glow began to lighten the sky over the eastern desert hills. The fellows knew dawn was near. Slowly they began to head back toward the beach.

In the dim gray light they could see the flickering flames of a small fire on the pebble beach. Someone was moving around it. Suddenly He cupped His hands around His mouth and shouted to them across the quiet waters.

"Lads, have you had any luck?" The sounds came to them clearly, amplified by the smooth surface of the water.

"No!" was the abrupt reply. This was followed by low, muted, mumbled sounds of grumbling.

"Then shoot your net to starboard!" the stranger shouted. "There's a school of fish there."

Without protesting or arguing they flung the net fiercely with their tired arms. It arced out in a beautiful circle, falling in a perfect pattern on the still lake. There was a gentle splash as it sank swiftly beneath the surface. Then almost instantly the fishermen could feel the tug and strain of big strong fish thrashing about in the mesh.

The great weight of fish struggling in the net was an exciting sensation. Seldom if ever had any of the men felt such a strain on their gear. What a tremendous catch! It was impossible to even haul aboard!

This was an absolute miracle!

What all their old tricks of the trade, all their skills and techniques, all their toil and labor had failed to achieve, this stranger on the shore had accomplished at a single stroke.

Suddenly it dawned on John.

"It's the Lord!" he ejaculated to Peter. "It's bound to be the Master!"

Immediately Peter knew John was right. It had to be Jesus. In his usual impetuous way he grabbed up his rough tunic, flung it on and jumped overboard. The boat was only about a hundred yards from the beach. Peter went thrashing towards the shore with powerful strokes. The other six fellows struggled at the oars to haul the net gradually to shallow water, dragging it on the bottom.

For Peter this was the pinnacle of his lifetime career as a fisherman. He had never, never known such a haul. Stunned, silent, saying nothing, he stood quietly beside the glowing embers with his Master. It was a moving moment. The last time he had been beside a small fire he had bitterly denied this One who was with him now.

It didn't seem to matter how much one abused Him, He still

came back. He was still there to forgive and forget and restore. This could only be God!

By now the six struggling lads in the boat had brought the catch right into the gently shelving beach. "Go out and help bring them in," the Master nodded, His head turned toward the boat. Peter complied at once. Wading out to his waist, he grabbed the net in his huge strong fists and drew it up onto the beach. It was an incredible sight. The silver horde thrashed about furiously, but the net was not torn. Though it was dragged on the bottom, not a fish escaped—nor did a single skein separate under the strain.

The fishermen's faces were flushed with excitement. Their eyes glowed with wonder as they grabbed up fish after fish to free it from the net. Every one was a prize catch. There was not an undersized fish in the lot. One hundred and fifty-three superb tilapia lay stretched out on the shore, glistening silver in the rising sun.

The young men, inwardly excited, were outwardly subdued. They had never seen anything like it. Gently they pulled their boat up on the beach. Then they carefully rinsed their scaly hands in the lake.

"Come and have some breakfast!" Jesus motioned them toward the fire, a gentle smile playing across His face. There was fish baked to a beautiful brown, and warm fresh bread for them to feast on. What a banquet for ravenous young men.

The seven men were really very shy. It seemed strange. They knew who their host was, yet somehow the former familiarity was no longer appropriate. Their usual banter and bravado were subdued and gone. They were dining with the Master. He was no longer just their Jesus of Nazareth—He was their Lord of Glory, their *Living Lord:* God very God. *Rabboni!*

In His usual, gracious, gentle, humble way Jesus moved amongst His friends serving them the delicious fish and fragrant bread. None of them dared ask point-blank if He really was the Lord of Glory—because they knew. They knew unmistakably that only He could or would ever arrange things so wonderfully. Only He cared so much for them. Only He fully understood their fallible natures. Only He could draw out the best in them. Only He could now call them to a new life of commitment from which they would never flinch again.

It was on this warm spring morning, beside this beautiful lake, that at last they were prepared to abandon forever all that they loved and held dear.

Several times before the Master had called them from this lake. Their response had always been a positive one. They had left their lake, their boats, their nets, and even their families to follow Him. Yet somehow, in a peculiar way, they had inevitably drifted back again. But now no more. This morning they had crossed their Rubicon. There was no more going back . . . no more turning back. The lake had played them false and let them down that night. But the Master, as always, made good on His commitment to them. Again He had proved totally trustworthy.

"Simon Peter," Jesus addressed the big fisherman directly, "Peter, do you love Me? Do you love Me more than anything else?" Three times the searching question was put to the bold, bluff fellow. He sat on a boulder, tossing small pebbles into the lake, half ashamed, half glad, awkward in answering.

Three times Peter protested his affection and utter devotion to the Master. It was not easy to be scrutinized this way. "Yes, Lord!" he reiterated three times, "You know I love You." The third time Peter was grieved. "Lord," he protested vehemently, his eyes filling with scalding tears, "You know all things; You know all my strengths, all my weaknesses; You know the worst; You know the best about me. You know I really, really do love You!"

Peter's great heart of love and affection was full and overflowing for the Master that morning. He was drawn out to the Christ in utter self-abandonment that he had never known before. He was willing to abandon the boat, the fishing, the lake, his gentle life in Galilee, his very self for his Lord.

It no longer mattered to Peter now what he was asked to do or where he was asked to go. He would no longer be the blustering fisherman. He was to become the strong shepherd who was to care for a little flock. He would no longer spend his life in the gentle atmosphere of Galilee. He would be the champion of the emerging new Church that would grow underground in the grim ghettos of Jerusalem, Rome, and the dreadful cities of Asia Minor.

The Master tried to prepare the strong-muscled man for this:

"No longer will you just buckle up your big belt and wander where you like as before, Peter." Jesus put a hand on his strong shoulder. "Rather, under the direction and impulse of My Presence, by My Spirit, you will be carried into all kinds of impossible places to achieve great, impossible things you would never volitionally choose to do yourself!"

That still, warm morning beside the shiny lake, Peter and his companions absolutely and irrevocably abandoned themselves to Christ. He in turn abandoned Himself to them for all time.

CHAPTER FORTY-FIVE

The Commissioning

At least twice during the interval between His Resurrection and His final Ascension, our Lord took care to commission His men with their lifework. The supernatural enterprise which He had initiated on earth was to be carried on and expanded under them. There was to be a splendid, ongoing continuity to the divine endeavor of God to redeem men.

This was no random arrangement. Rather it was a plan conceived carefully in the councils of heaven. It was God the Father's own unique and wondrous scheme whereby His work in the world from now on would be achieved, not by His Son as a single servant to suffering humanity but by many servants indwelt by His own gracious Spirit.

The Master made this very clear the first night in Jerusalem when He appeared to His ten frightened friends. Thomas was absent that evening. After reassuring them who He was, Jesus spoke to them earnestly and clearly about their responsibilities: "As the Father has sent Me into the world, so likewise now, I am sending you out into the society of men."

Of course it is not hard to understand why they would find this assignment somewhat overwhelming. At this point they were a rather pathetic little group of timid, frightened men. Their very lives were in jeopardy. Their strong, great leader had left them very much on their own. Instead of His life culminating in a glorious coronation, it had appeared to terminate tragically on a tree. Rather than becoming the outstanding leaders of a victorious, revolutionary new earthly empire, they found themselves a harried band of believers viewed as vagabonds. The outlook was anything but promising, the future very fragile, and their aspirations exceedingly tenuous.

That evening in that borrowed room their Christ had commissioned them for an assignment far surpassing their wildest dreams. Had they known then what the next few weeks would produce, their hopes would have soared and their spirits would have been electrified. But some of them still doubted.

The Master looked around at them with enormous empathy. They had tried so hard to be loyal to Him. They had shown Him so much affection in their own crude, rough way. They had demonstrated to a degree that they were capable of greatness. He had brought out the best in their behavior by His presence with them. He had shared so many of the exciting aspects of His own hopes and desires for the world with them. A new order of righteousness was being established on earth. The kingdom of God, the gracious government of God by His Spirit, was being initiated in human hearts.

Gazing upon them He sighed deeply. The momentous hour for the commencement of this new spiritual empire had come. Without fanfare or display He simply breathed upon them the very breath of His own being: "Receive the Holy Spirit. Receive My very own Spirit. Receive the Spirit of God."

He whom they were receiving was none other than the Sovereign of heaven. He it was who now would rule in their affairs as He had in the affairs of the Master. It was under His monarchy that they would move. It was under His control that they would carry out enormous conquests. It was under His energizing that they would become the initiators of a brand-new, revolutionary society of men: the Church.

It would have its birth and beginning here in Jerusalem, expand outward into Judea, stretch to Samaria, and finally reach out to embrace the farthest outposts of the world.

Half in disbelief, half in hope, His men had trekked back to Galilee. They vacillated violently from one day to the next. They swung between noble new aspirations on one hand to the mundane ruts of their former life on the other. At times they felt like they were on a wildly swinging pendulum. It took them from the highest hopes and most ecstatic joy, when the Master was with them, to the depths of despondency and despair when He was absent. Some occasions were bright with delight. Others were black with despair. They seemed torn between doubt and adoration. They would worship yet wonder.

It was in this mood that He again appeared amongst all of them on a hill in Galilee. It was a prearranged rendezvous. The end of His earthly sojourn amongst them was near. It could very well be that it was the same favorite hill from which He had first spoken to them years before about His new ideas. In that initial sermon on the mount He had shared profound insights with them about the sort of life He wanted men to live. It was the loftiest standard ever set before men. They had seen it lived out in His own character and conduct. The question was, Could it be carried out in common men like themselves? He assured them it could, and would be, as they were empowered by His Presence, through His Spirit.

The parallel between this encounter and the initial contact God had with man was remarkable. God had breathed upon the first man, Adam, capable of communion with Himself, and he became a living soul, of the earth, earthy. Now He came a second time to breathe upon these humble men of Galilee, imparting to them His eternal breath. He gave them His very life, that of His own divine Spirit, that they might become quickened, living spirits. They were born from above, energized from on high. Regenerated in spirit, they in turn would represent His life on earth. The capacity to achieve this came from Him.

"All power is given unto Me." The words were like thunderbolts from above: *"All power, all energy, all the resources of heaven above and earth below are vested in Me."*

He the Christ had simply reclaimed what was ever, always His. From before the emergence of planet earth even, all the principalities and powers of the universe had been lodged in Him. All things had been created by Him and for Him. He was before all things, and by virtue of His very being they were conserved and sustained up to this instant in time.

It was in no way presumptuous of Him to pass on a portion of this power now to His people. It was His unique privilege to dispense His enormous energies as He wished. And that He deigned to do this to a small fistful of frightened, feeble fellows is part of the grand pageantry of God at work in the world.

This was no less a miraculous display of His deity than had been His own humble life cloaked in human flesh and form. Deliberately of His own free will He—God, very God—had divested Himself of His divine form. He had set aside His supernatural existence to enter the company of men as a man. Willingly and freely He had assumed the role of a poor person, prepared to serve His fellows in the most menial manner. But beyond this He had endured enormous suffering, even tasting death itself to deliver His fellows from the fear and clutch of death and the devil.

His had been a magnificent achievement.

Men at this stage of history could not fully grasp it.

It would take the benefit of hindsight and the illumination of God's own Spirit for men to comprehend the enormous conquest of evil and victory over Satan achieved by Christ.

Yet now He stood calmly and quietly amongst them on this hill in Galilee. There was no ostentation, no parading of His might. He declared in simple, unadorned terms, *"All power is Mine."*

It would be in the strength of His energy that they would go from here to turn the world upside down. It would be in the endowment of His might that they would proclaim all over the earth the good news of His salvation for lost men. It would be in the authority of His prestige and presence that they would introduce others into this new community of men—the Church—His band of believers.

This commissioning was not something they could possibly achieve under their own initiative. It was an impossible assignment but for His empowering. The dynamic energy needed to do it would be His. It would be transmitted and imparted to them by His presence through His Spirit. They would be men endowed with enormous powers, not their own but a portion of His. The remarkable achievements they would realize were the result of His resources being made available to them.

Always, ever, the key was *"Lo, behold—be aware: I am with you . . . always!"*

Even though they, like we, were common men and common clay, fashioned from the frail material of the human family, they would become a formidable force upon the planet. Though some of them feared, some of them doubted, still *He would be with them always.*

His assurance and His commitment to them in giving them this charge could not be surpassed.

"I am with you: to be your wisdom—your love—your strength—your insight—your courage—your hope—your good cheer—your energy . . . ."

The work of God in the world would go on!

It was He who would do it, as always—but through His people.

What they learned that day was that anyone who is commissioned by Christ is no longer a freewill agent. No longer could they just do as they wished. They could not just casually gravitate back to their old life-style. They were remade men. Their lives would be redirected into new areas of service. The lake and the hills and the boats and the dear old life of Galilee would remain only as memories . . . happy memories.

They were men who would be on the move.

They would become ambassadors of the King.

Their will was to do the Master's will.

Their work was His work.

Their words were His.

Their whole thrust and surge of spiritual life would make an enormous impact on civilization. Never again would the world be quite the same. The good news of God's rescue operation would be proclaimed everywhere. It was bound to polarize people, just as the life of their Lord had polarized His contemporaries. Some would accept it gladly. Others would be enraged by it.

Because of this, some of them would be loved and adored by their fellows. Others would be hated and persecuted with enormous suffering because of their allegiance to the Christ.

From timid, frightened, wavering men they would be transformed into fearless warriors, endowed with enormous energy, motivated by God's own might.

The strength and force with which they would fan out across the face of the earth were not their own but those of the Master.

He had risen from the grave.

He was at work amongst them.

He was the Living Lord.

And they were glad . . . rejoicing in His presence with them.

CHAPTER FORTY-SIX

The Conqueror Returns

The last forty days of Christ's visitation to His followers were finally concluded. Again and again He had appeared amongst them at various times and in varying locations. In His own quiet, winsome way the Master had shown Himself to His friends in such convincing reality that they now had infallible proof of His living reality amongst them.

He was no longer an apparition to be feared. He was not a ghostlike form who made them uneasy and unsure. He had talked with them in plain language they could comprehend. He had shared meals with them, laid a fire and served them delicious food prepared with His own hands. He had taken long walks with them, conversing about current events as well as things yet to come. In short, they had sensed and known Him as a living person with whom they could communicate by means of all their faculties—physical, mental, emotional, and spiritual.

There had been reestablished between them a wondrous interpersonal relationship of positive assurance. He—*Rabboni*—was their Master: their Messiah, their Lord, their God. They saw Him. They heard Him. They met with Him. They touched Him. They talked with Him. They adored and worshiped Him. They loved Him intensely. In truth He was totally theirs, and they in turn were totally His. Bonds of loyalty stronger than steel had now been forged between Him and His friends.

Nothing in heaven or earth could ever again separate them from the awareness of His love for them. Despite their own disastrous performance in the past, His loyalty to them had never wavered. Irrespective of their fluctuating feelings, His devotion to them remained undiminished. He had conquered all their misgivings, banished all their doubts, and captured their hearts completely.

It was His last great conquest.

The thirty-three-odd years of His earthly interlude had come to an end. Everything He had entered human history to achieve had been accomplished. His assignments, self-imposed, had been consummated with incredible detailed perfection of which only deity is capable.

His every performance upon the puny stage of Palestine had been executed with faultless finesse. Not that it was playacting. It was not; far from it. It was the drama of deity in human guise depicting the very character of the divine. His sojourn on the planet had been the eternal demonstration of God's own life and love and light in terms unmistakable to stumbling, groping, selfish earth children.

His humble birth in a crude cave: His carefree boyhood on the warm hills of Galilee: His long years as a craftsman at the carpenter's bench: His tremendous teaching with such enormous authority: His mighty miracles amongst the thronging masses: His conquest of all that was vile, of sin and Satan and selfishness, on the hill of Calvary: His glorious Resurrection from the rock tomb where neither death, decay, nor decomposition could hold Him—all had been executed with mounting splendor and growing grandeur.

And though now but a handful of human beings were acutely aware of His glory, in the unseen world His return as the conquering hero was awaited with enormous expectation.

He had come to a planet and a people struggling in their sins, their selfishness, and their despair. He had in utter selflessness identified Himself with suffering men and women in their dilemma and darkness. He had demonstrated irrevocably that God in man could overcome evil with good: that light does dispel darkness: that love does drive out despair: that life does vanquish death: that because God became man, men can become Godlike.

Nothing in human history had ever happened to rival this revelation. It was a program of such magnitude that only God Himself could have conceived it. Yet it was executed in such exquisite beauty and simplicity that even an earth child could comprehend its meaning. In fact the more childlike one's perspective of this majestic performance, the more meaningful it becomes.

The Master had discussed all of this with His friends. He had taken them back carefully to the ancient Scriptures. He had shown how every forecast made of old about Him had been fulfilled down to the most minute detail. He Himself, speaking through the poets, prophets, and seers of former times, had tried to prepare His audience for His own appearance. But even then they were not ready to receive Him. And when He did come, but for this tiny handful, He had been rejected and repudiated.

Still, this had not deterred Him in His grand designs. The performance had gone on as programmed in the councils of eternity. All that had been prearranged even before ever the earth was formed had now been accomplished. It had been an amazing achievement demonstrating the enormous generosity and graciousness of God to men, in spite of all their objections and adverse reactions. He had come and He had conquered.

In firm but gentle ways the Master weaned His friends from their familiar haunts and homes in Galilee. He made them see their future lay not in the north but in the very heart of the great city that had done its utmost to obliterate His presence from the world He had come to redeem.

It was back in Jerusalem that He prepared them for the next great act in God's unfolding drama on the planet. Now they would share center stage with Him in His acts. Empowered by His presence, energized by His own Spirit, endowed with His wisdom, they would witness the emergence of a mighty movement amongst all men of all nations. His Church, His people, would come into being before their wondering eyes.

They would have to be patient just a little longer.

They would have to wait quietly for a visitation from on high.

They would have to be of one heart, one mind, one spirit.

It was God who would act. But it was through them He would act. They would see the actual visible establishment of their longed-for kingdom of God on earth. It would come sweeping in on the great wind of His own Spirit. Under the sovereignty of that Spirit the glorious government of God would be set up in ten thousand times ten thousand waiting souls, waiting down the centuries to receive Him as royalty from above.

All of this was possible now because the epoch hour had come for Him to be received back to glory with great acclaim. He who had willingly set aside all of His own privileges and power as God very God in order to be made a man, was now to reclaim that position. He who had gladly become a servant obedient even to death, was now setting aside His earthly trappings to take on Him again the full-orbed glory of the Godhead. He who had been despised and rejected of men was now to be received with honor, praise, glory, and adulation by the uncounted hosts of heaven.

The suffering servant of men was to become again the Supreme Sovereign of the Universe.

He who had known poverty, labor, sweat, sorrow, weariness, tears, and the cruel tortures of His contemporaries on earth was now to be crowned King of Kings and Lord of Lords. In the royal chambers of the Unseen World from which He had come there would be celebrations of such splendor and magnitude that no mortal could comprehend them. The puny minds and finite faculties of mere men could not bear the glory or ineffable brightness of that celestial coronation. It was a celebration beyond man's comprehension. The Conqueror returned!

Evidence that this had happened would come to earth. The Spirit He would dispense to His waiting friends in Jerusalem would bear witness to the fact that their Lord was now at His pinnacle of power, seated in great glory at the Father's right hand. As He had promised them: "I will send you My Spirit. I will come to you. If a man loves Me and complies with My wishes, My Father will love him, and *We* will come to him and take up residence with him."

It was all tremendously exciting.

They stood on the threshold of a new era.

He had done everything possible to prepare them for the dynamic dawning of a new day in the dramatic events of God.

Quietly and without any unusual display, the Master led His little band out of Jerusalem on this warm spring morning. They passed the great temple porches where He had so often created such a stir.

Some of the fellows winked at each other as they recollected the riots when He drove out the hucksters. They strolled along the dusty streets that had been stained with blood from His wounded, lacerated back as He carried His cruel cross as far as He could. They were solemn with the agonizing memory. Up the path that wound over the Mount of Olives He led them. Every step brought into sharp focus the days and nights they had shared here: the triumphal march into the city with His riding an unbroken colt: the dreadful night in the garden: the lynching by the mob: the quiet nights they slept here under the stars. All these and many more scenes tumbled through their emotions.

Now they came over the crest of the ridge. Below them lay Bethany. Away to the east, far as the eye could see, were the wild hills gashed by the deep rift of the Jordan Valley. What a multitude of memories all this region held for them. Their years together tramping across this tumbled terrain had been filled with awesome miracles and wondrous adventure. It had been so stimulating to share life with the Master.

Gently He turned toward them. Lifting His arms, He stretched out His hands upon them in the ancient blessing of His people:

The Lord bless thee, and keep thee: the Lord make his face shine upon thee, and be gracious unto thee: the Lord lift up his countenance upon thee, and give thee peace.

Numbers 6:24–26

As the last words—*give thee peace*—fell from His lips, He was lifted triumphantly from them. In an aura of stillness, strength, and serenity He was received up in a cloud of radiant splendor.

His exit had been as silent as His entry.

Two angels assured His watching friends that in due time He would in truth return again to earth in visible form. But when He did, it would be in power and with great glory. In fact every eye would see Him. Every knee would bow before Him. Every tongue would confess that He is Lord.

The disciples and their companions were not disturbed by His going. He had so prepared them for this departure that their spirits were ecstatic with jubilation.